Drawn *to* Birds

A NATURALIST'S SKETCHBOOK

Jenny deFouw Geuder

Adventure Publications
Cambridge, Minnesota

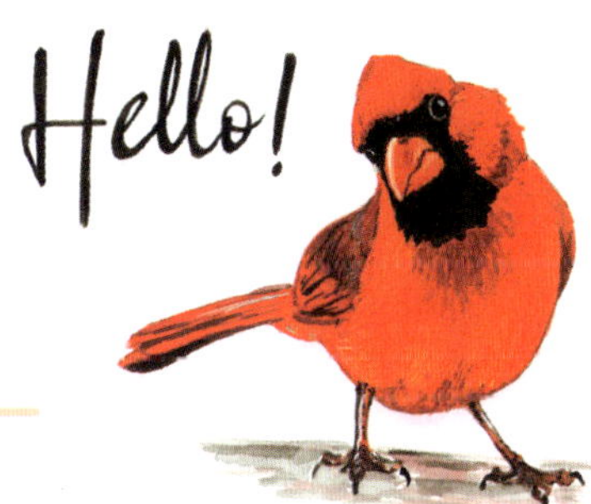

Cover and book design by Jonathan Norberg

Edited by Brett Ortler

Proofread by Emily Beaumont

Cover images copyright by Jenny deFouw Geuder except feather by pikepicture/Shutterstock.com.

Interior images copyright by Jenny deFouw Geuder except author photo on pg. 144 by Josh Knap/Peninsula Photography.

Photo Credits:

Reference photos purchased or sourced from the following stock sources: Dreamstime, Pixabay, Unsplash, Morguefile, and Pixy.

White-throated sparrow reference photo courtesy of National Park Service staff (public domain).

Reference images for the following list of watercolors are used with the permission of their respective photographers:

Goldfinch, Barbara Hymer; Heron, Hummingbird, and Sharp-Shinned Hawk, Cindy Fry; Indigo Bunting, Elizabeth May; Loon, Elena Austin; Purple Finch, Cal Kimola Brown; Red-tailed Hawk, David Salter; Robin and babies, Ernie Griffith; Peregrine Falcon stoop image inspired by Gowree, E.R., Jagadeesh, C., Talboys, E. et al. Vortices enable the complex aerobatics of peregrine falcons. Commun Biol 1, 27 (2018), licensed via Creative Commons 4.0 Attribution license (http://creativecommons.org/licenses/by/4.0/). Original image available here: https://doi.org/10.1038/s42003-018-0029-3

10 9 8 7 6 5 4 3 2 1

Drawn to Birds: A Naturalist's Sketchbook

Published by Adventure Publications
An imprint of AdventureKEEN
310 Garfield Street South
Cambridge, Minnesota 55008
(800) 678-7006
www.adventurepublications.net

Printed in China
ISBN 978-1-64755-225-1 (pbk.); ISBN 978-1-64755-226-8 (ebook)

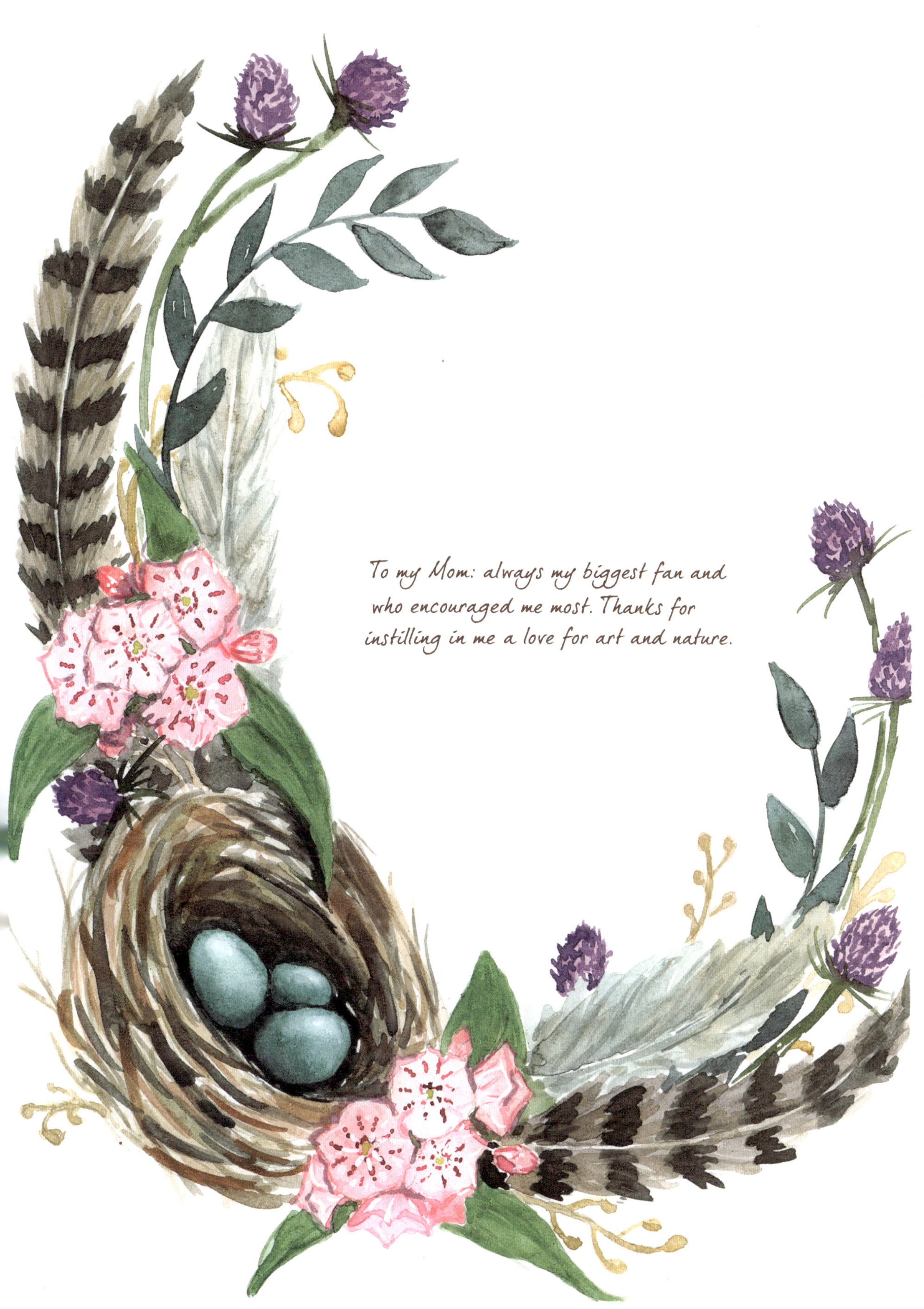

To my Mom: always my biggest fan and who encouraged me most. Thanks for instilling in me a love for art and nature.

Explore This Book

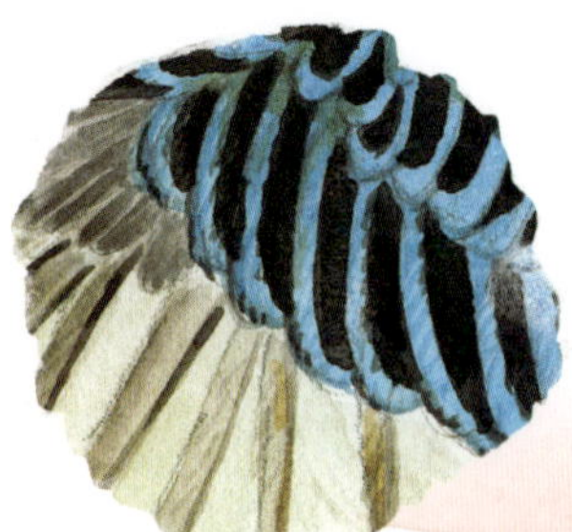

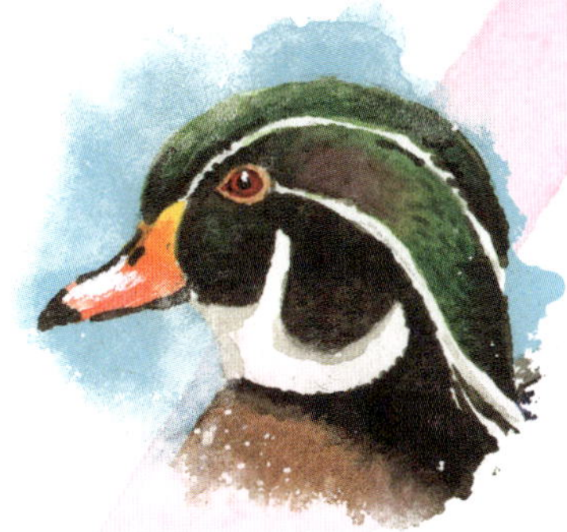

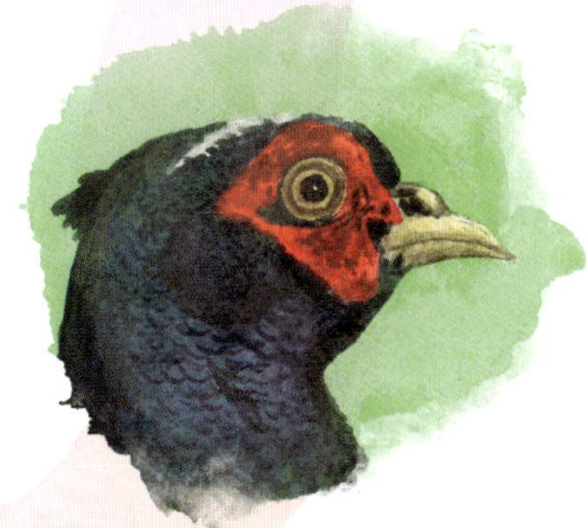

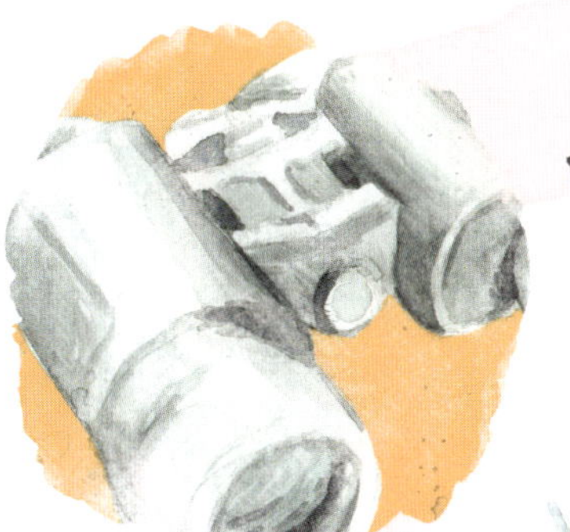

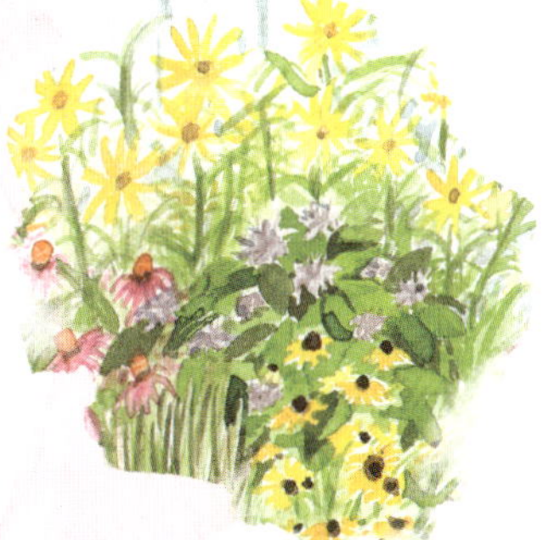

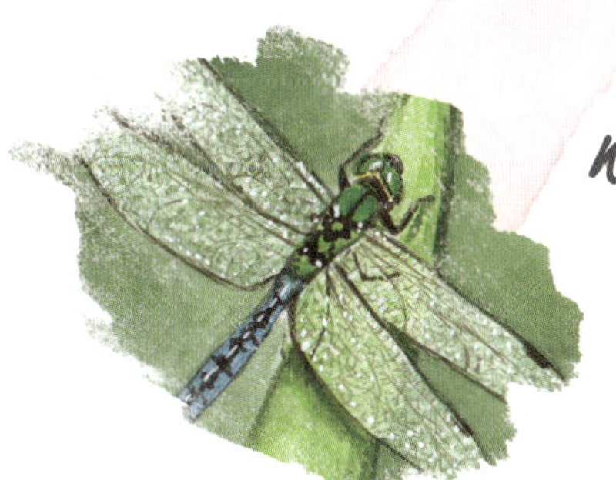

Garden!

Doodle!

Notice details, color.

Take photos!

How to Use this Book

Identify species.

Take notes, write observations.

1. Go outside! Look around you. Listen. Breathe.

2. Be inspired! Find out more about a bird you love, or one you know nothing about. Have fun!

Whatever you do,
it doesn't have to
be "perfect."

Don't compare your art,
photos, doodles, or garden
to anyone else's.

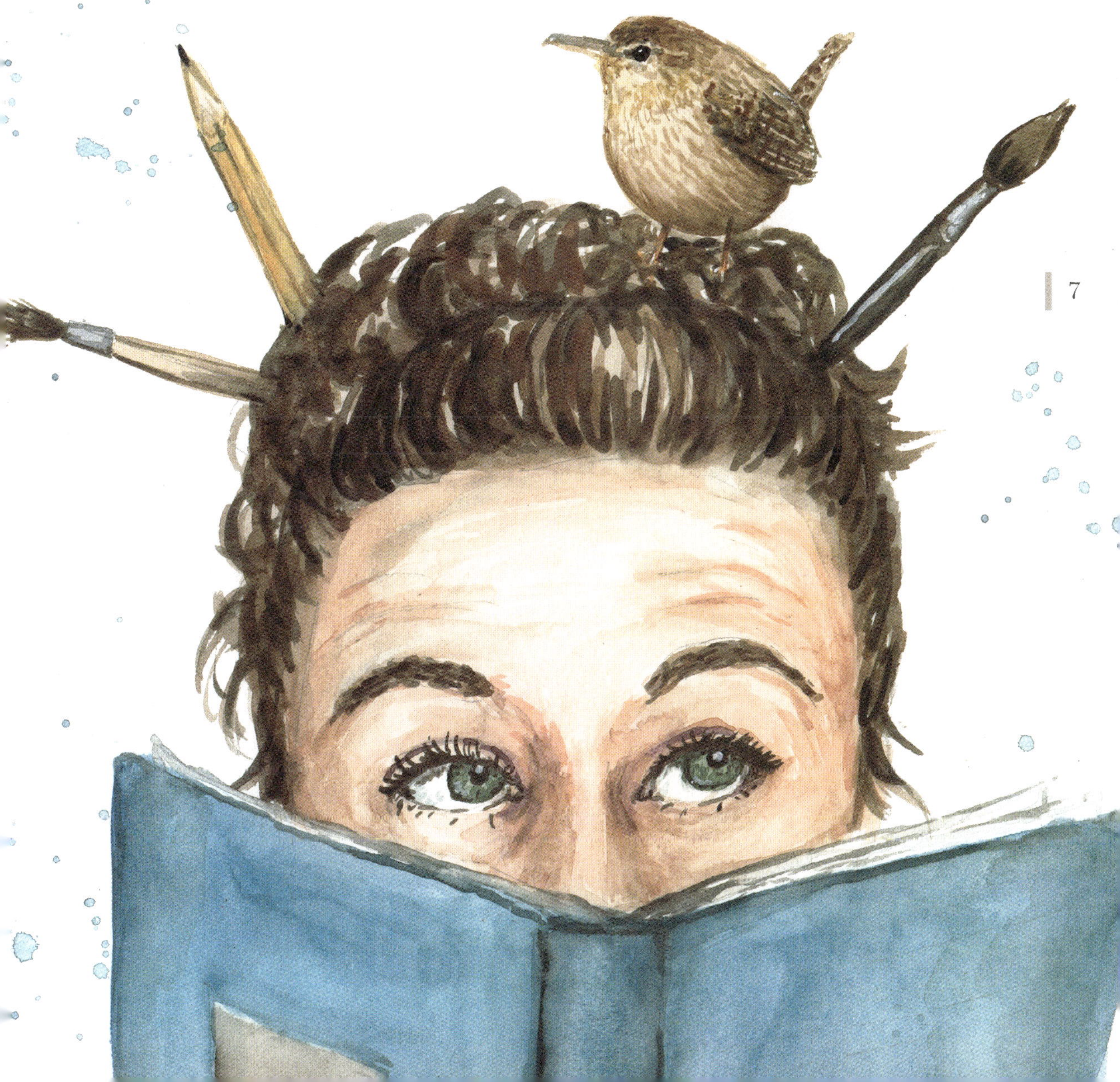

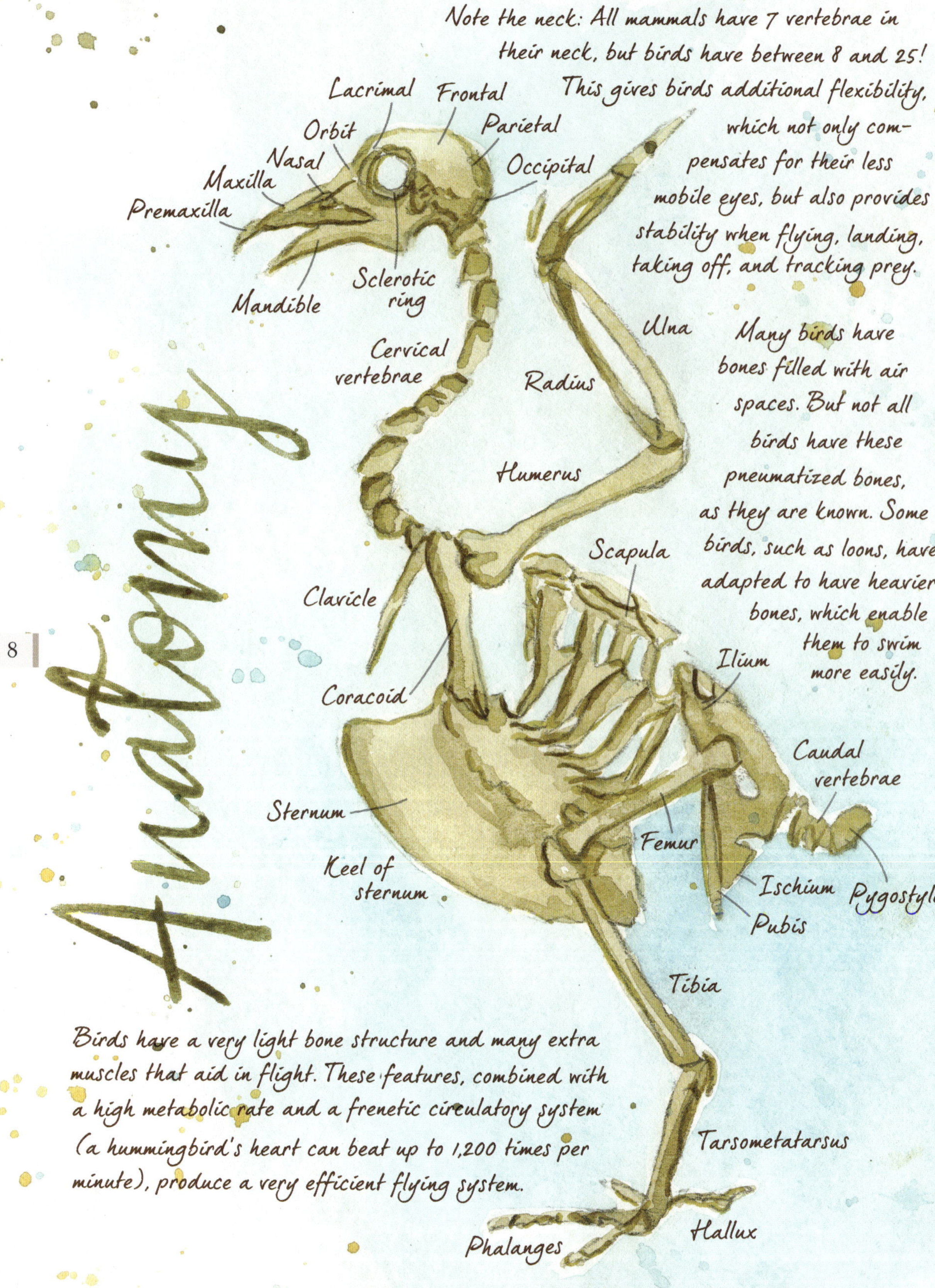
Anatomy
Note the neck: All mammals have 7 vertebrae in their neck, but birds have between 8 and 25! This gives birds additional flexibility, which not only compensates for their less mobile eyes, but also provides stability when flying, landing, taking off, and tracking prey.
Lacrimal
Frontal
Orbit
Parietal
Nasal
Occipital
Maxilla
Premaxilla
Sclerotic ring
Mandible
Cervical vertebrae
Ulna
Radius
Many birds have bones filled with air spaces. But not all birds have these pneumatized bones, as they are known. Some birds, such as loons, have adapted to have heavier bones, which enable them to swim more easily.
Humerus
Scapula
Clavicle
Ilium
Coracoid
Caudal vertebrae
Sternum
Femur
Keel of sternum
Ischium
Pygostyle
Pubis
Tibia
Birds have a very light bone structure and many extra muscles that aid in flight. These features, combined with a high metabolic rate and a frenetic circulatory system (a hummingbird's heart can beat up to 1,200 times per minute), produce a very efficient flying system.
Tarsometatarsus
Hallux
Phalanges

Feet

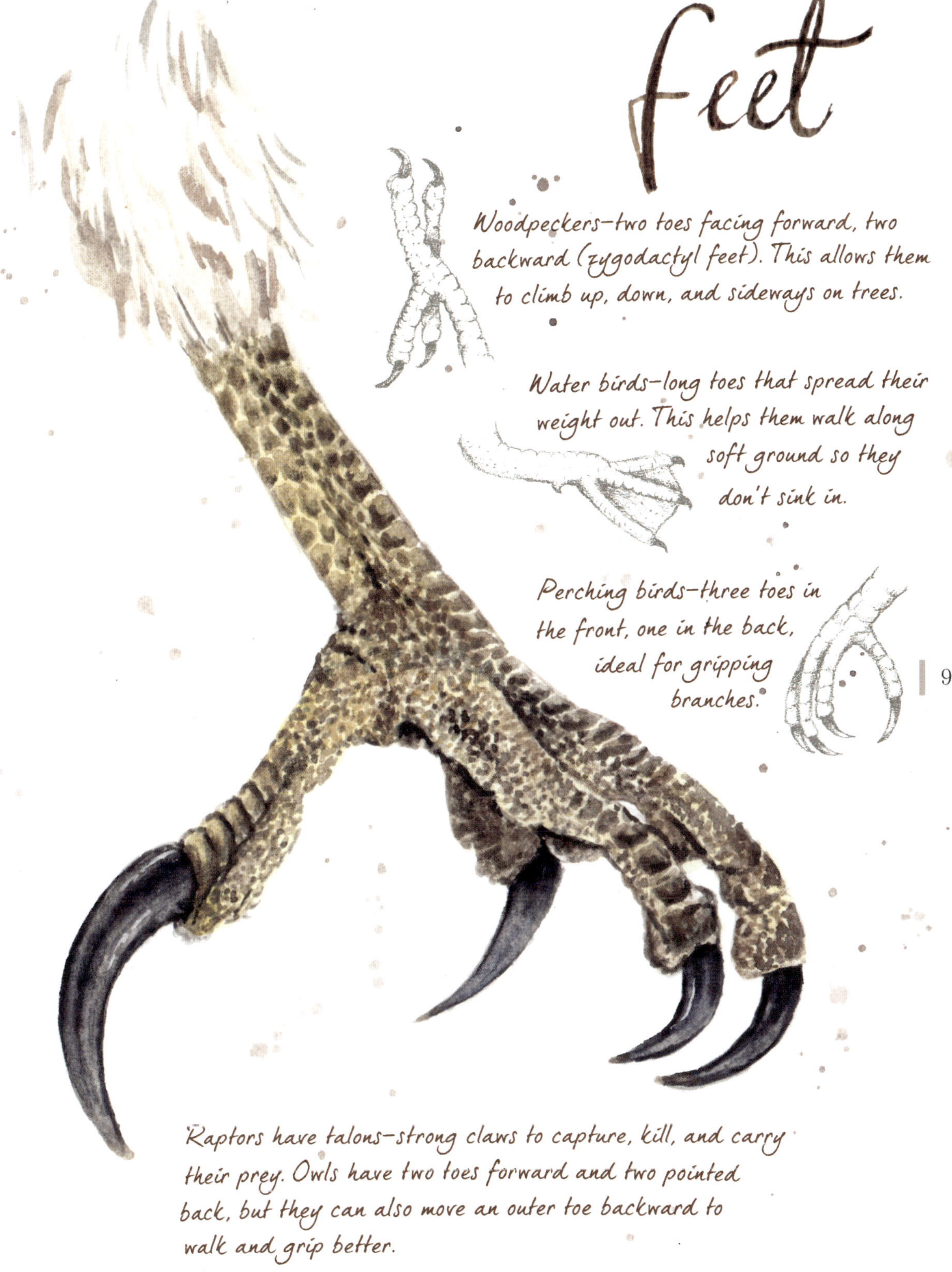

Woodpeckers—two toes facing forward, two backward (zygodactyl feet). This allows them to climb up, down, and sideways on trees.

Water birds—long toes that spread their weight out. This helps them walk along soft ground so they don't sink in.

Perching birds—three toes in the front, one in the back, ideal for gripping branches.

Raptors have talons—strong claws to capture, kill, and carry their prey. Owls have two toes forward and two pointed back, but they can also move an outer toe backward to walk and grip better.

Feathers

*Feathers not to scale!

There are seven types of feathers.

Feathers do so much! They...

- blanket
- cushion
- provide shade
- protect skin
- distract attackers
- camouflage
- attract attention
- help birds float
- help birds glide
- provide lift

4) Tail feathers—usually with more rounded edges, strong ato help steer in flight

3) Wing feathers —asymmetrical, with a shorter, less-flexible leading edge

Goldfinch

Red-tailed Hawk

1) Bristle feathers—usually on head, protect eyes/face

2) Plume feathers— fuzzy; closest to body to trap heat

5) Filoplume feathers—whisker-like; help sense position

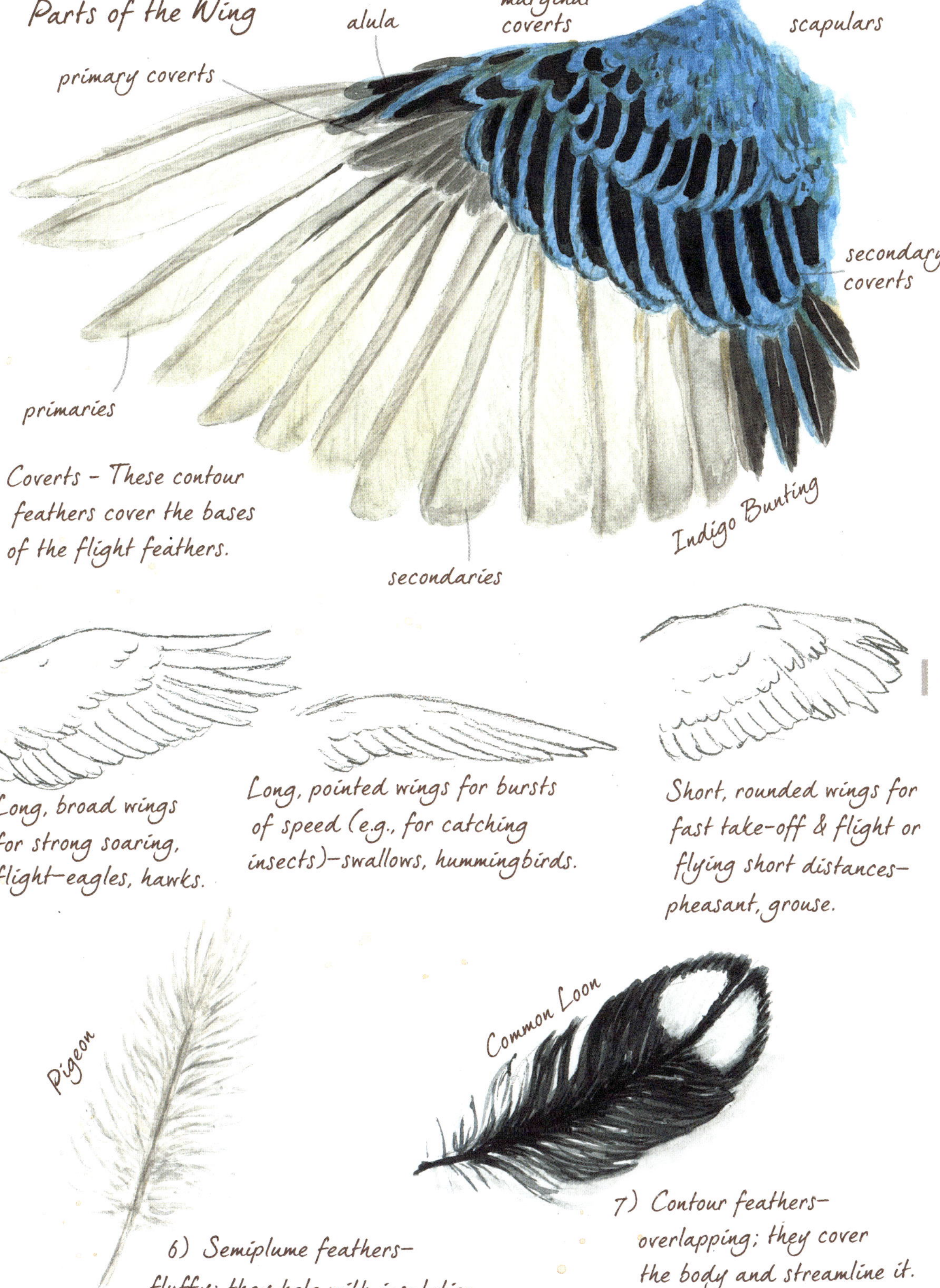

Parts of the Wing
alula
marginal coverts
scapulars
primary coverts
secondary coverts
primaries
Coverts - These contour feathers cover the bases of the flight feathers.
Indigo Bunting
secondaries
Long, broad wings for strong soaring, flight—eagles, hawks.
Long, pointed wings for bursts of speed (e.g., for catching insects)—swallows, hummingbirds.
Short, rounded wings for fast take-off & flight or flying short distances—pheasant, grouse.
Pigeon
Common Loon
6) Semiplume feathers—fluffy; they help with insulation.
7) Contour feathers—overlapping; they cover the body and streamline it.

Beneficial Beaks

Bird beaks are often well adapted for specific food sources.

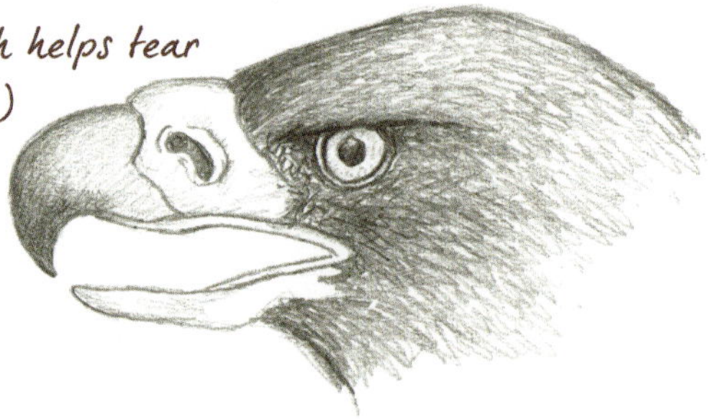

Raptor; notch helps tear into meat (eagle)

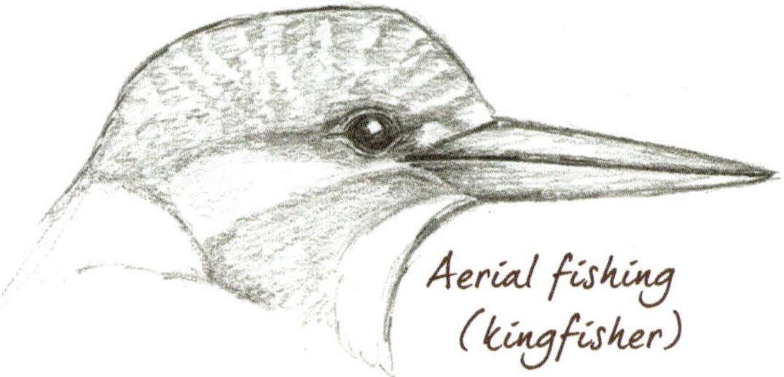

Aerial fishing (kingfisher)

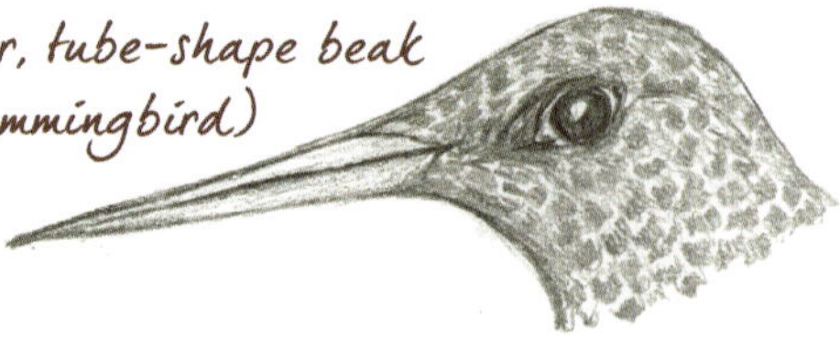

Nectar, tube-shape beak (hummingbird)

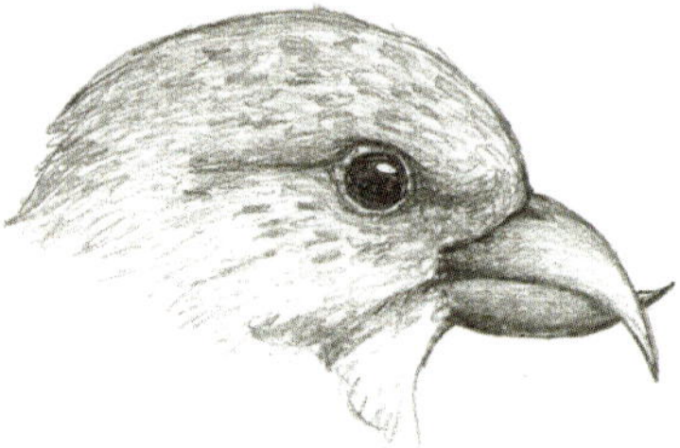

Crossbill

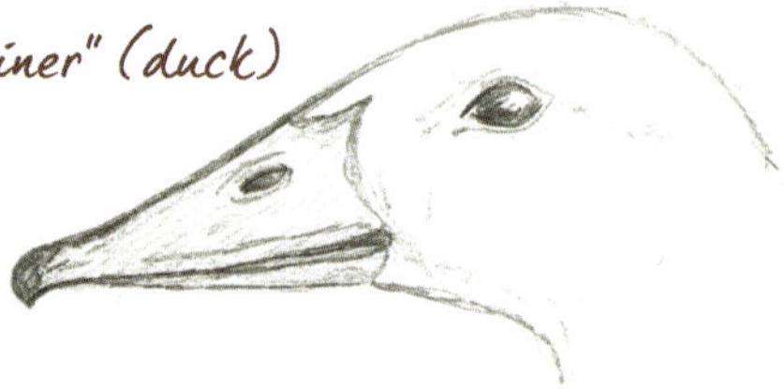

"Strainer" (duck)

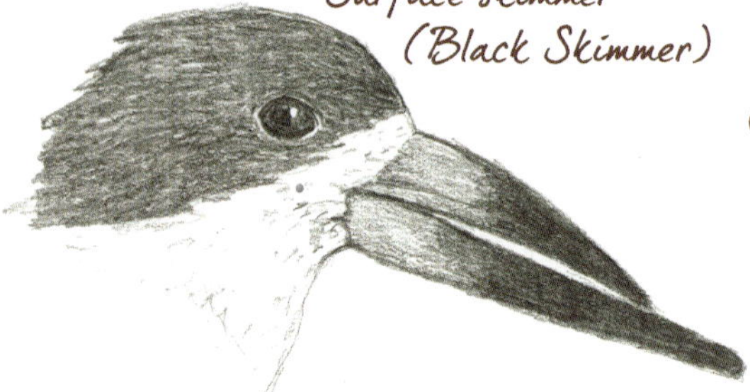

Surface skimmer (Black Skimmer)

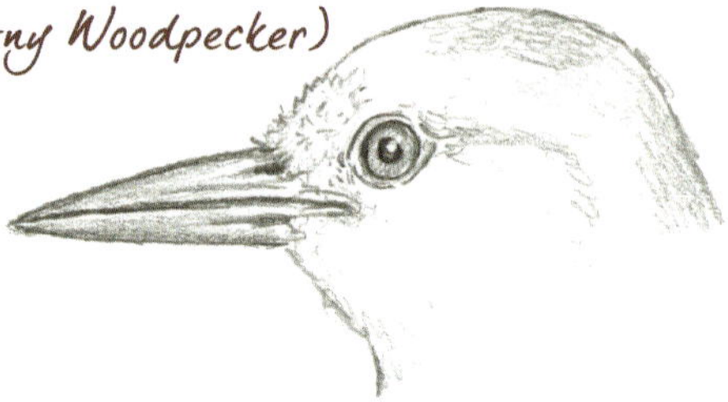

Chisel-beak for woodpecker (Downy Woodpecker)

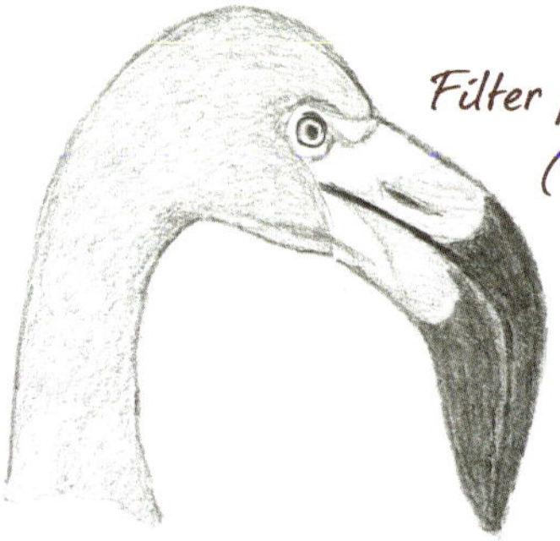

Filter feeding (Flamingo)

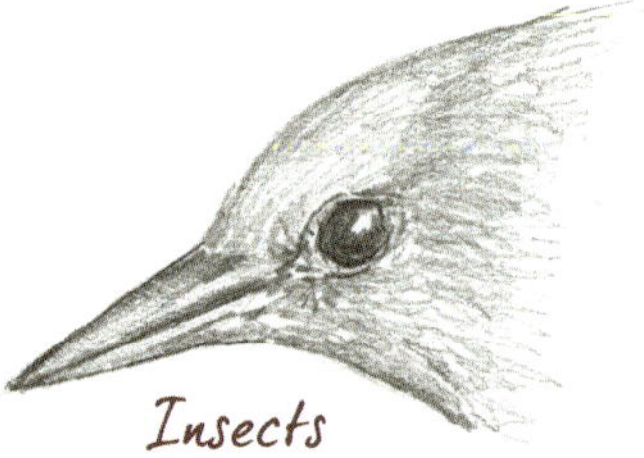

Insects (Black Phoebe)

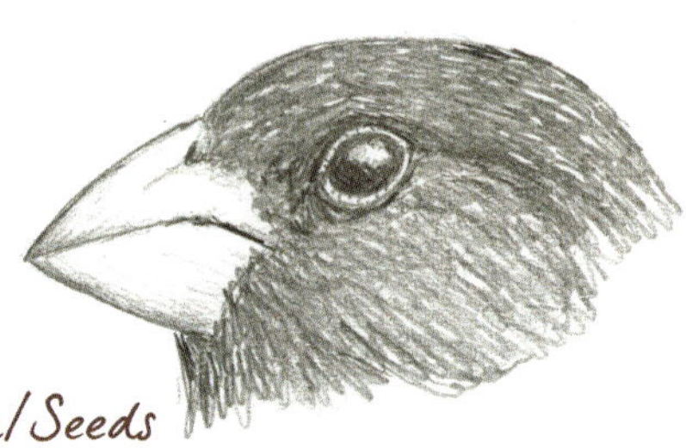

Grain/Seeds (Rose-breasted Grosbeak)

Eyes

Raptors have amazing eyesight—they can see their prey from over a mile away.

Birds all have three eyelids—an upper one, a lower one, and a nictitating membrane that helps clean and protect the eye.

retina
sclerotic ring
choroid
iris
sclera
lens
fovea
cornea
muscle

Bird eyes are a lot like human eyes, but with some distinct adaptations. Most birds can't move their eyes much, if at all. They turn their heads to move their eyes. This is because a bird's eyes are quite large compared to the size of its head.

Raptors have their eyes situated toward the front: they don't have very good peripheral vision (another reason many raptors are injured on roadways). An owl can turn its head about 200 degrees but can't move its eyes at all! Smaller birds have eyes situated on the sides of the head; this provides good peripheral vision, enabling them to see much of their surroundings.

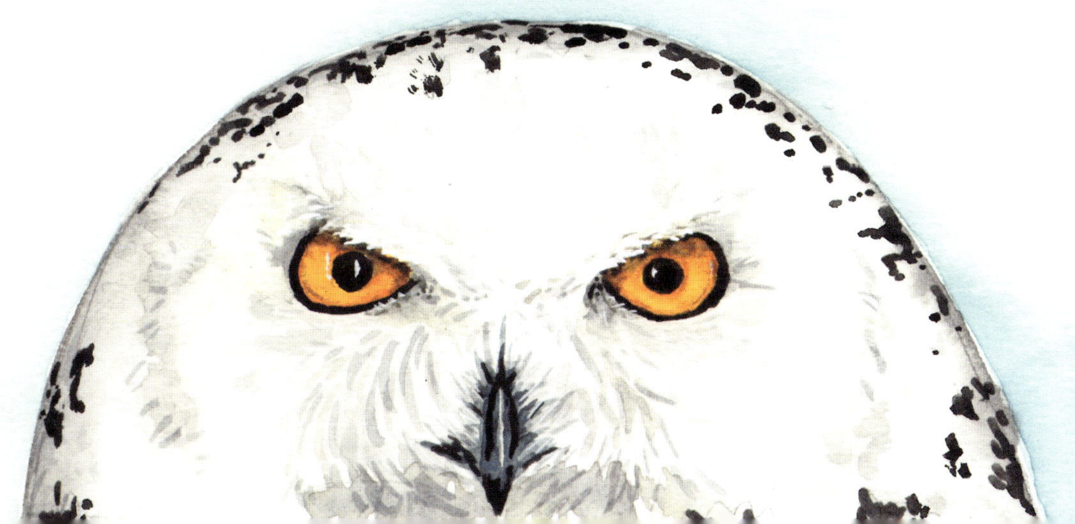

Whose Nest is This?

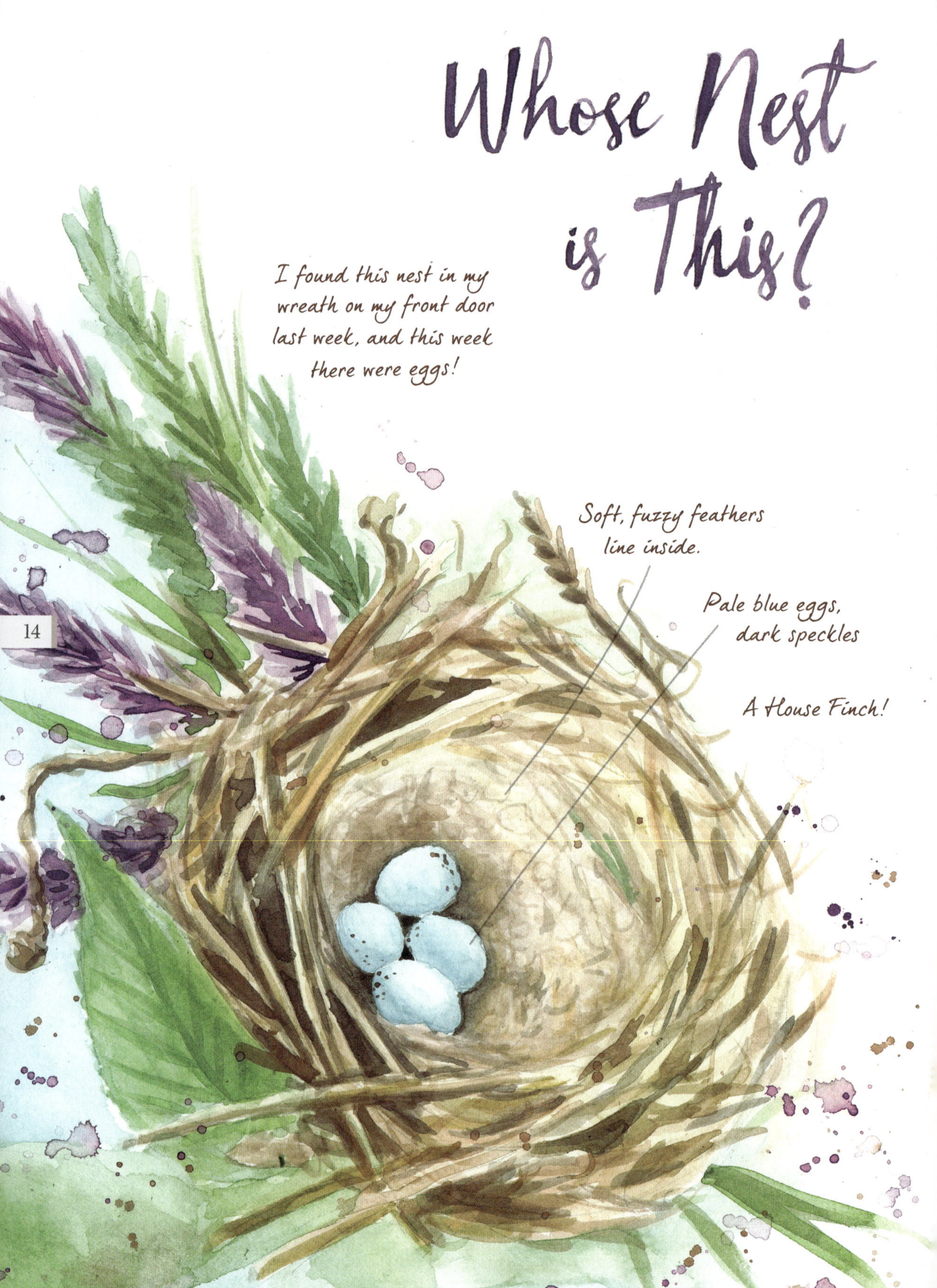

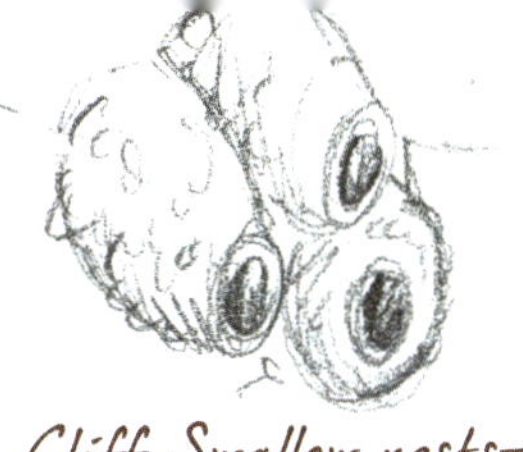

Cliff Swallow nests—mud!

Nest Notes

Baltimore Oriole!
Socklike or "pendant" Nest

Be a detective. If active—leave a nest a lot of space—binoculars are handy. Write a description of the birds and their activities; take notes!

Location and time are key. Migratory birds have separate territories versus "resident" birds. A nest found earlier in the spring is probably that of a resident bird rather than a migratory one. Keep track of where you have found it. Is it on the ground? On your house?

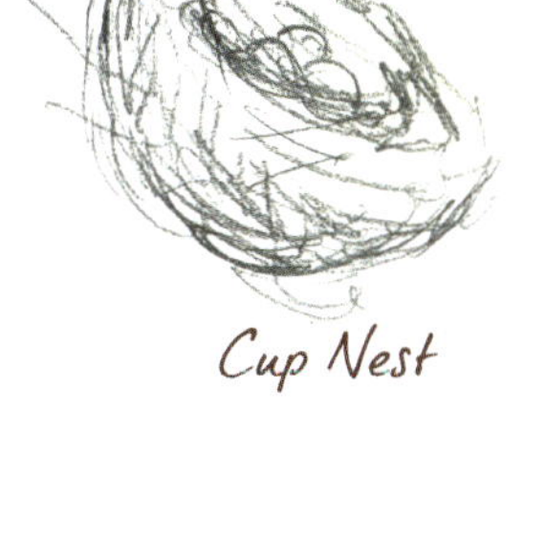

Cup Nest

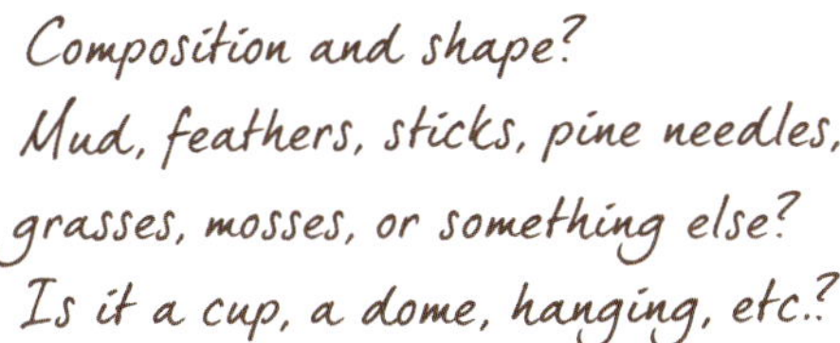

Composition and shape?
Mud, feathers, sticks, pine needles, grasses, mosses, or something else?
Is it a cup, a dome, hanging, etc.?

Eggs—size, shape, and color.
Markings and color can vary a lot, so don't base your investigation on this alone.

Platform Nest

Remember to leave a nest where you find it, even if you think it is not being used. Bird nests, even inactive ones, are often protected under federal law.

Cavity Nest

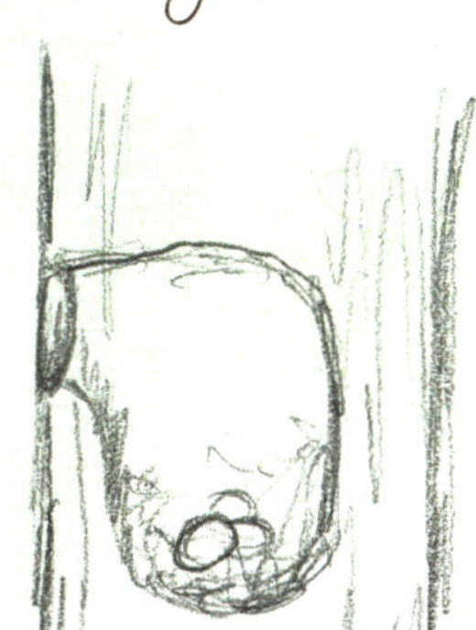

For fun, nest-related community science, visit nestwatch.org

Eggs

Goldfinch
Wren
Song Sparrow
Eastern Bluebird
House Sparrow
Oriole
Scarlet Tanager
Brown Thrasher
Cardinal
Gray Catbird
Mockingbird
Red-winged Blackbird
Meadowlark
European Starling
Flicker
American Robin
Killdeer
American Crow
Ring-necked Pheasant
Mallard

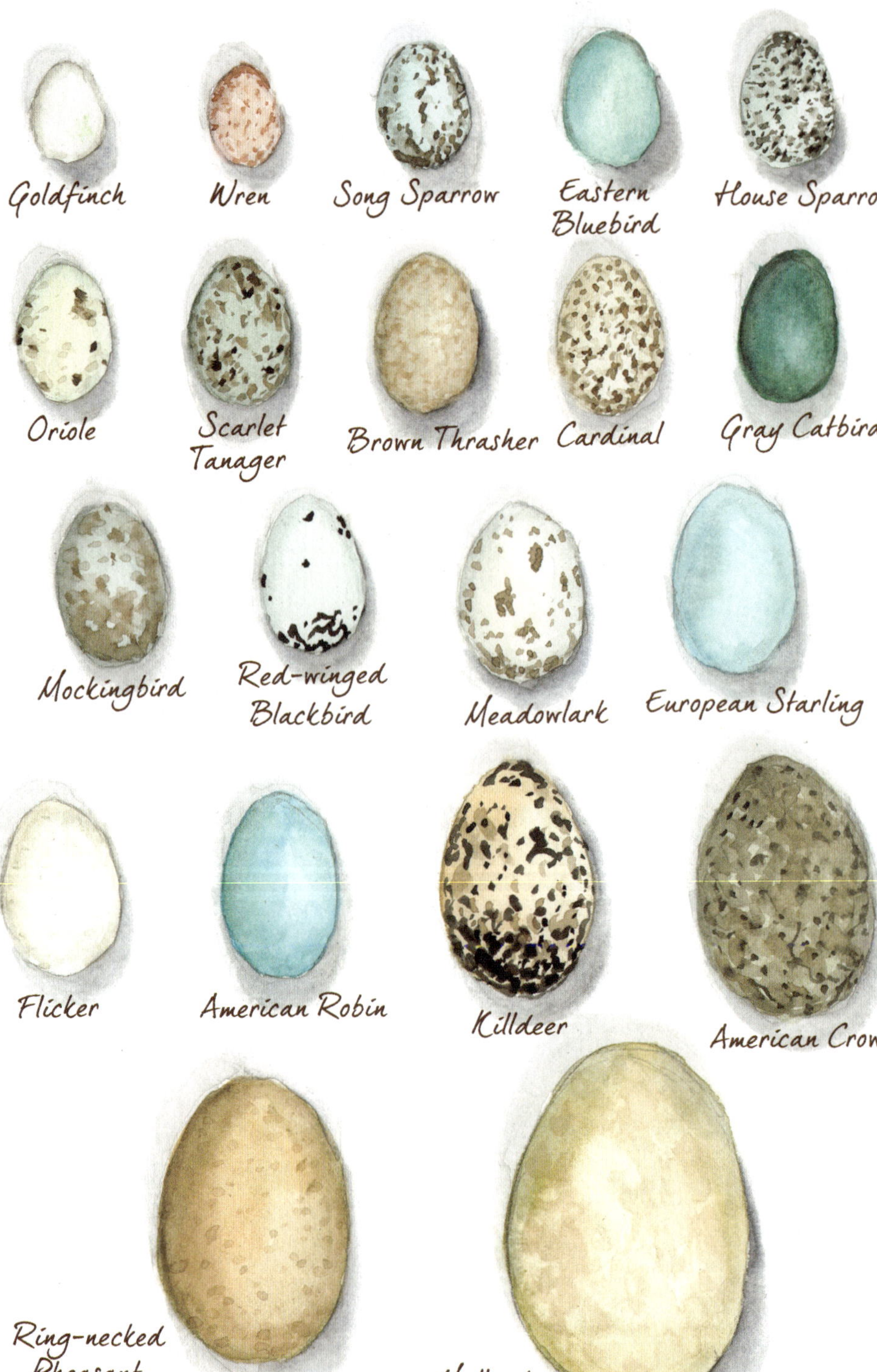

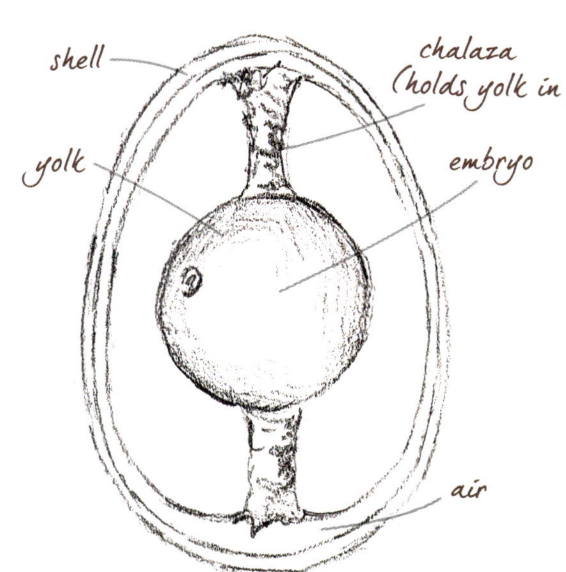

How many eggs: Depends! Some birds only lay one egg (condor), while others lay three (red-tailed hawk) or up to a lot more (wood duck can lay up to 17)! Most small songbirds lay about one egg a day until they reach the number they want. A clutch of eggs is the total number of eggs laid in one nest.

Egg shape: Recent research suggests that egg shape has to do with how good a flier a bird is: better fliers tend to have more asymmetrical eggs, maybe relating to fitting the babies in shapes better suited for sleeker, more aerodynamic bodies.

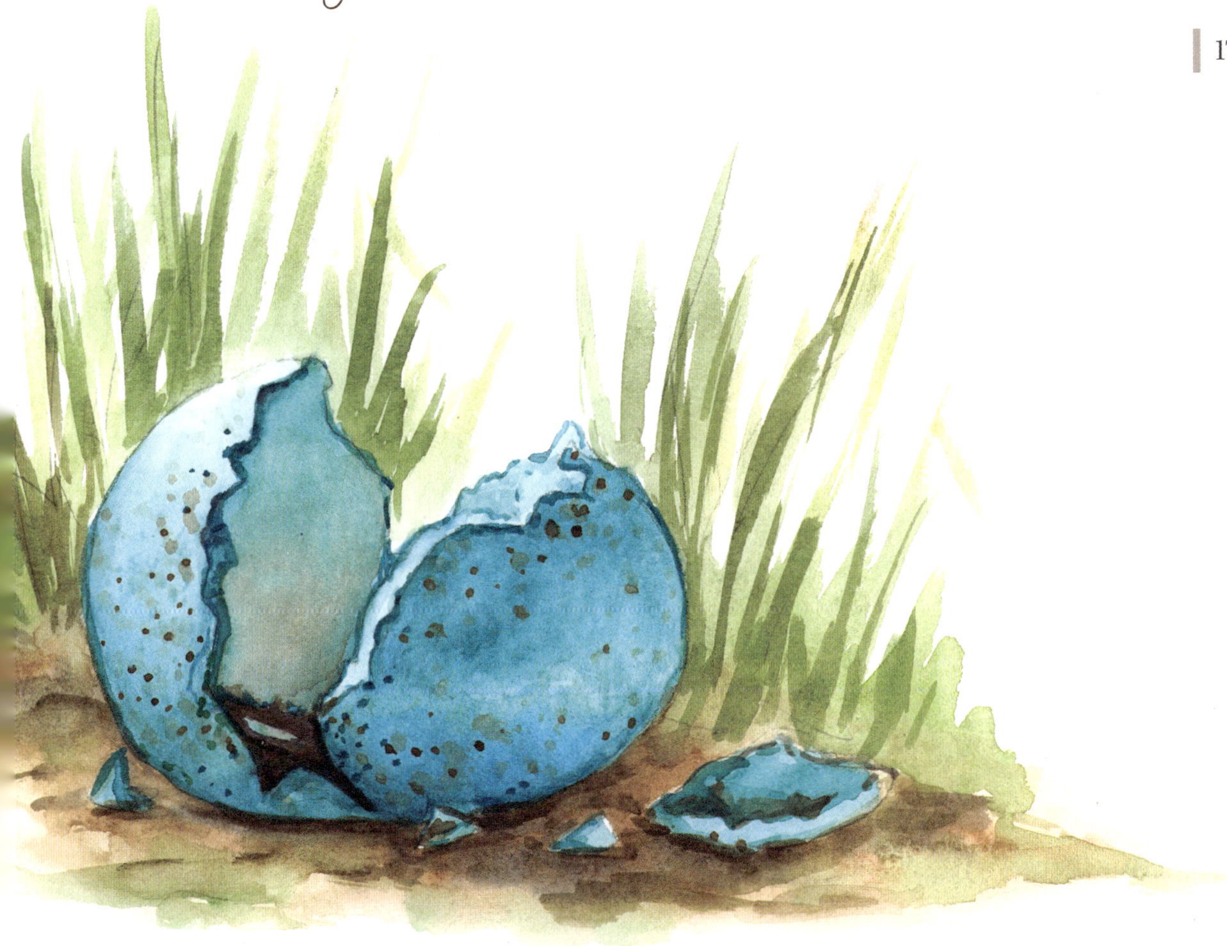

Hatchlings & Nestlings

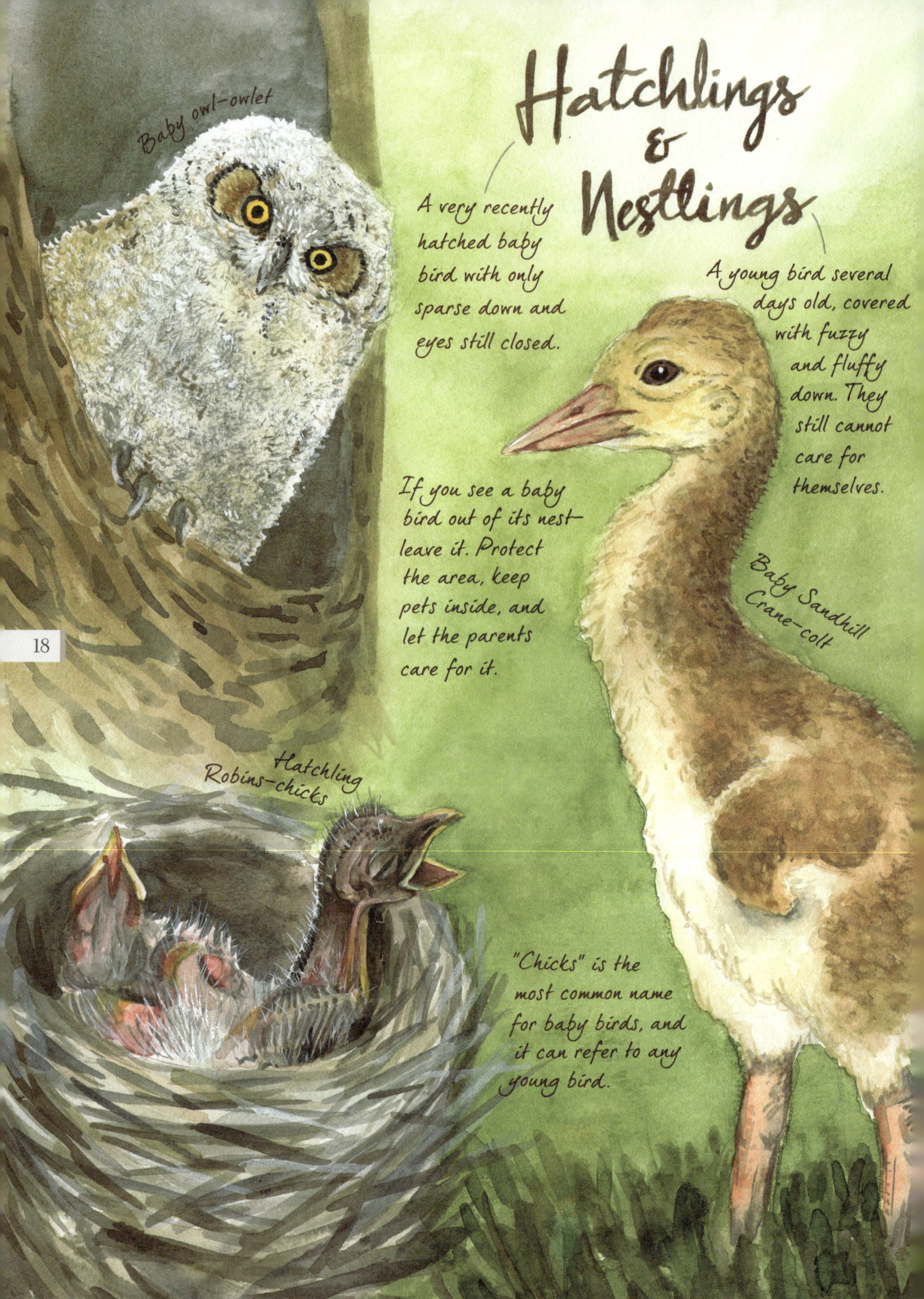

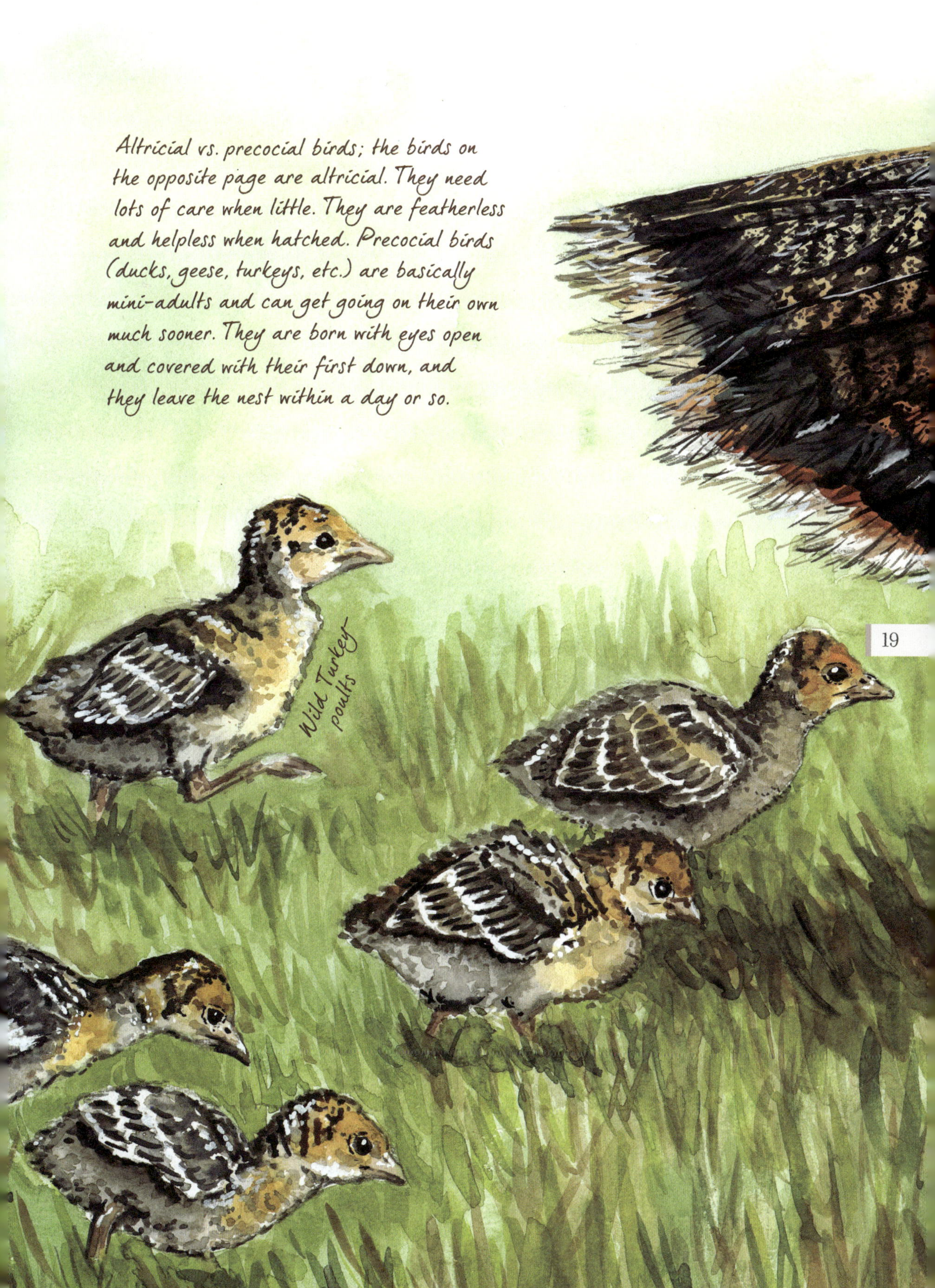

Altricial vs. precocial birds; the birds on the opposite page are altricial. They need lots of care when little. They are featherless and helpless when hatched. Precocial birds (ducks, geese, turkeys, etc.) are basically mini-adults and can get going on their own much sooner. They are born with eyes open and covered with their first down, and they leave the nest within a day or so.

A fledgling (juvenile) has its first coat of feathers and can move around on its own. Fledglings will start adventuring out on their own at this stage, but they still need their parents for food and safety. Often their colors are noticeably different than adults.

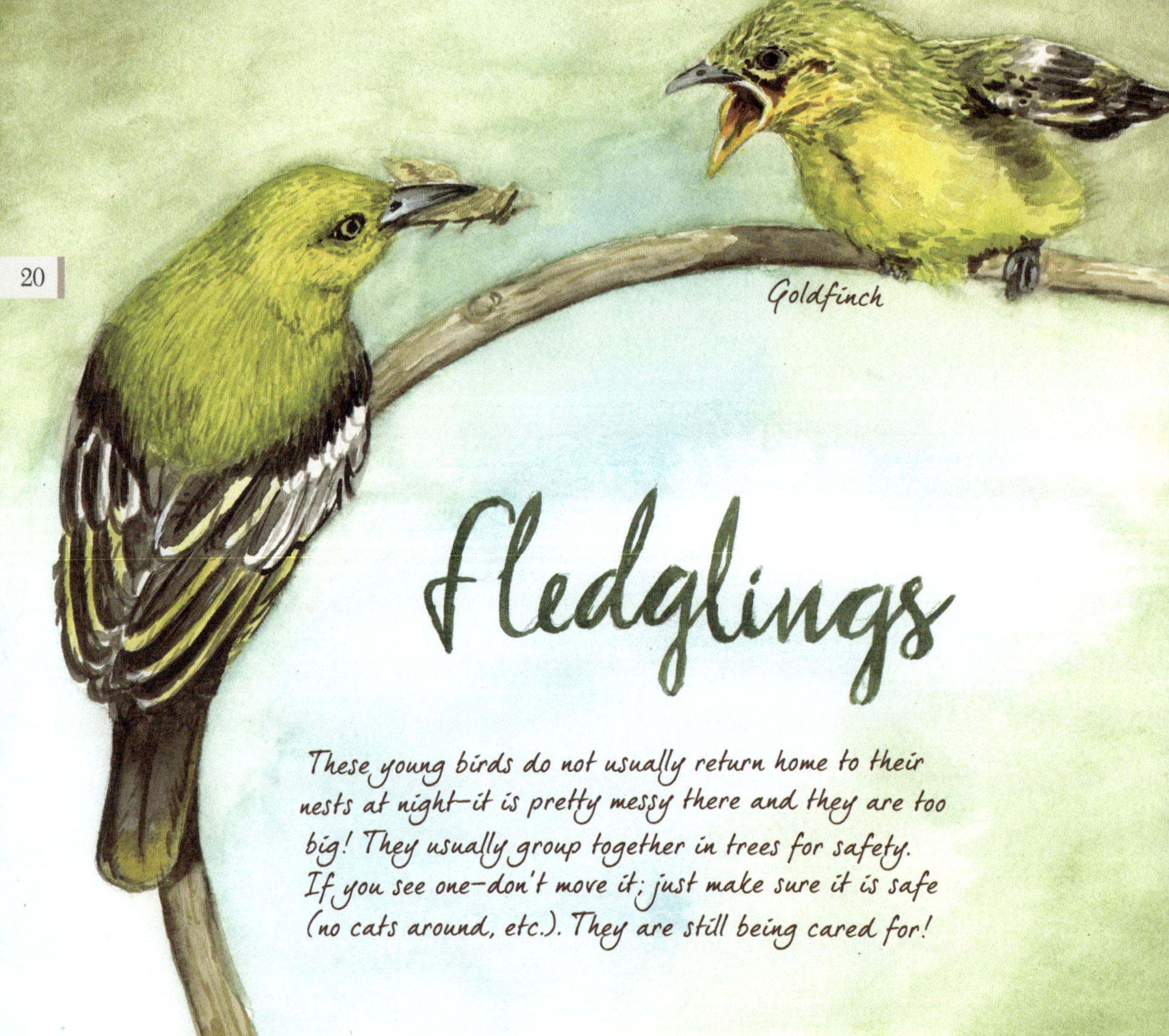

Fledglings

These young birds do not usually return home to their nests at night—it is pretty messy there and they are too big! They usually group together in trees for safety. If you see one—don't move it; just make sure it is safe (no cats around, etc.). They are still being cared for!

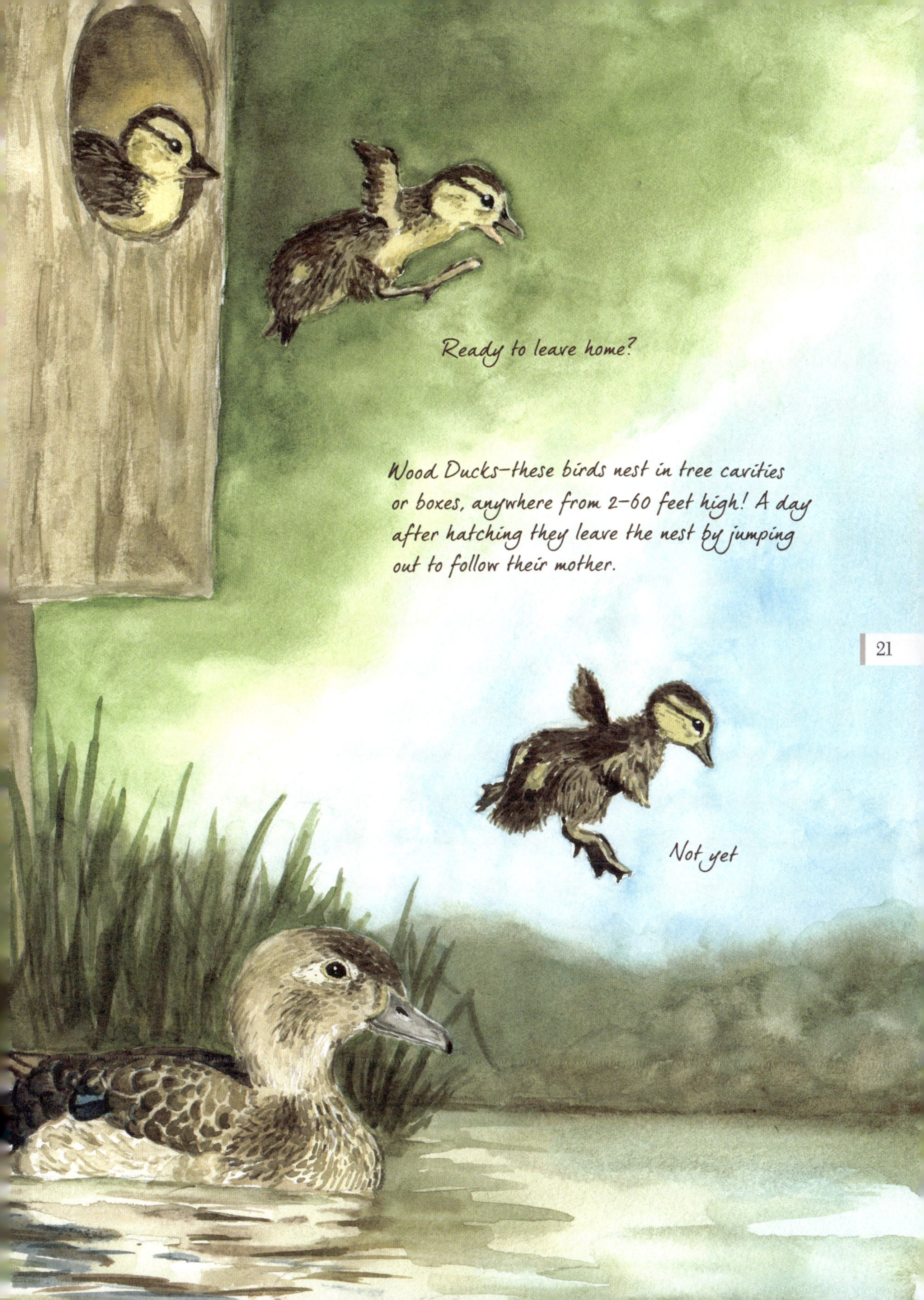
Ready to leave home?
Wood Ducks—these birds nest in tree cavities or boxes, anywhere from 2–60 feet high! A day after hatching they leave the nest by jumping out to follow their mother.
Not yet

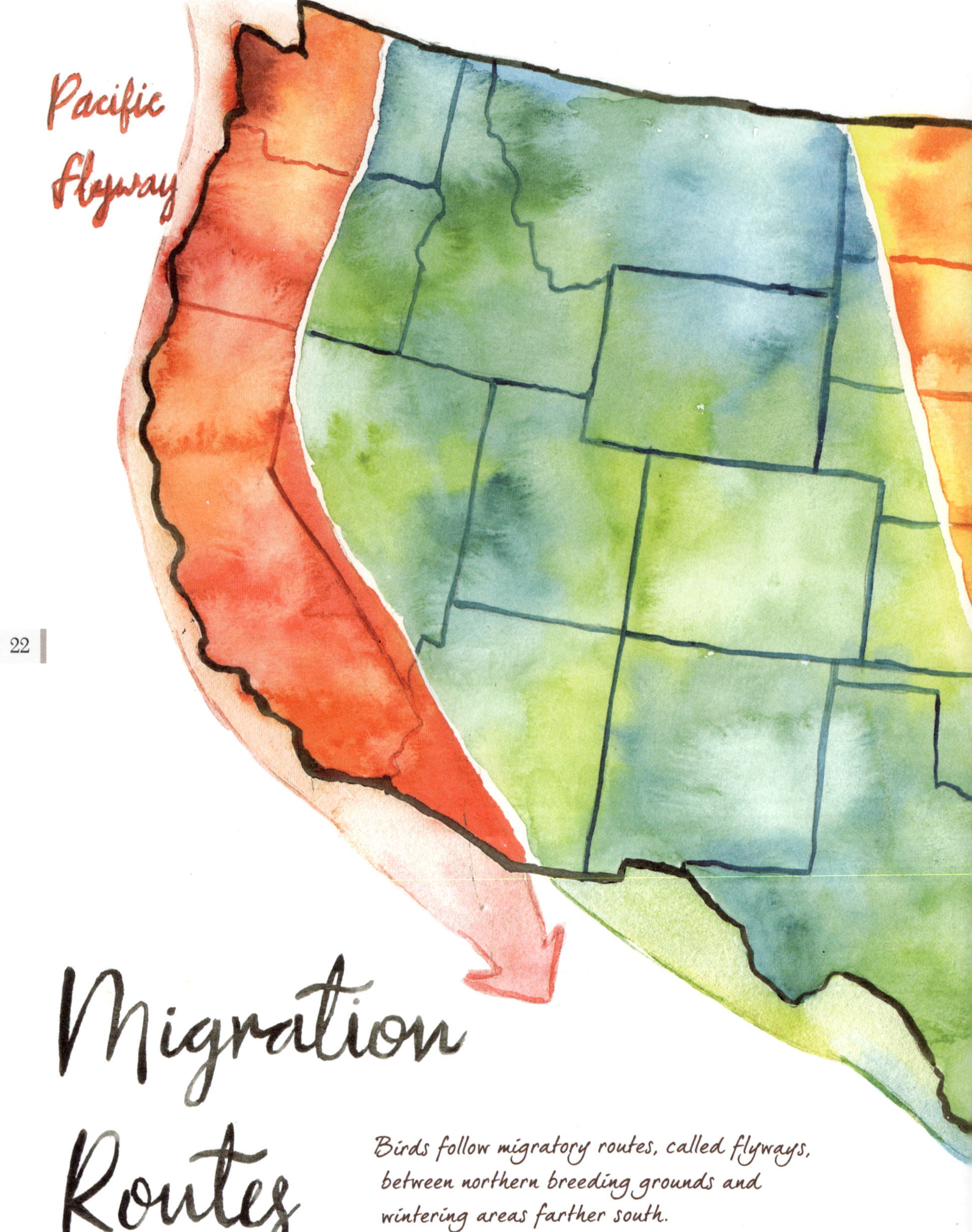

Migration Routes

Birds follow migratory routes, called flyways, between northern breeding grounds and wintering areas farther south.

Flyways are a little like highways in the sky, and their endpoints range greatly, from the Gulf of Mexico and the southern United States to Mexico and into South America. Some birds only migrate far enough as they need to. The Dark-eyed Junco breeds in far northern Canada but winters in Minnesota and other Midwestern states.

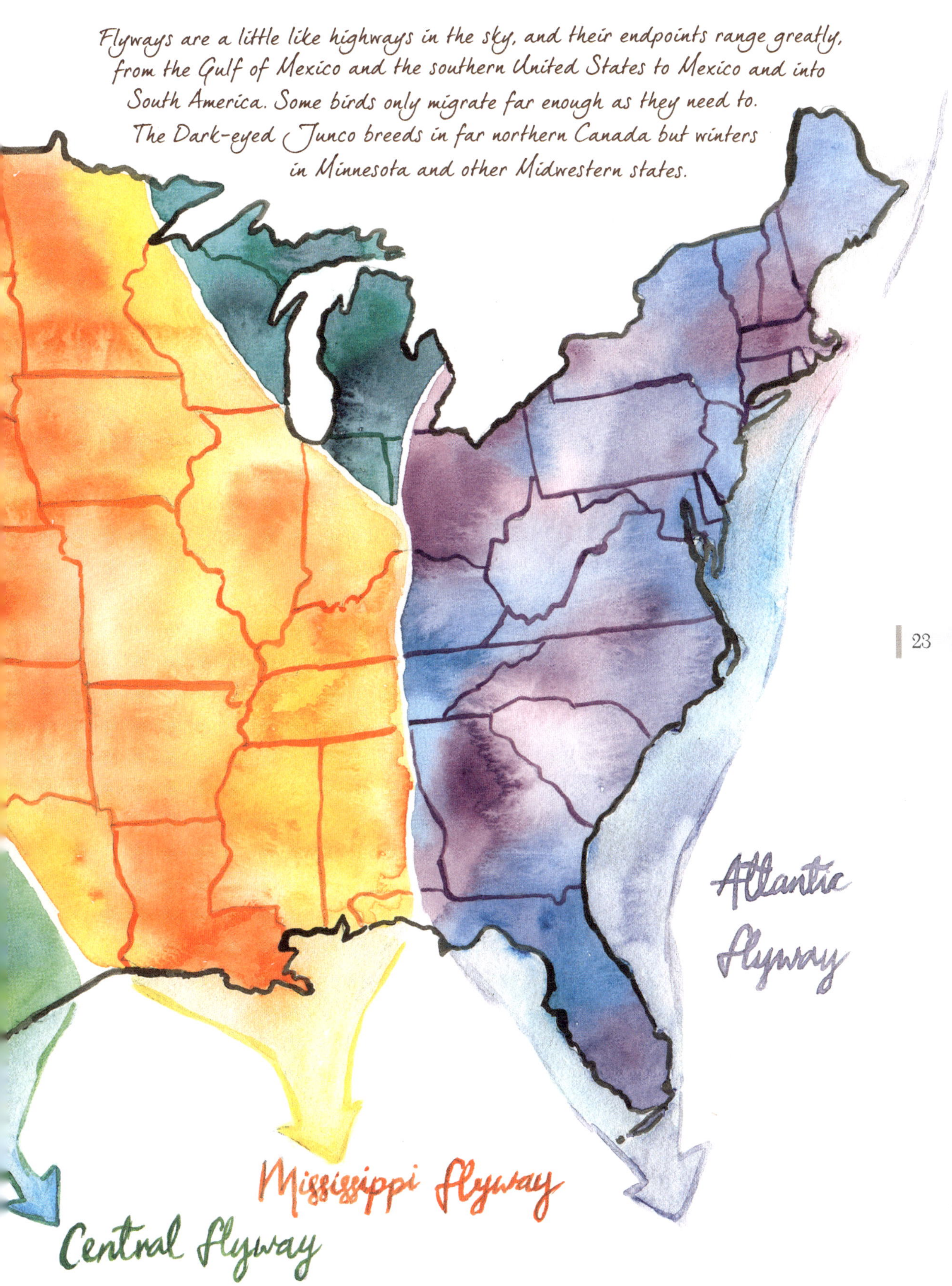

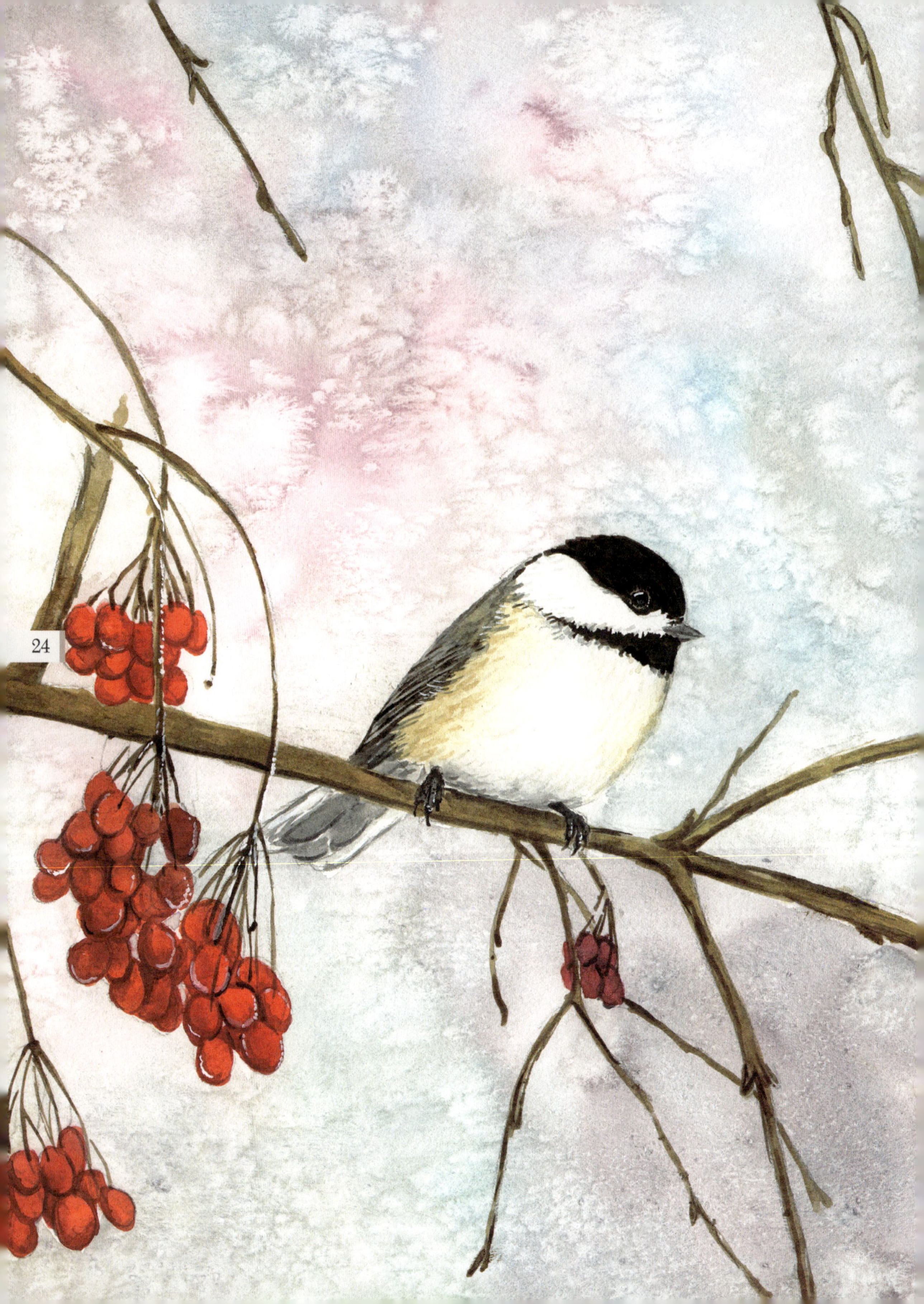

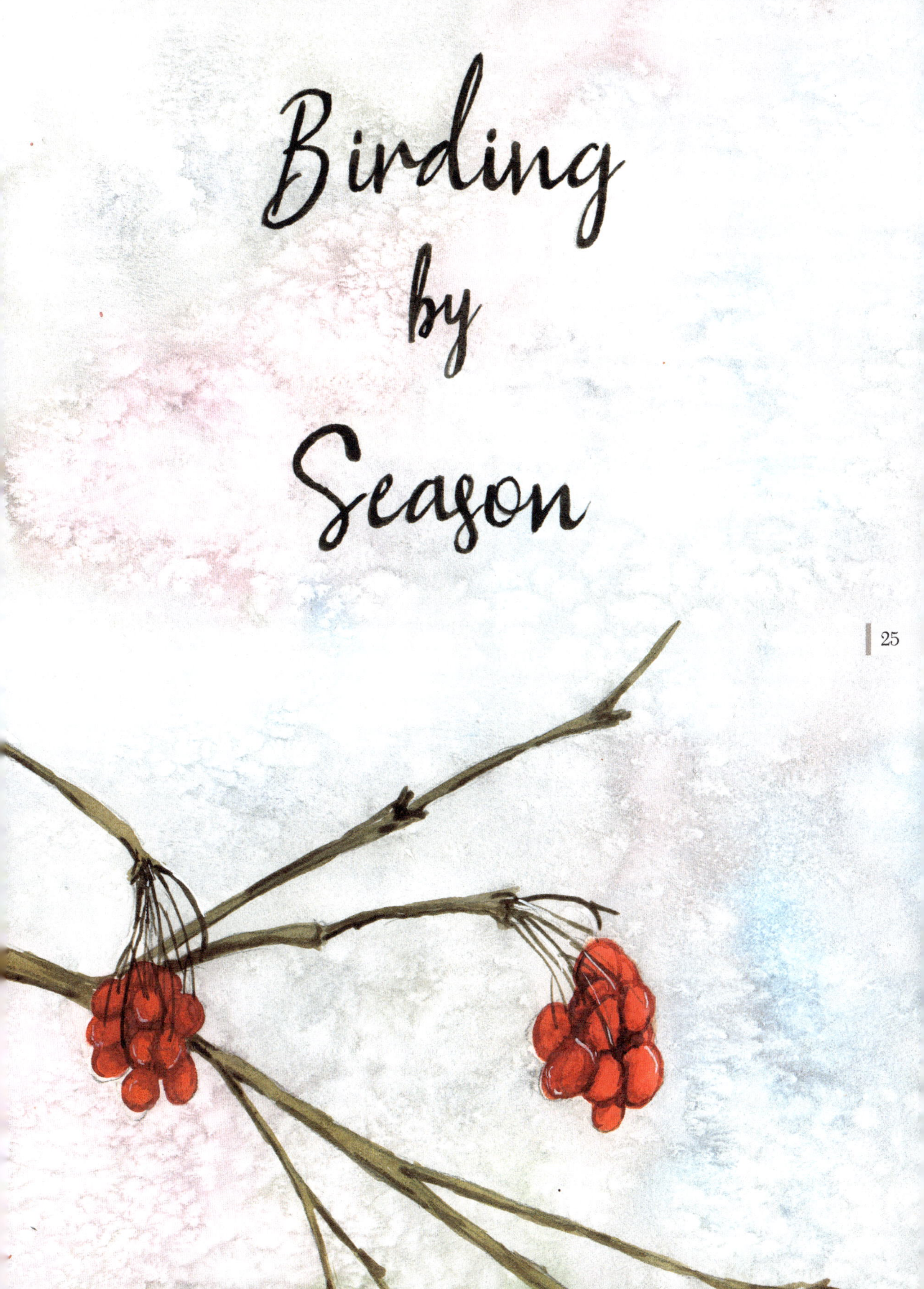
Birding
by
Season

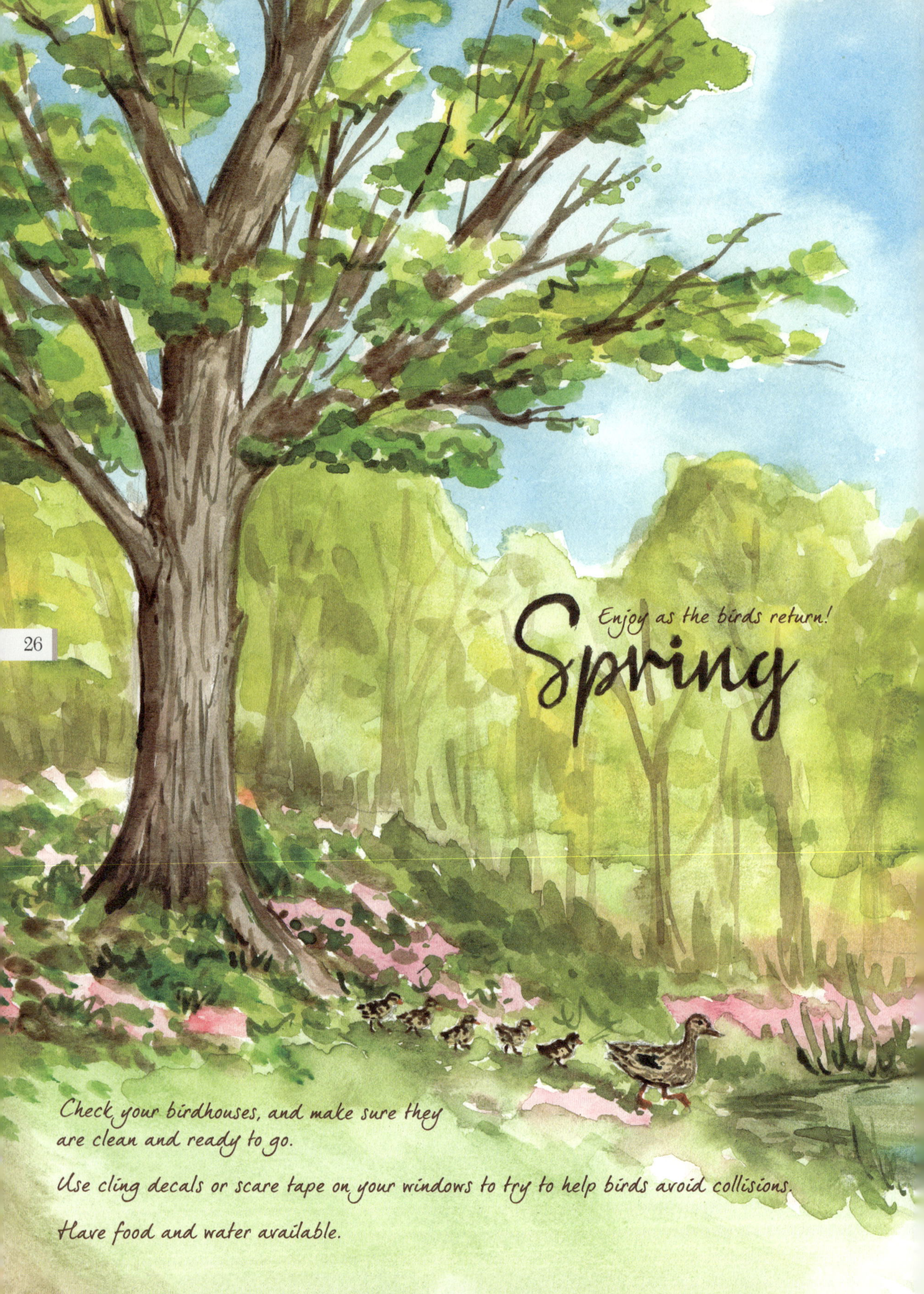

26
Enjoy as the birds return!
Spring
Check your birdhouses, and make sure they are clean and ready to go.
Use cling decals or scare tape on your windows to try to help birds avoid collisions.
Have food and water available.

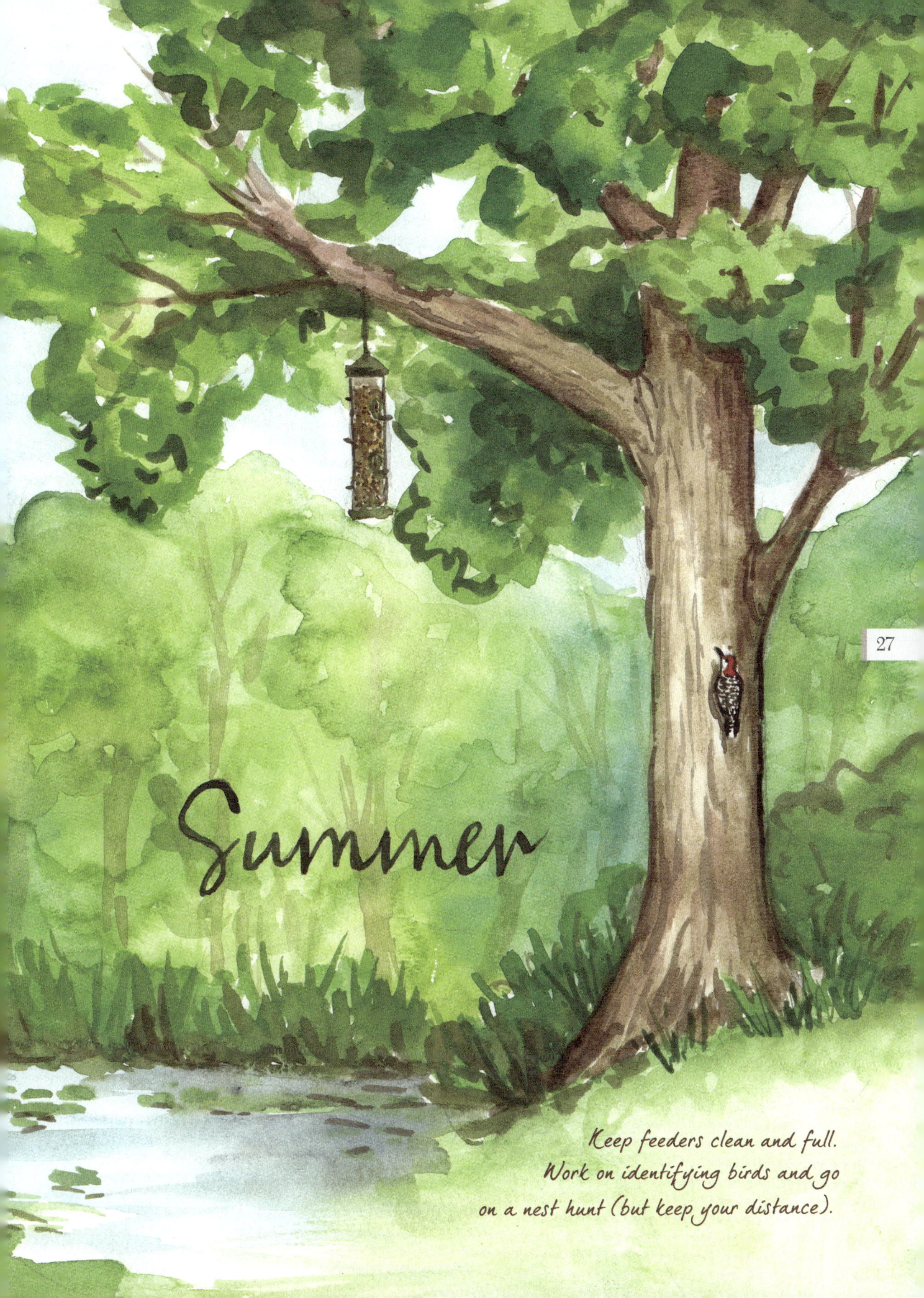
Summer
Keep feeders clean and full.
Work on identifying birds and go
on a nest hunt (but keep your distance).

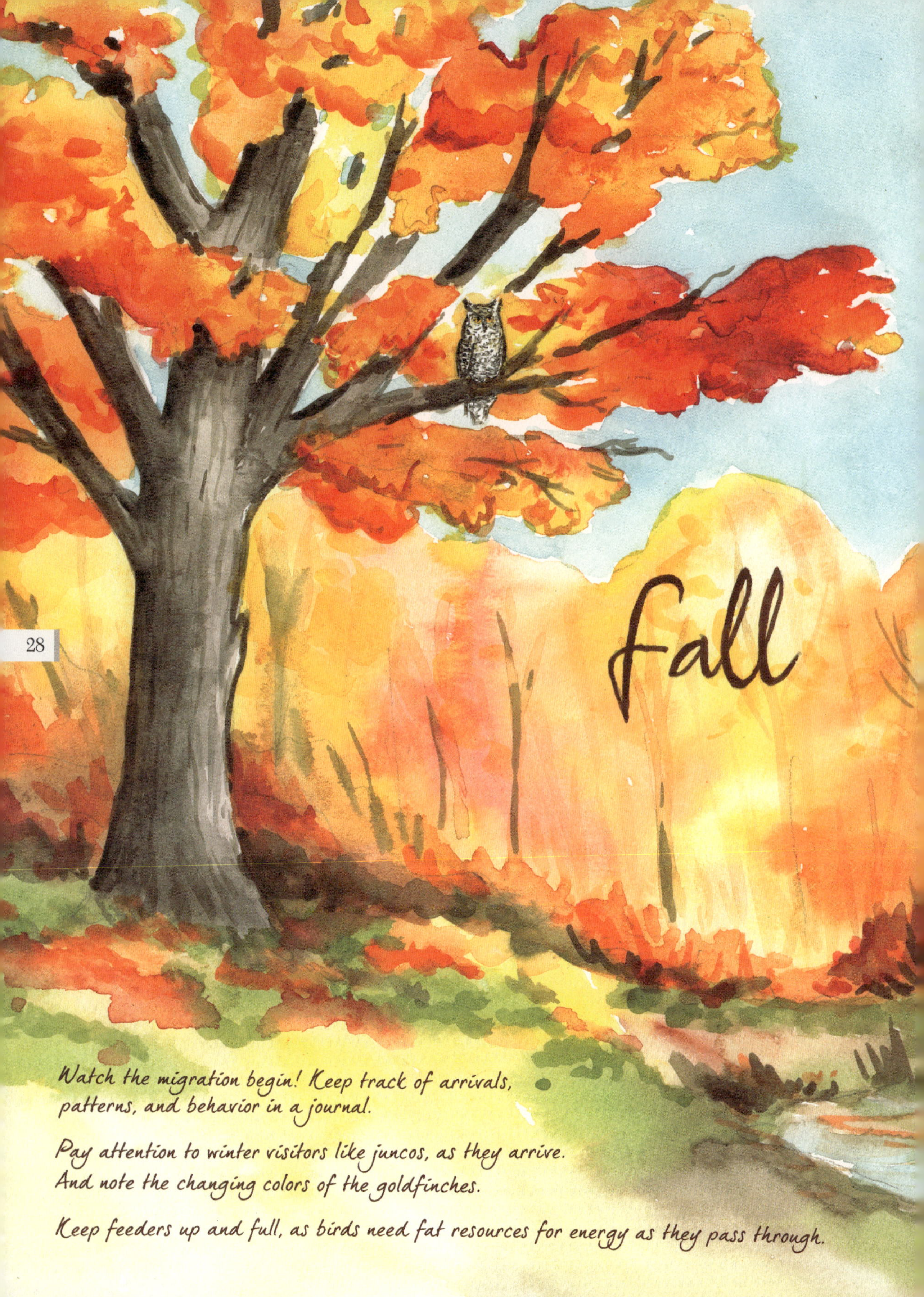

Watch the migration begin! Keep track of arrivals, patterns, and behavior in a journal.

Pay attention to winter visitors like juncos, as they arrive. And note the changing colors of the goldfinches.

Keep feeders up and full, as birds need fat resources for energy as they pass through.

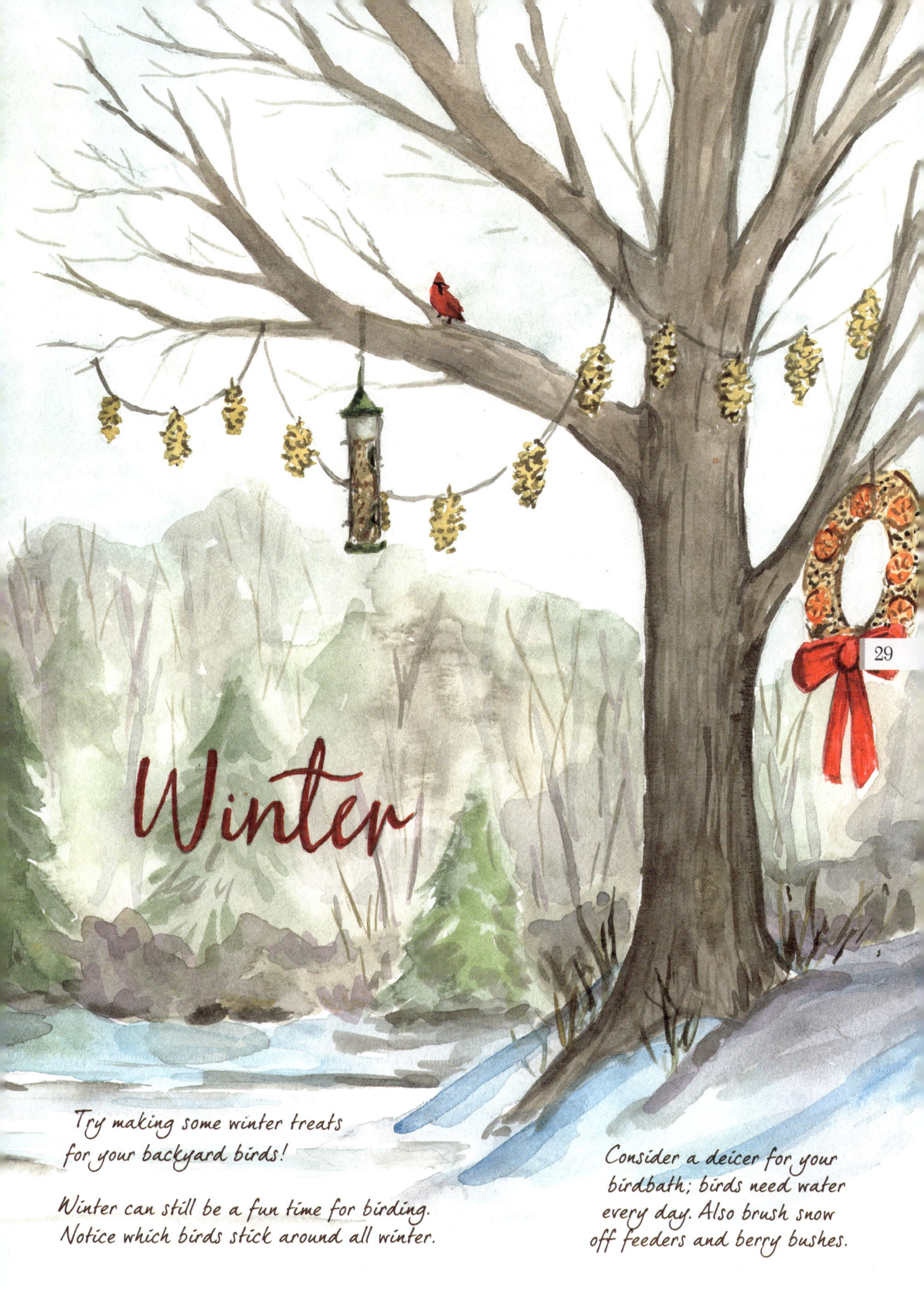
Winter
Try making some winter treats
for your backyard birds!
Winter can still be a fun time for birding.
Notice which birds stick around all winter.
Consider a deicer for your
birdbath; birds need water
every day. Also brush snow
off feeders and berry bushes.

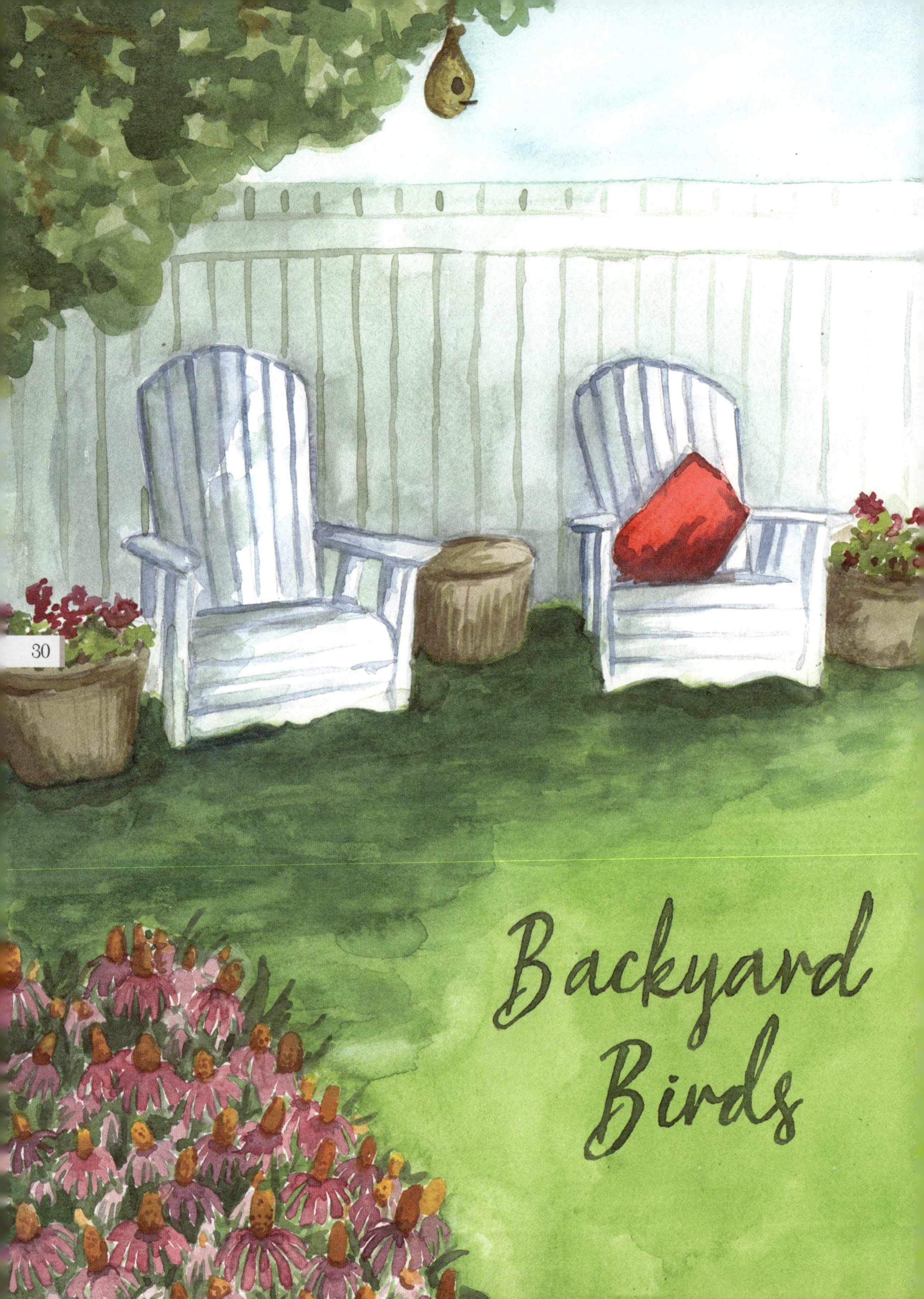
Backyard Birds

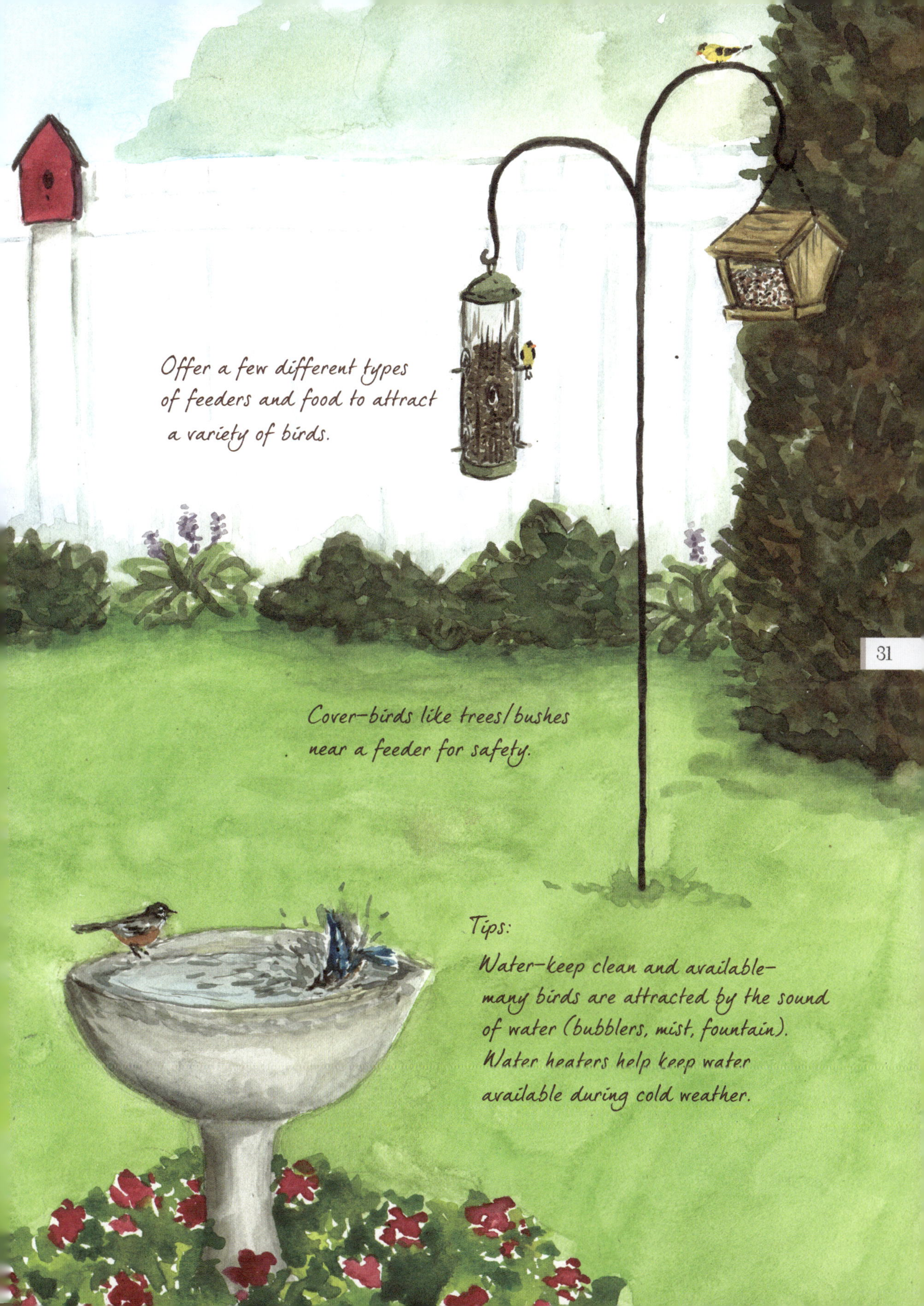
Offer a few different types of feeders and food to attract a variety of birds.
Cover-birds like trees/bushes near a feeder for safety.
Tips:
Water-keep clean and available-many birds are attracted by the sound of water (bubblers, mist, fountain). Water heaters help keep water available during cold weather.

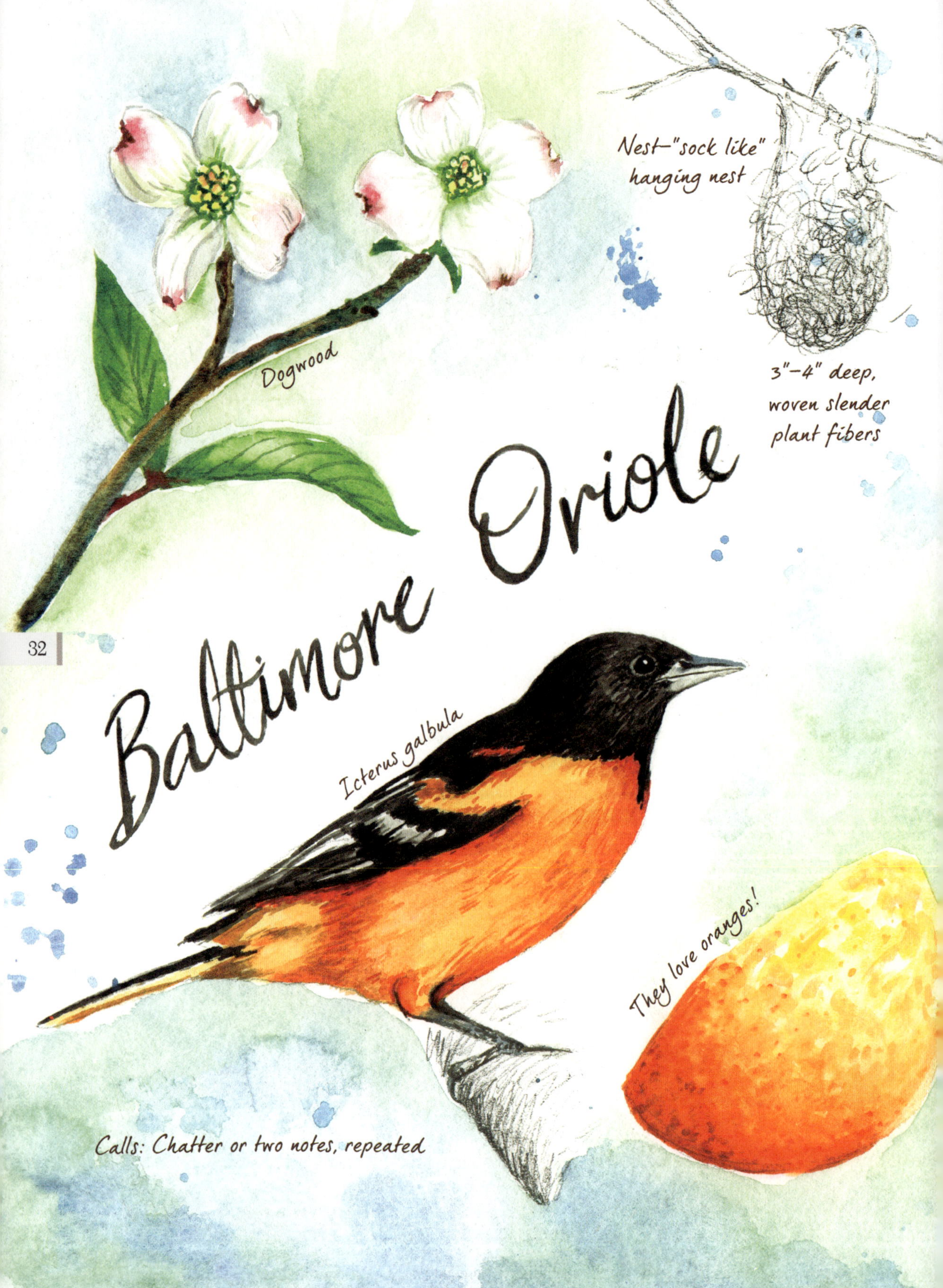
Nest-"sock like" hanging nest
Dogwood
3"–4" deep, woven slender plant fibers
Baltimore Oriole
Icterus galbula
They love oranges!
Calls: Chatter or two notes, repeated

Eastern Bluebird

A backyard favorite! They love open meadows near trees.

If you put up a house, you may get a pair to stay near you.

Great for your garden—they eat a ton of insects and pests. Plus, they are cheerful and charming.

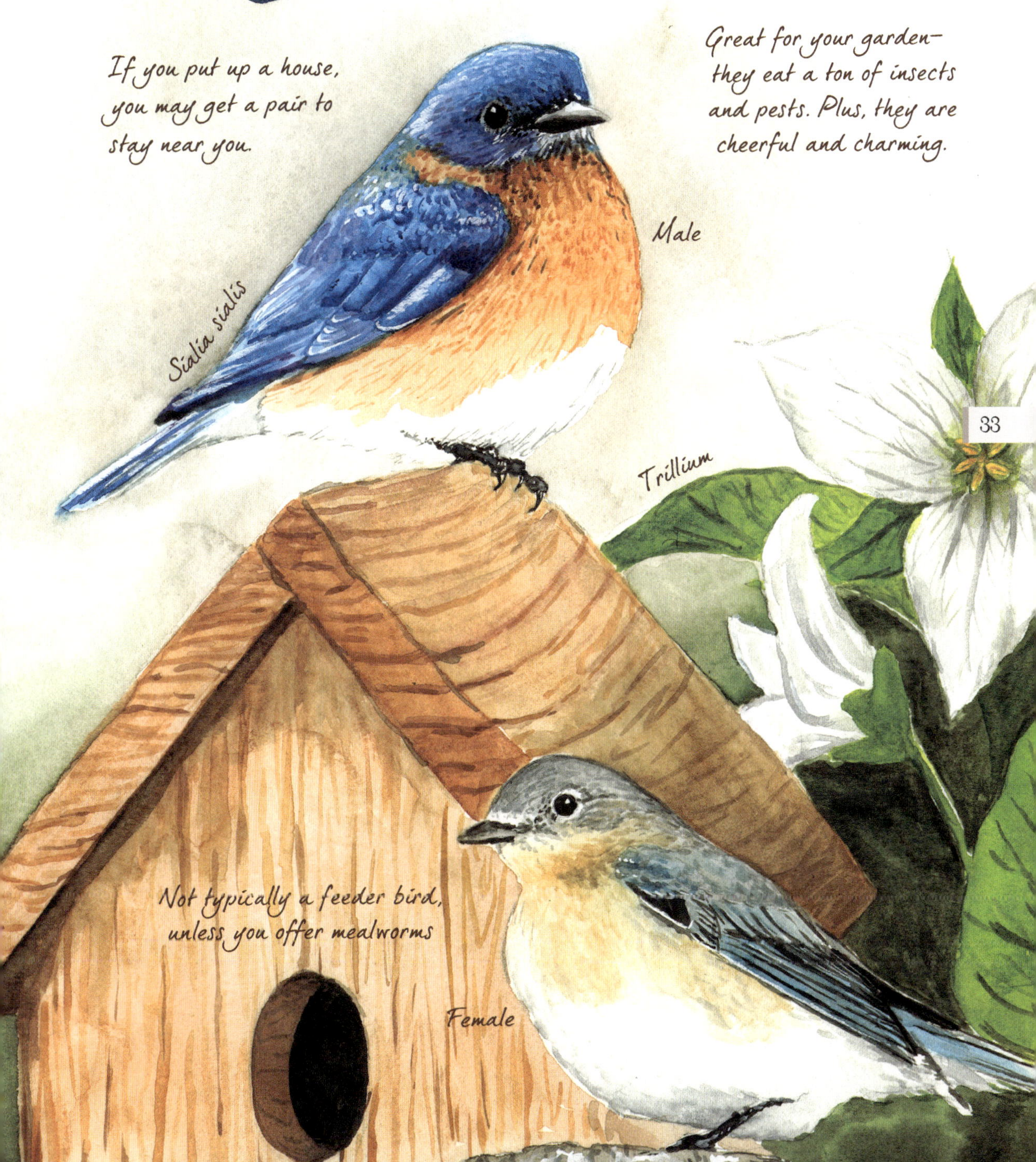

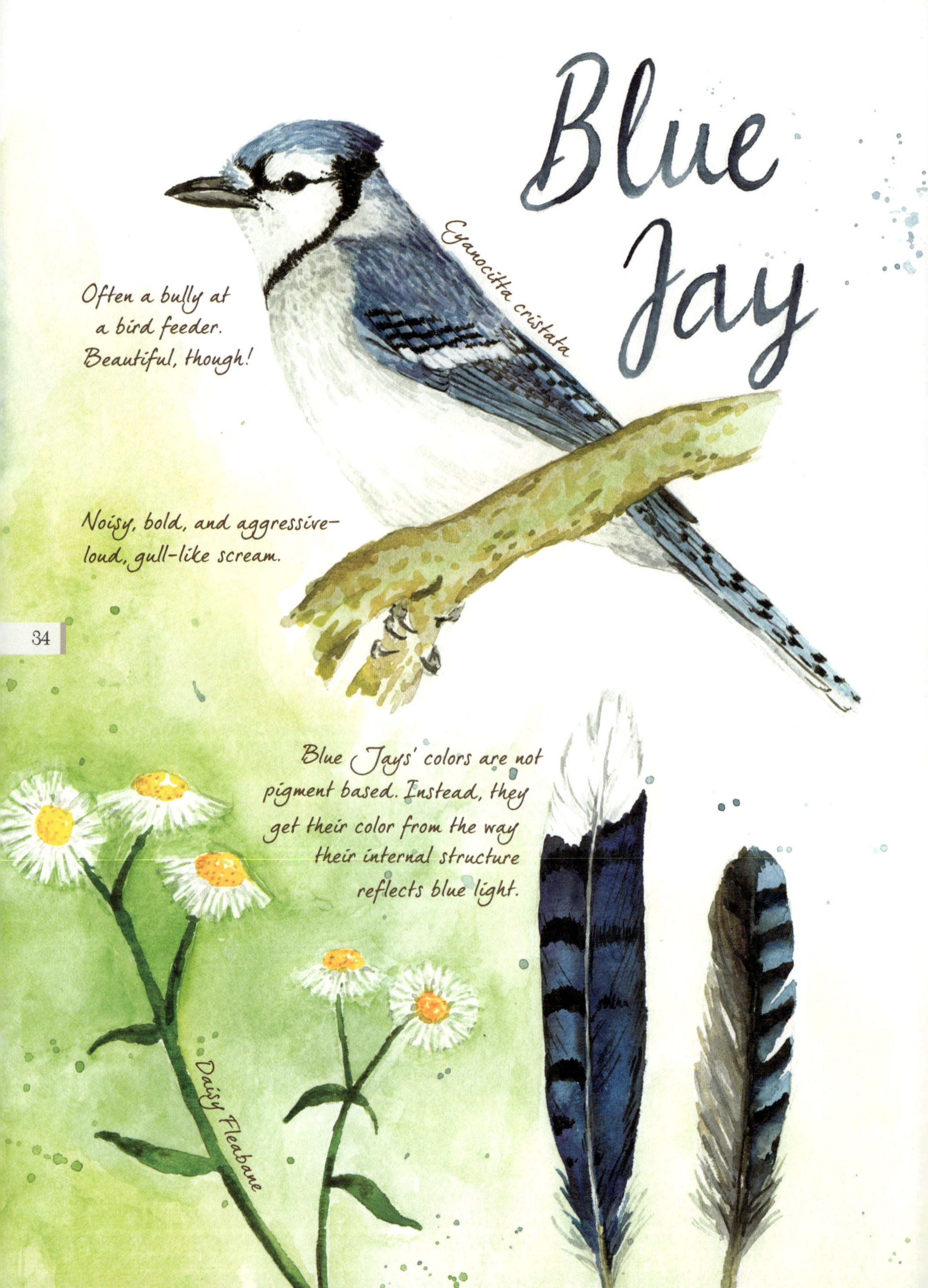
Blue Jay
Cyanocitta cristata
Often a bully at a bird feeder. Beautiful, though!
Noisy, bold, and aggressive-loud, gull-like scream.
Blue Jays' colors are not pigment based. Instead, they get their color from the way their internal structure reflects blue light.
Daisy Fleabane

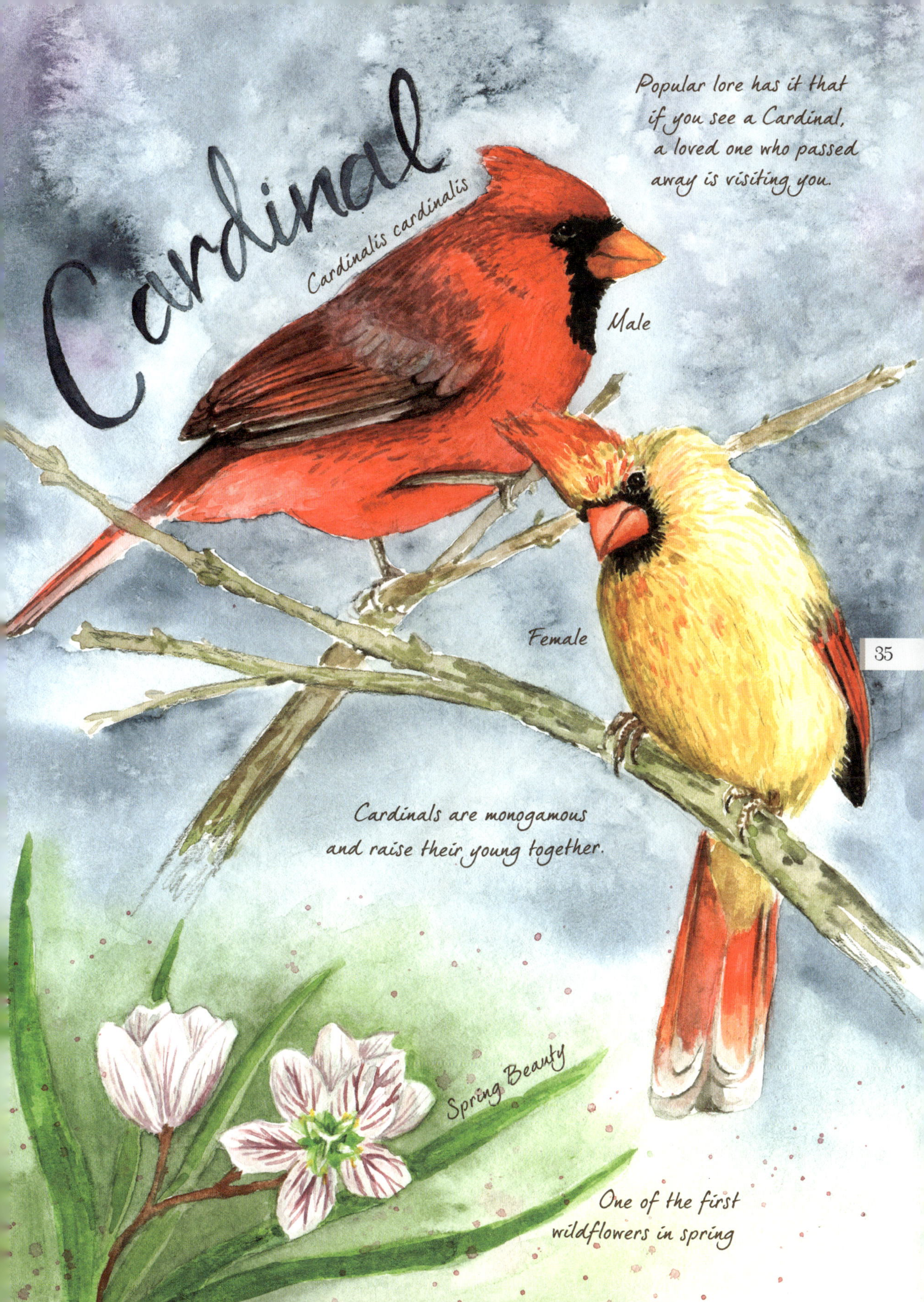
Cardinal
Cardinalis cardinalis
Popular lore has it that if you see a Cardinal, a loved one who passed away is visiting you.
Male
Female
Cardinals are monogamous and raise their young together.
Spring Beauty
One of the first wildflowers in spring

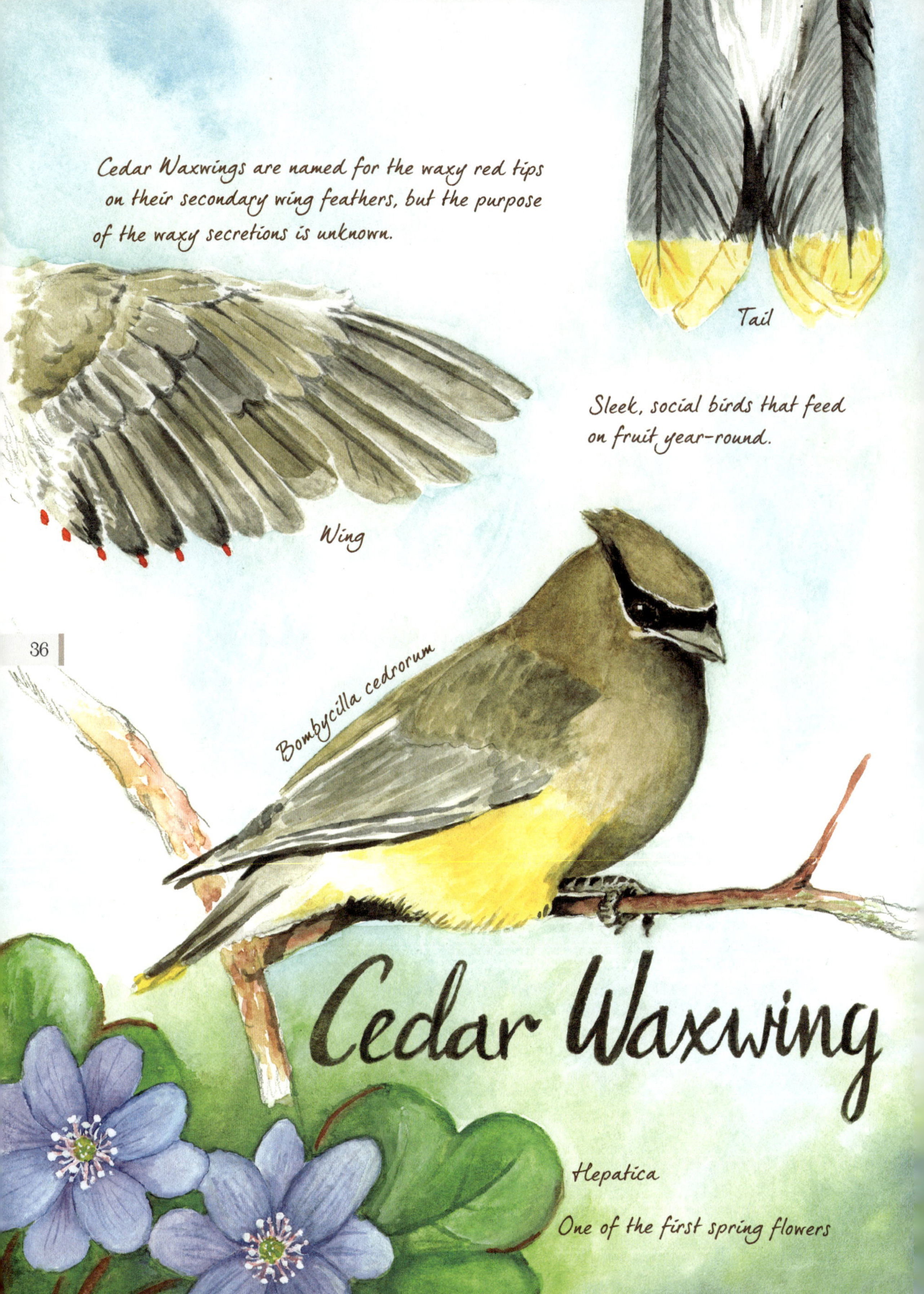

Cedar Waxwings are named for the waxy red tips on their secondary wing feathers, but the purpose of the waxy secretions is unknown.
Tail
Sleek, social birds that feed on fruit year-round.
Wing
Bombycilla cedrorum
Cedar Waxwing
Hepatica
One of the first spring flowers

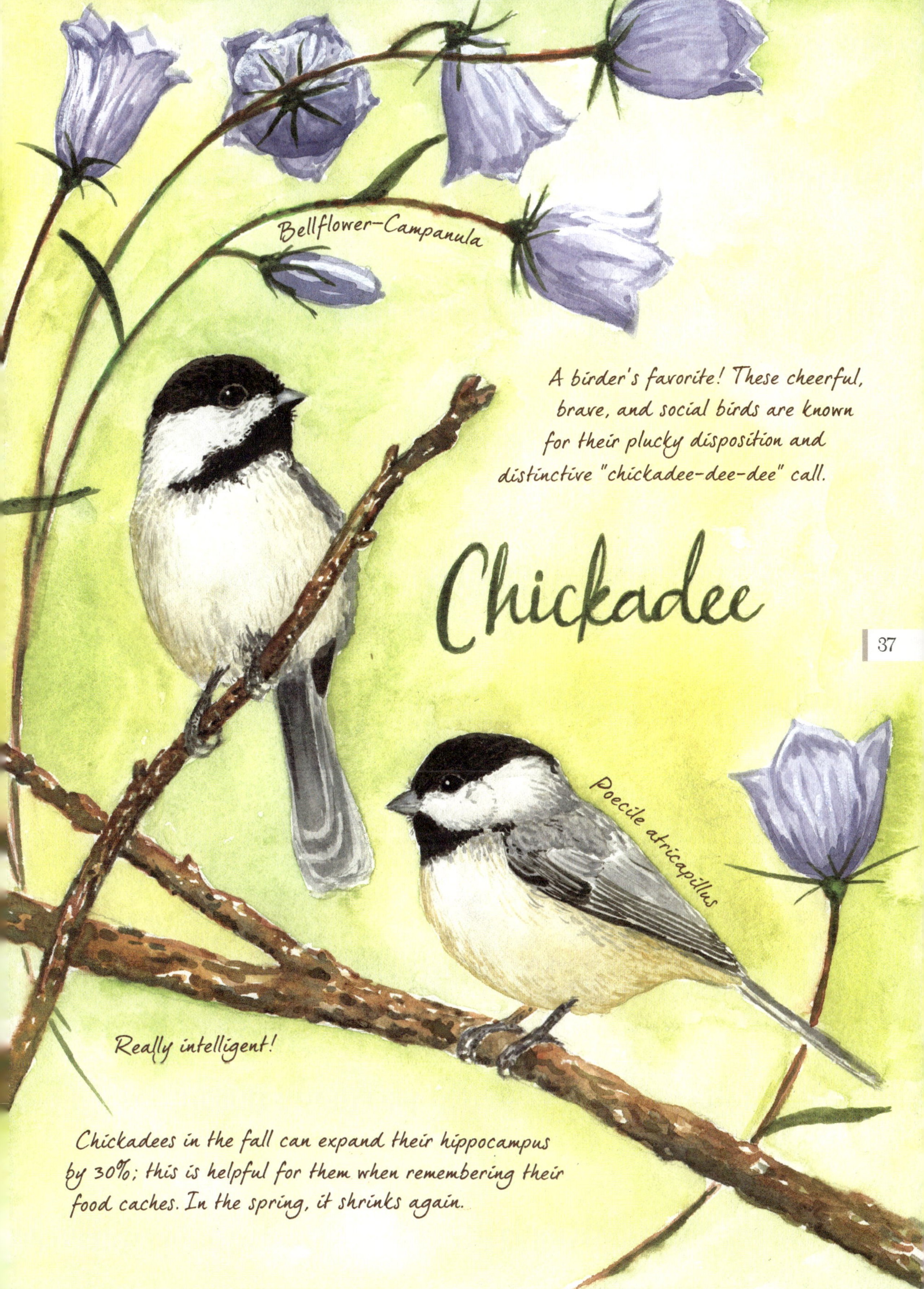
Bellflower–Campanula
A birder's favorite! These cheerful, brave, and social birds are known for their plucky disposition and distinctive "chickadee-dee-dee" call.
Chickadee
Poecile atricapillus
Really intelligent!
Chickadees in the fall can expand their hippocampus by 30%; this is helpful for them when remembering their food caches. In the spring, it shrinks again.

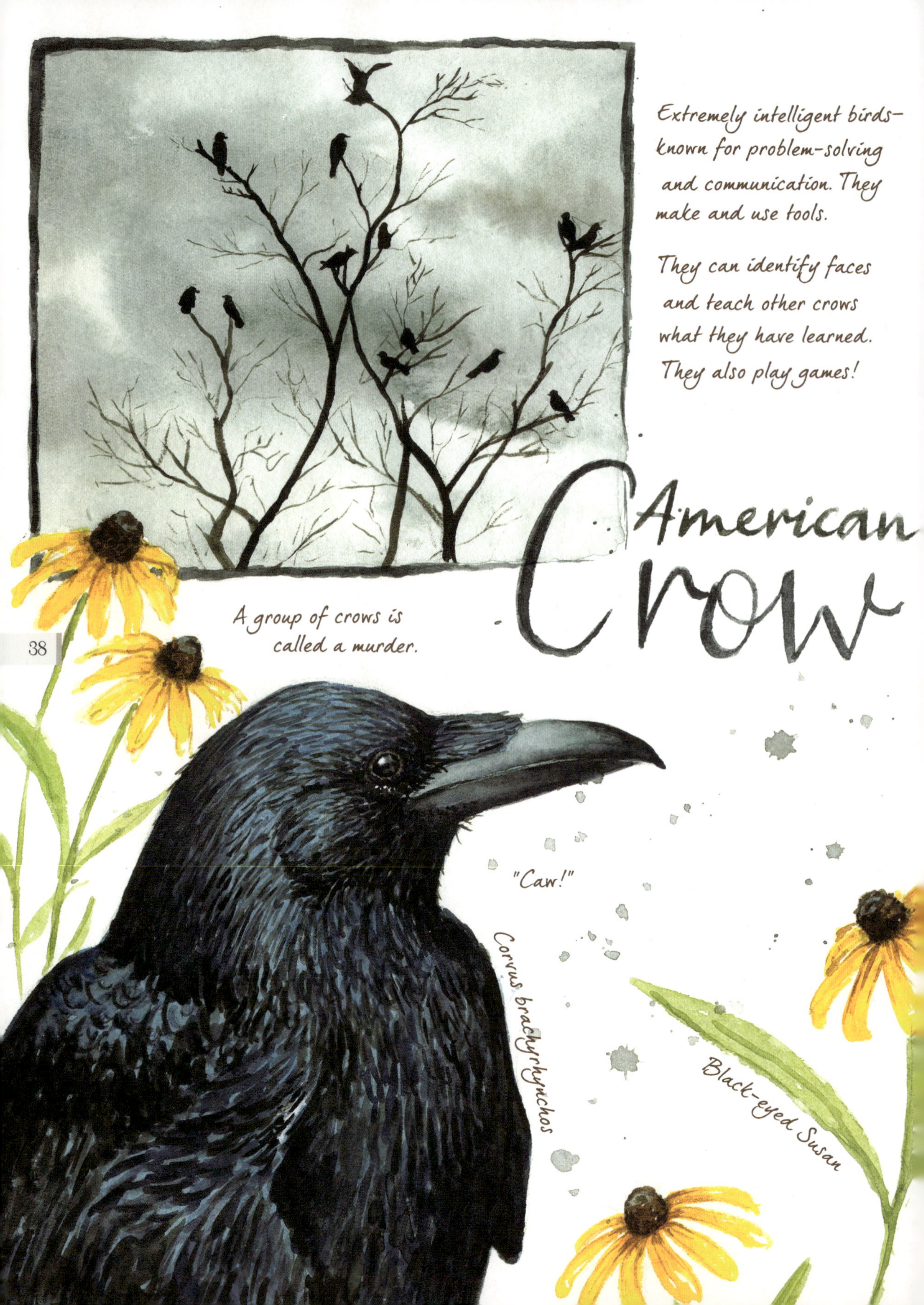
Extremely intelligent birds-known for problem-solving and communication. They make and use tools.
They can identify faces and teach other crows what they have learned. They also play games!
American Crow
A group of crows is called a murder.
"Caw!"
Corvus brachyrhynchos
Black-eyed Susan

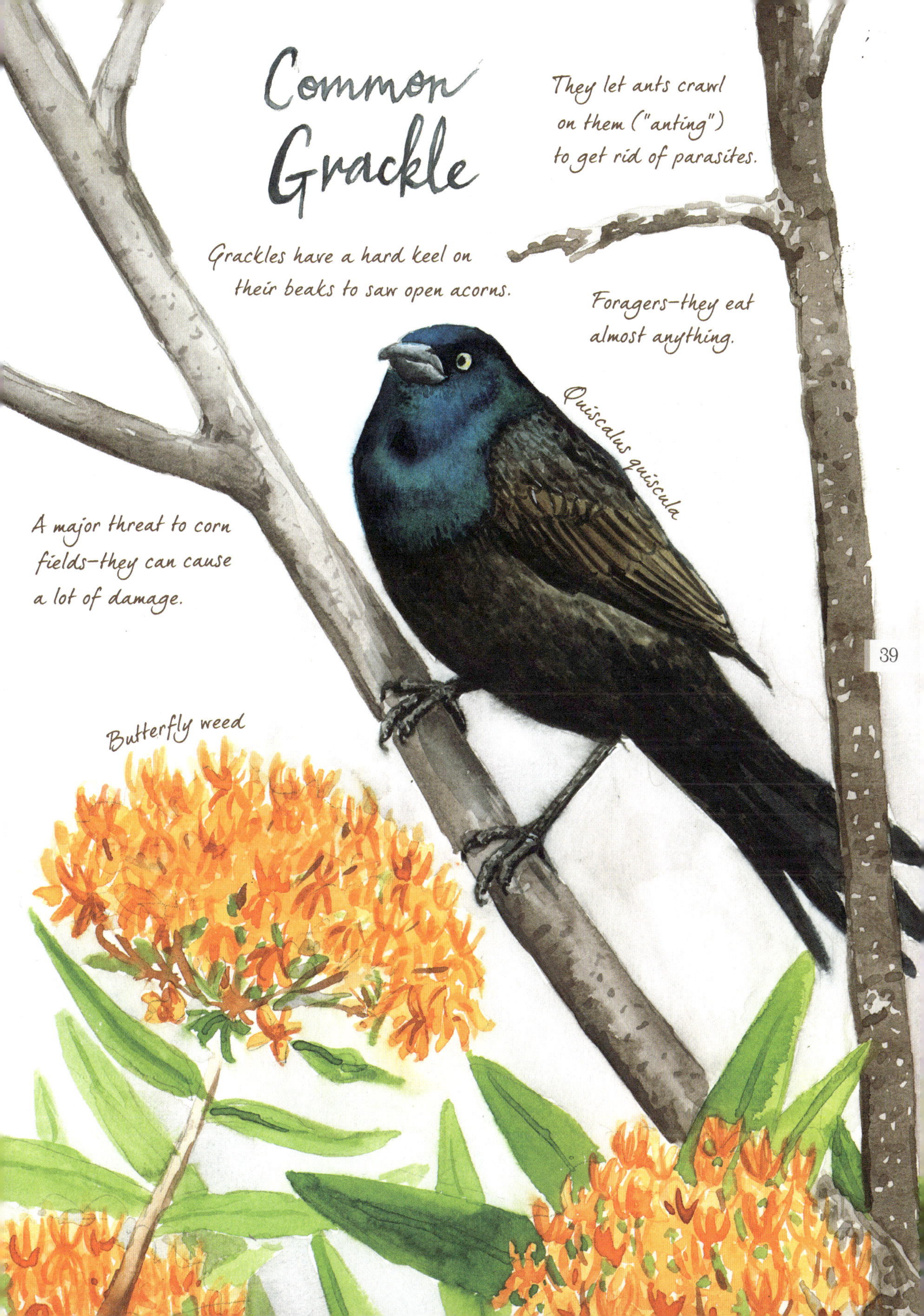
Common Grackle
They let ants crawl on them ("anting") to get rid of parasites.
Grackles have a hard keel on their beaks to saw open acorns.
Foragers–they eat almost anything.
Quiscalus quiscula
A major threat to corn fields–they can cause a lot of damage.
Butterfly weed

Rose-Breasted Grosbeak

Pheucticus ludovicianus

Males sing to establish territory and find a mate, and they are often very territorial.

Breeding pairs are monogamous and share in all the nesting duties.

A beautiful and flashy addition to your bird feeders (they prefer sunflower seeds, safflower, and peanuts).

They construct loose nests in the forks of trees—sometimes so loosely woven you can see the eggs from underneath.

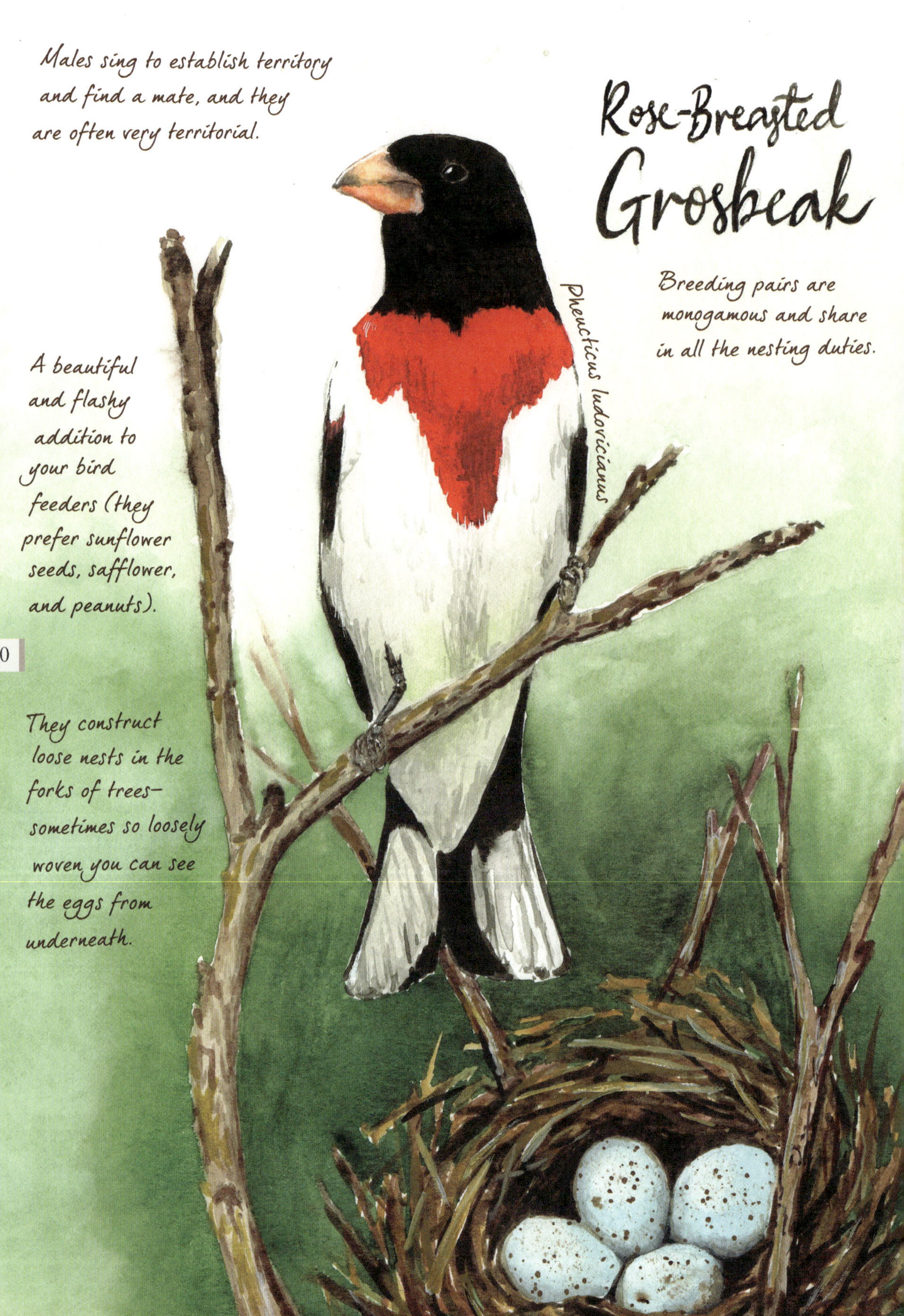

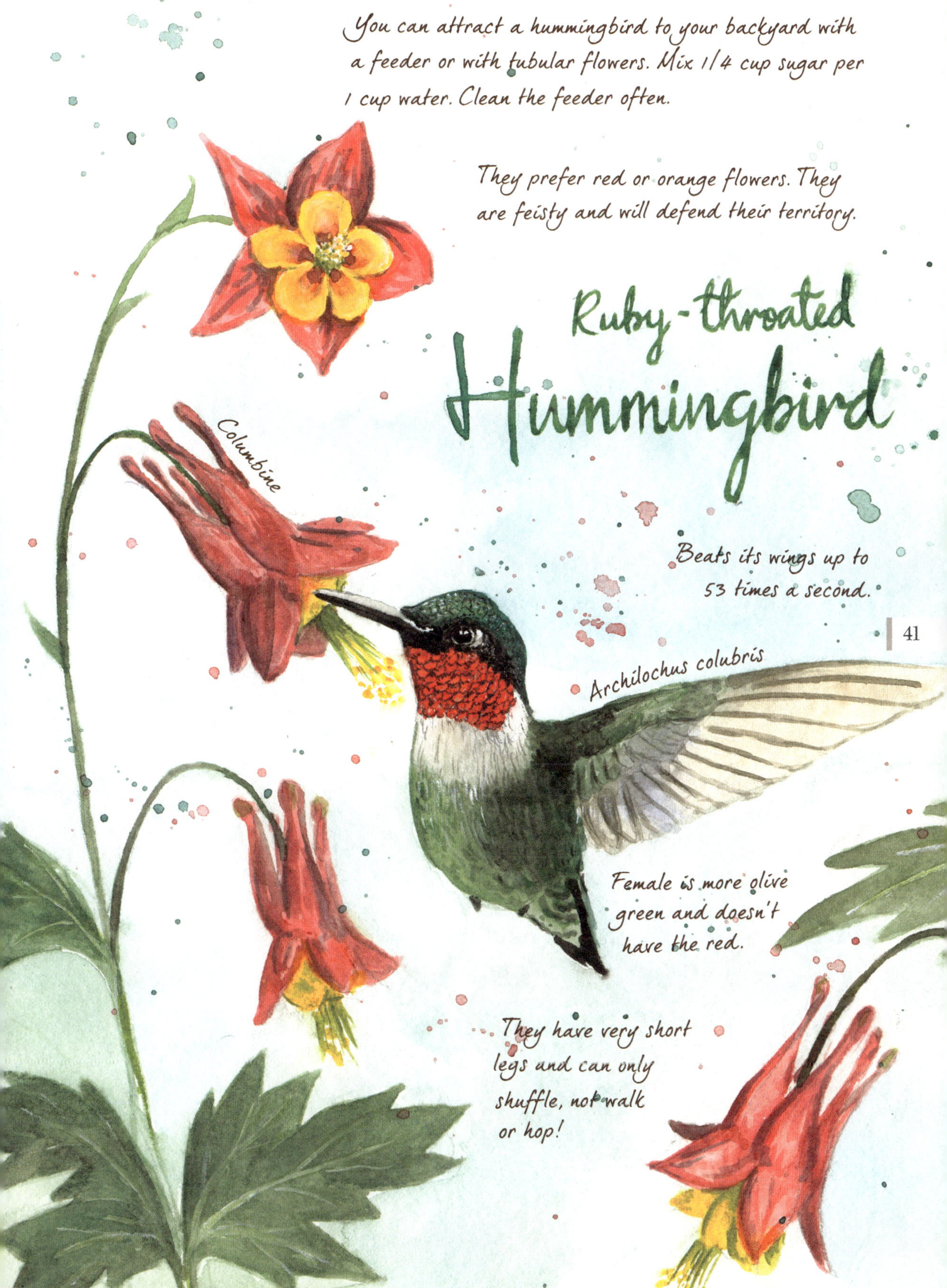
You can attract a hummingbird to your backyard with a feeder or with tubular flowers. Mix 1/4 cup sugar per 1 cup water. Clean the feeder often.
They prefer red or orange flowers. They are feisty and will defend their territory.
Ruby-throated Hummingbird
Columbine
Beats its wings up to 53 times a second.
Archilochus colubris
Female is more olive green and doesn't have the red.
They have very short legs and can only shuffle, not walk or hop!

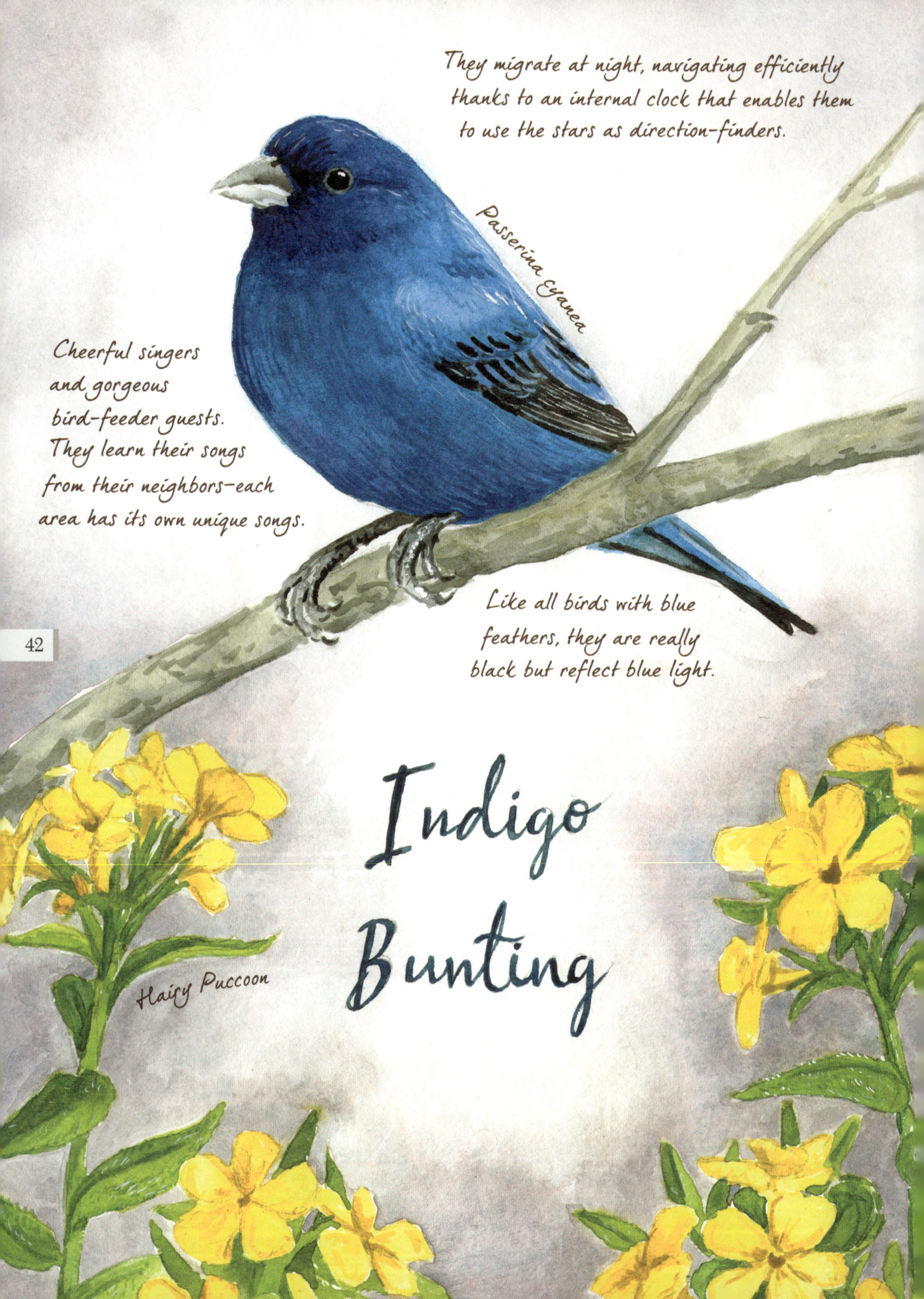
They migrate at night, navigating efficiently thanks to an internal clock that enables them to use the stars as direction-finders.
Passerina cyanea
Cheerful singers and gorgeous bird-feeder guests. They learn their songs from their neighbors—each area has its own unique songs.
Like all birds with blue feathers, they are really black but reflect blue light.
Indigo Bunting
Hairy Puccoon

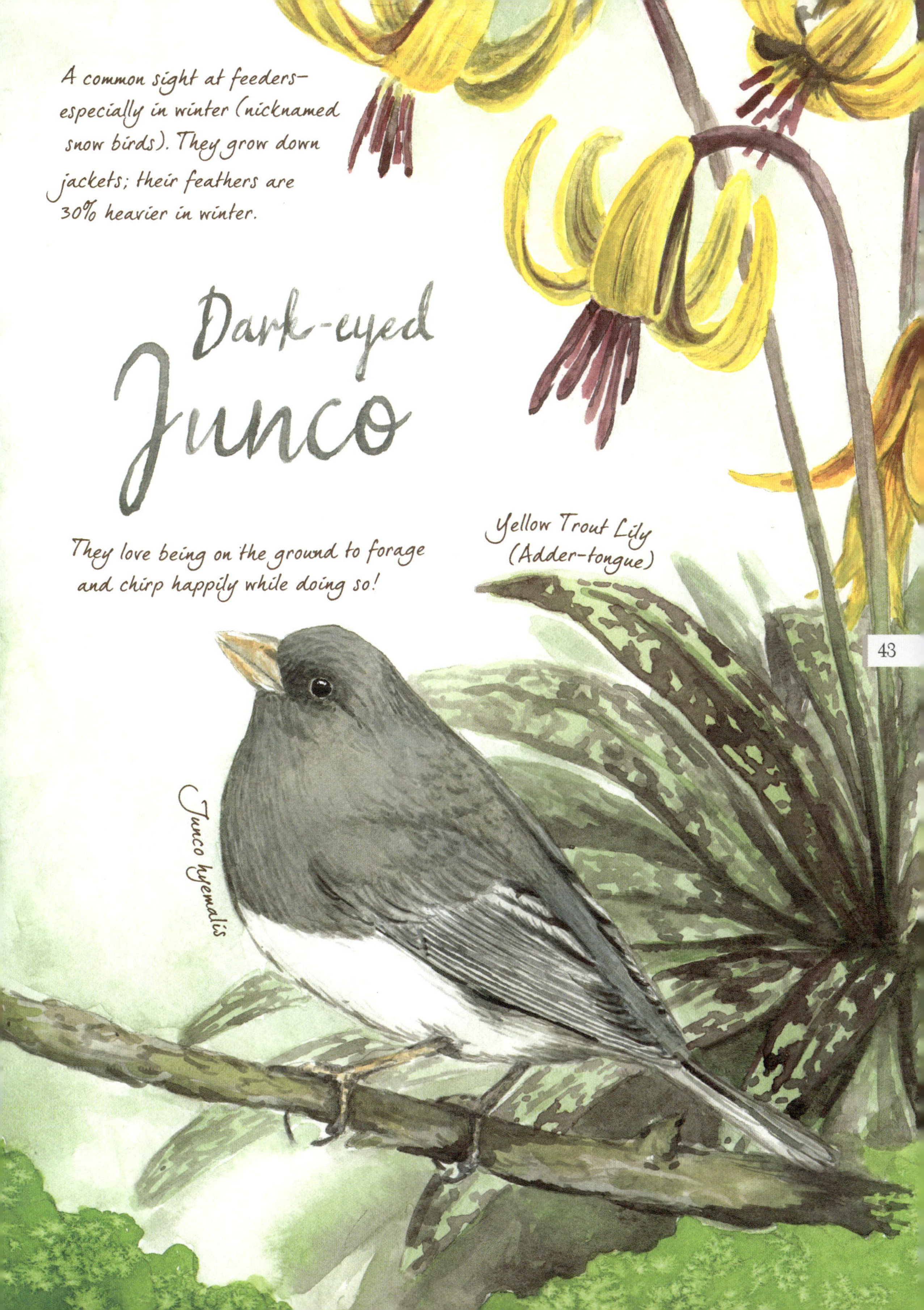
A common sight at feeders—
especially in winter (nicknamed
snow birds). They grow down
jackets; their feathers are
30% heavier in winter.
Dark-eyed
Junco
Yellow Trout Lily
(Adder-tongue)
They love being on the ground to forage
and chirp happily while doing so!
Junco hyemalis

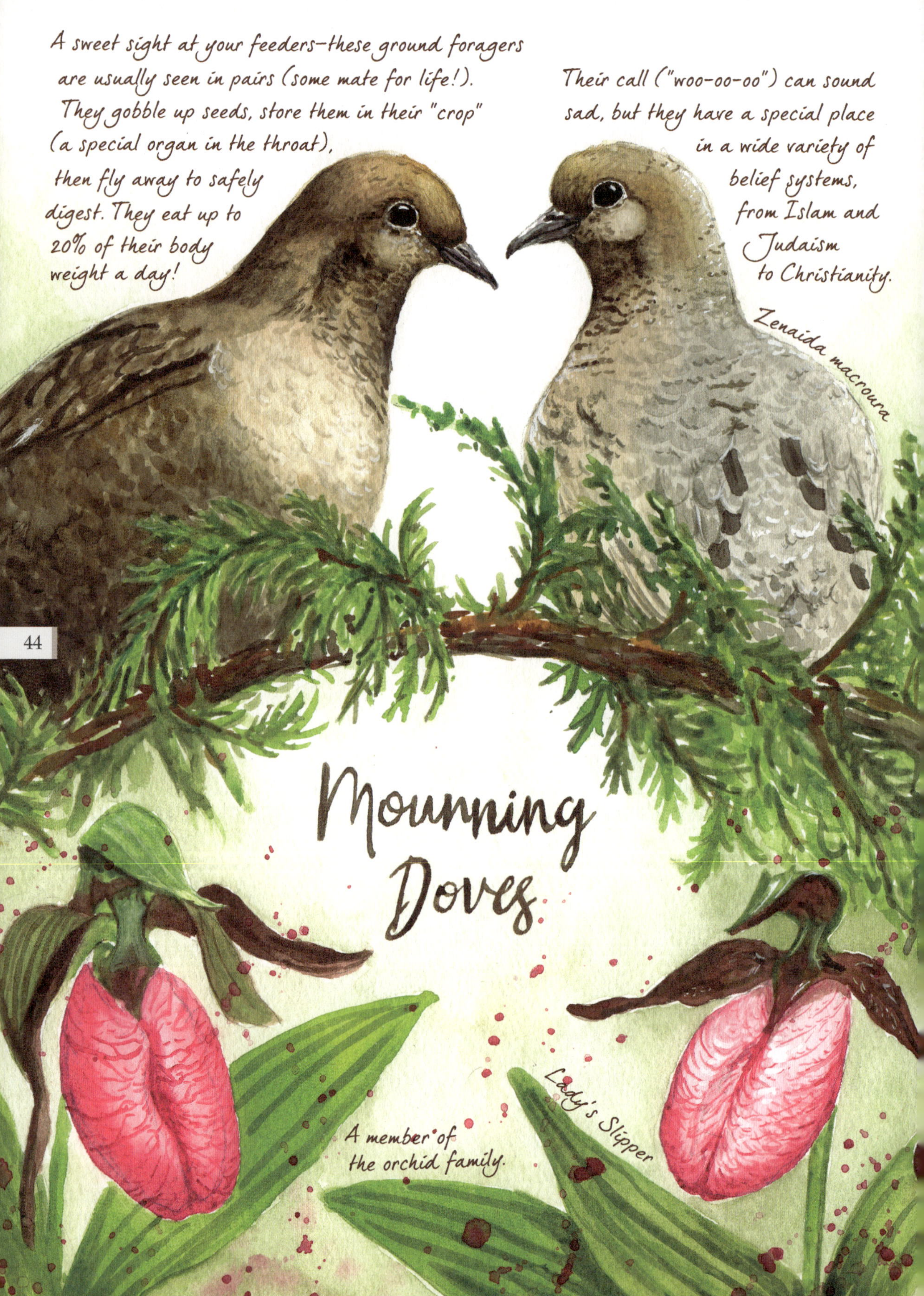
A sweet sight at your feeders—these ground foragers are usually seen in pairs (some mate for life!). They gobble up seeds, store them in their "crop" (a special organ in the throat), then fly away to safely digest. They eat up to 20% of their body weight a day!
Their call ("woo-oo-oo") can sound sad, but they have a special place in a wide variety of belief systems, from Islam and Judaism to Christianity.
Zenaida macroura
Mourning Doves
Lady's Slipper
A member of the orchid family.

Sparrows

Passerellidae

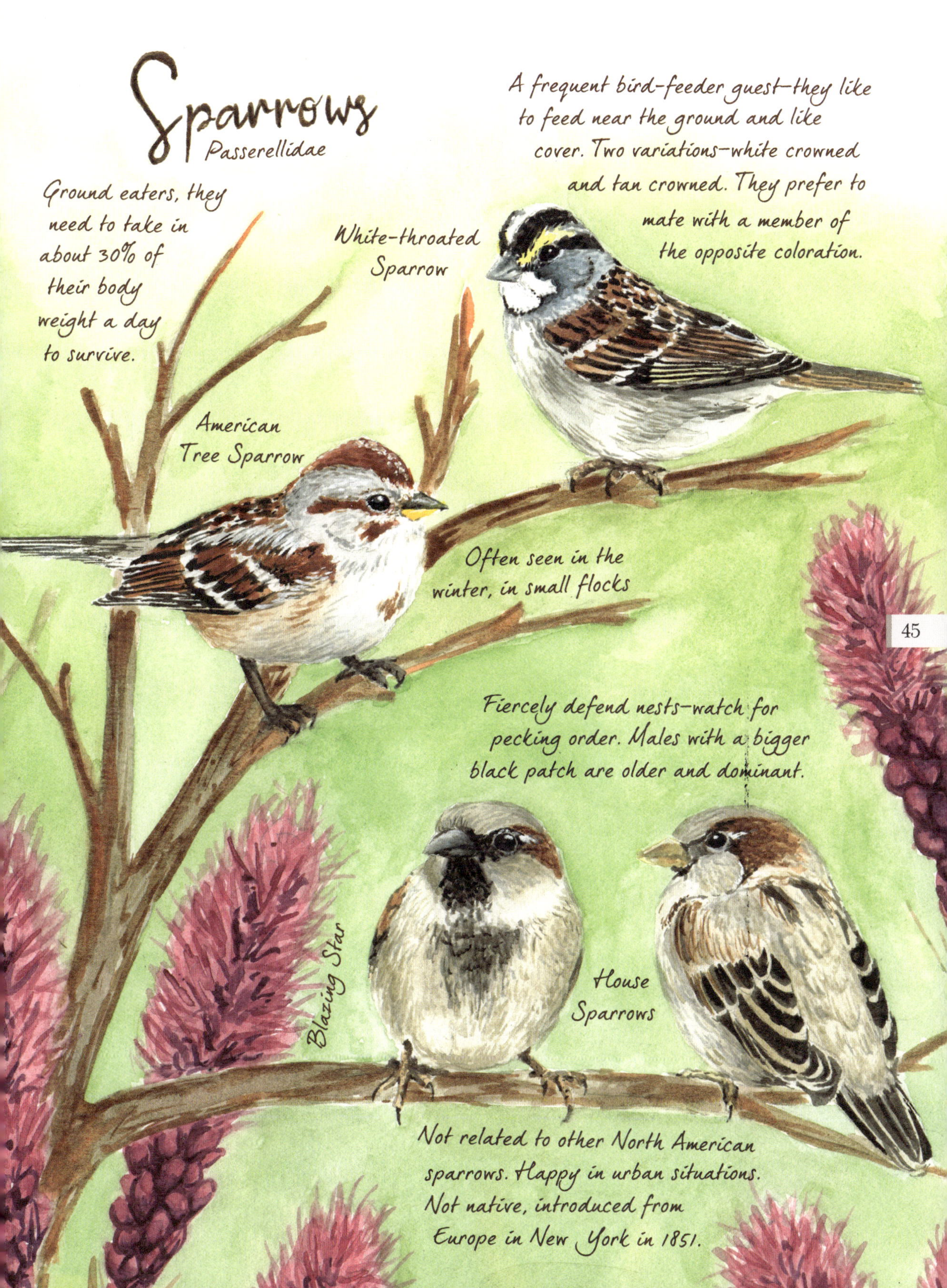

Finches

Fringillidae (the Finch family)

They love black-oil sunflower seeds.

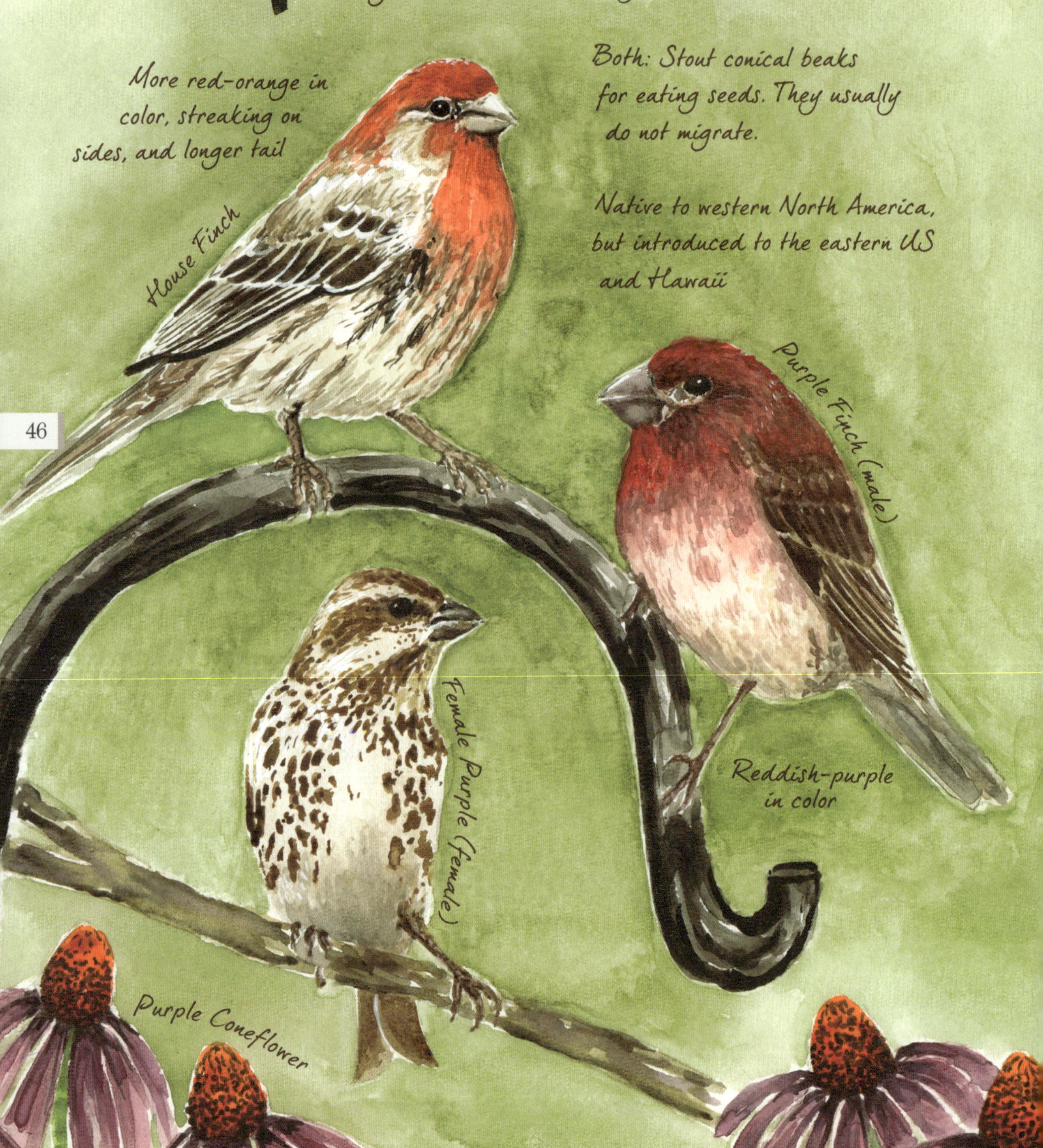

46

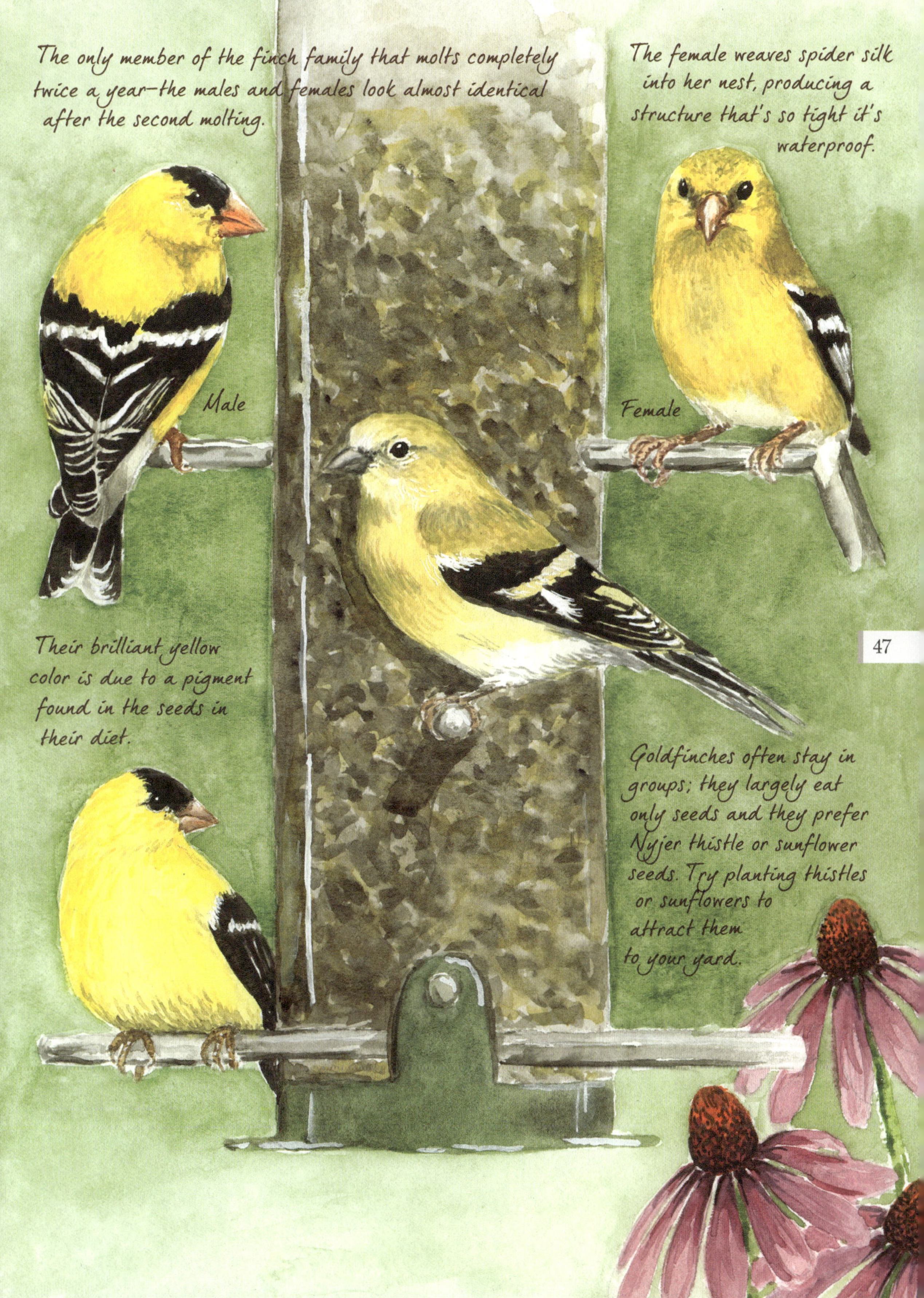

The only member of the finch family that molts completely twice a year—the males and females look almost identical after the second molting.
The female weaves spider silk into her nest, producing a structure that's so tight it's waterproof.
Male
Female
Their brilliant yellow color is due to a pigment found in the seeds in their diet.
Goldfinches often stay in groups; they largely eat only seeds and they prefer Nyjer thistle or sunflower seeds. Try planting thistles or sunflowers to attract them to your yard.

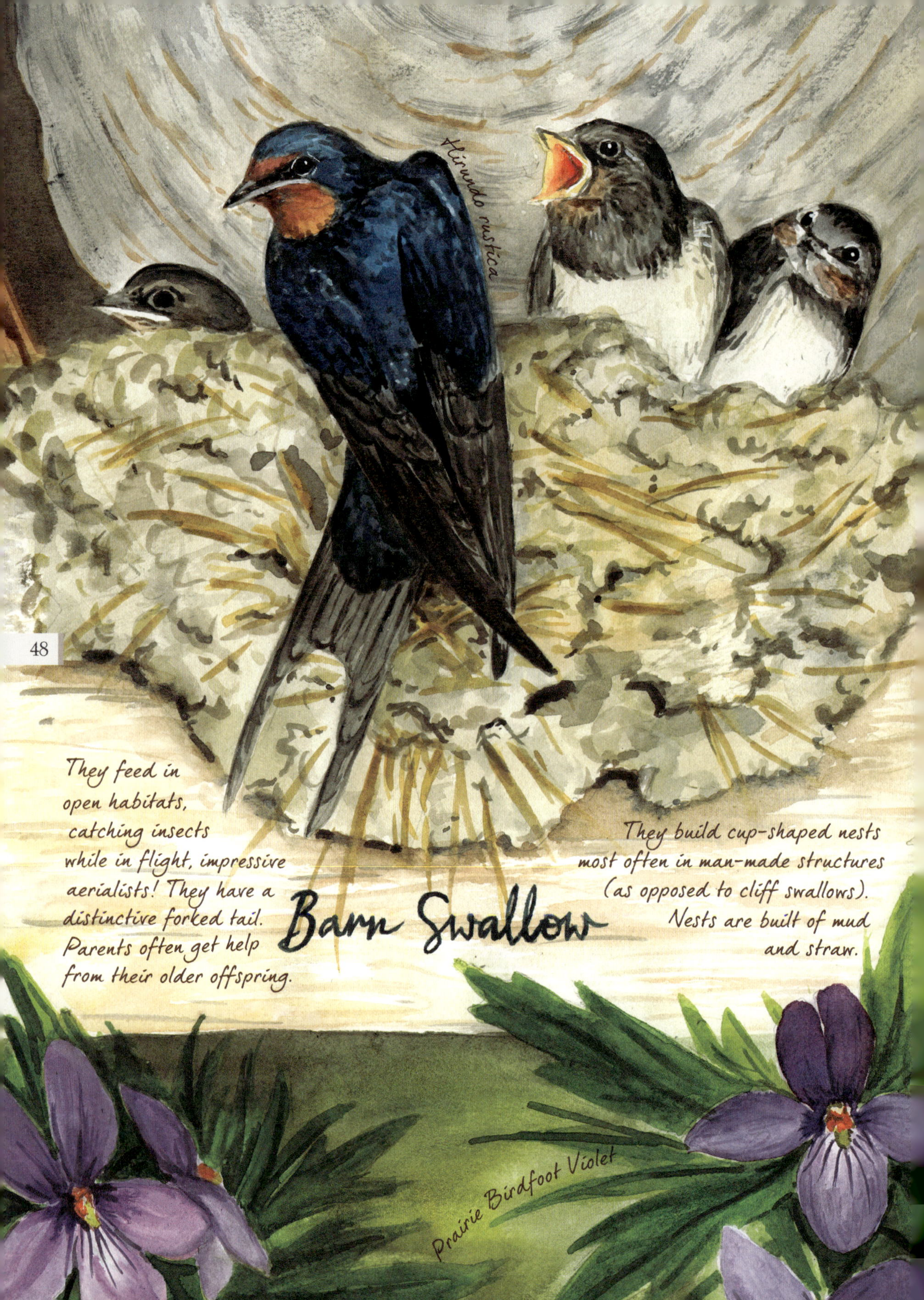
Hirundo rustica
They feed in open habitats, catching insects while in flight, impressive aerialists! They have a distinctive forked tail. Parents often get help from their older offspring.
Barn Swallow
They build cup-shaped nests most often in man-made structures (as opposed to cliff swallows). Nests are built of mud and straw.
Prairie Birdfoot Violet

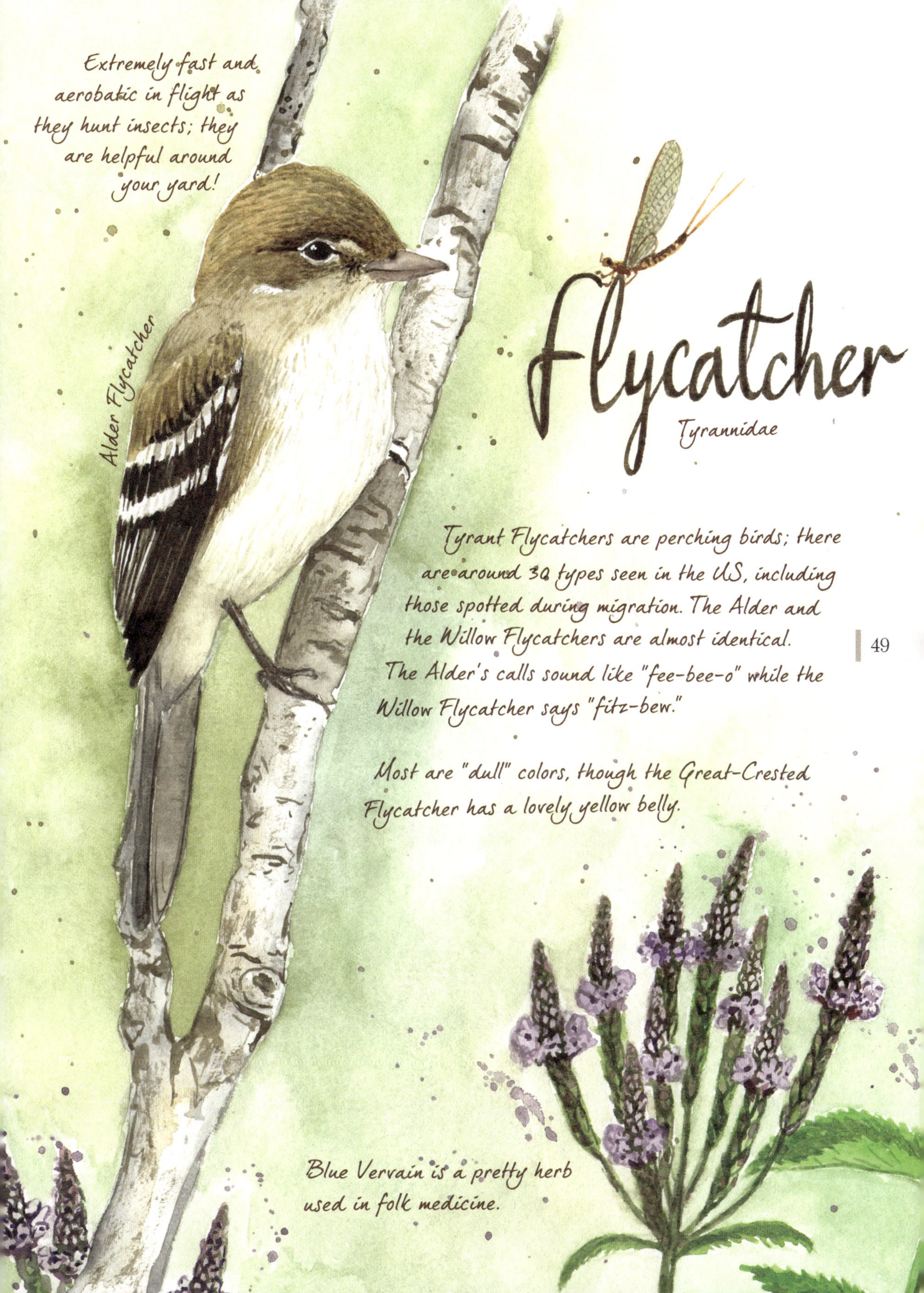

Flycatcher

Tyrannidae

Tyrant Flycatchers are perching birds; there are around 30 types seen in the US, including those spotted during migration. The Alder and the Willow Flycatchers are almost identical. The Alder's calls sound like "fee-bee-o" while the Willow Flycatcher says "fitz-bew."

Most are "dull" colors, though the Great-Crested Flycatcher has a lovely yellow belly.

Blue Vervain is a pretty herb used in folk medicine.

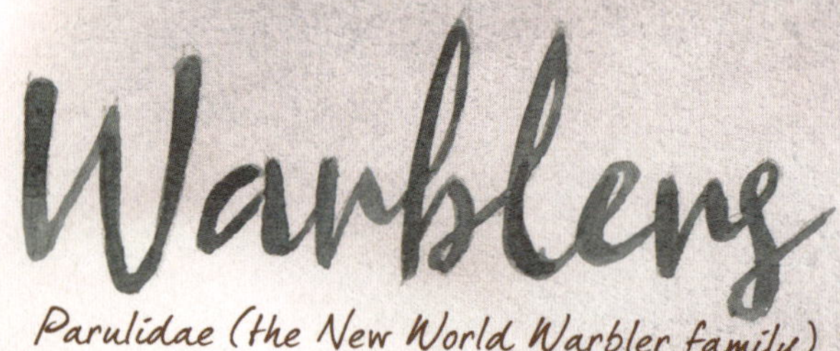

Warblers

Parulidae (the New World Warbler family)

Small, vocal insect-eaters

The Kirtland's Warbler (also known as Jack Pine bird) is coming back from near extinction. They require young stands of jack pine, which often grow after fires. Once the trees get too big, they leave.

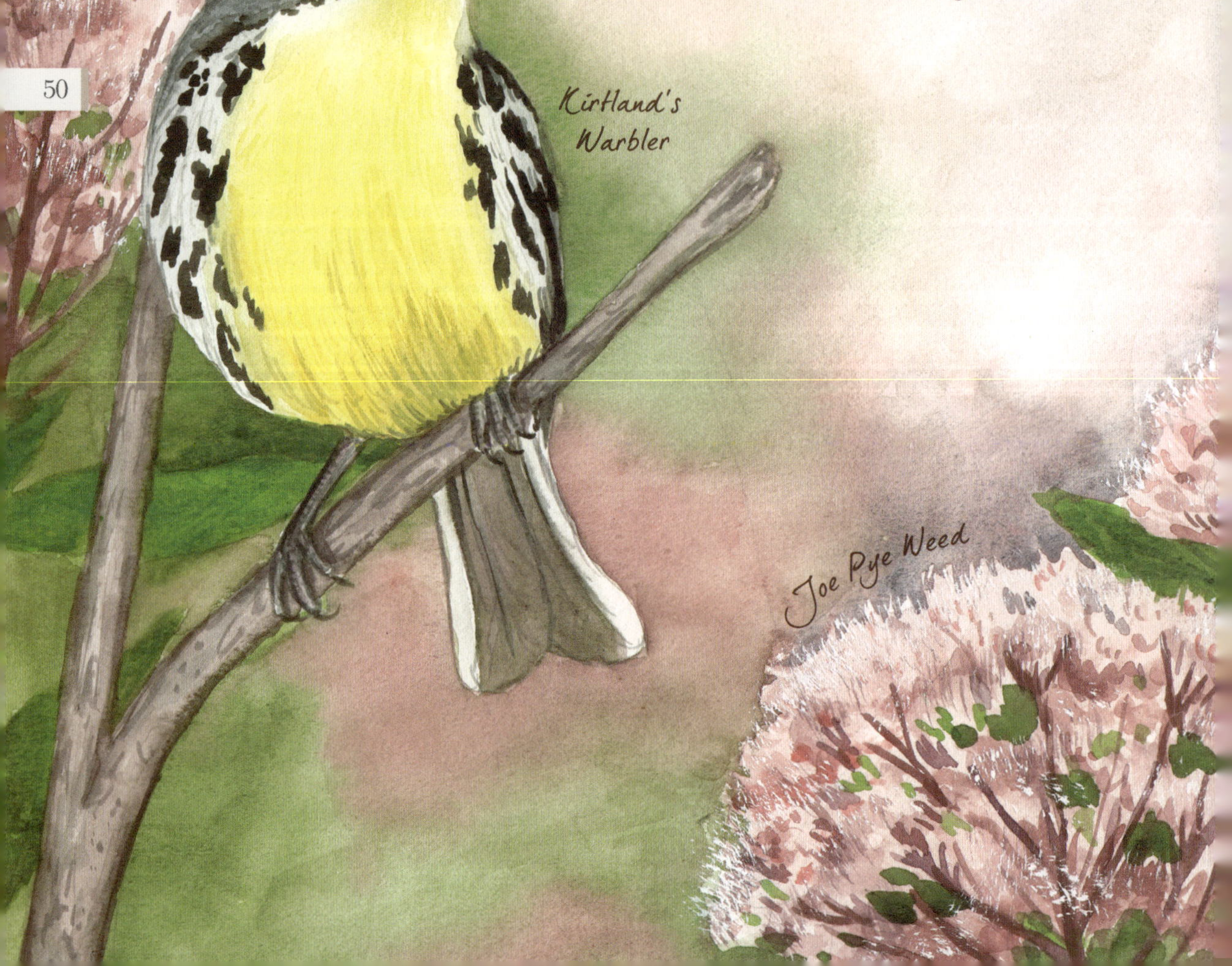

Kirtland's Warbler

Joe Pye Weed

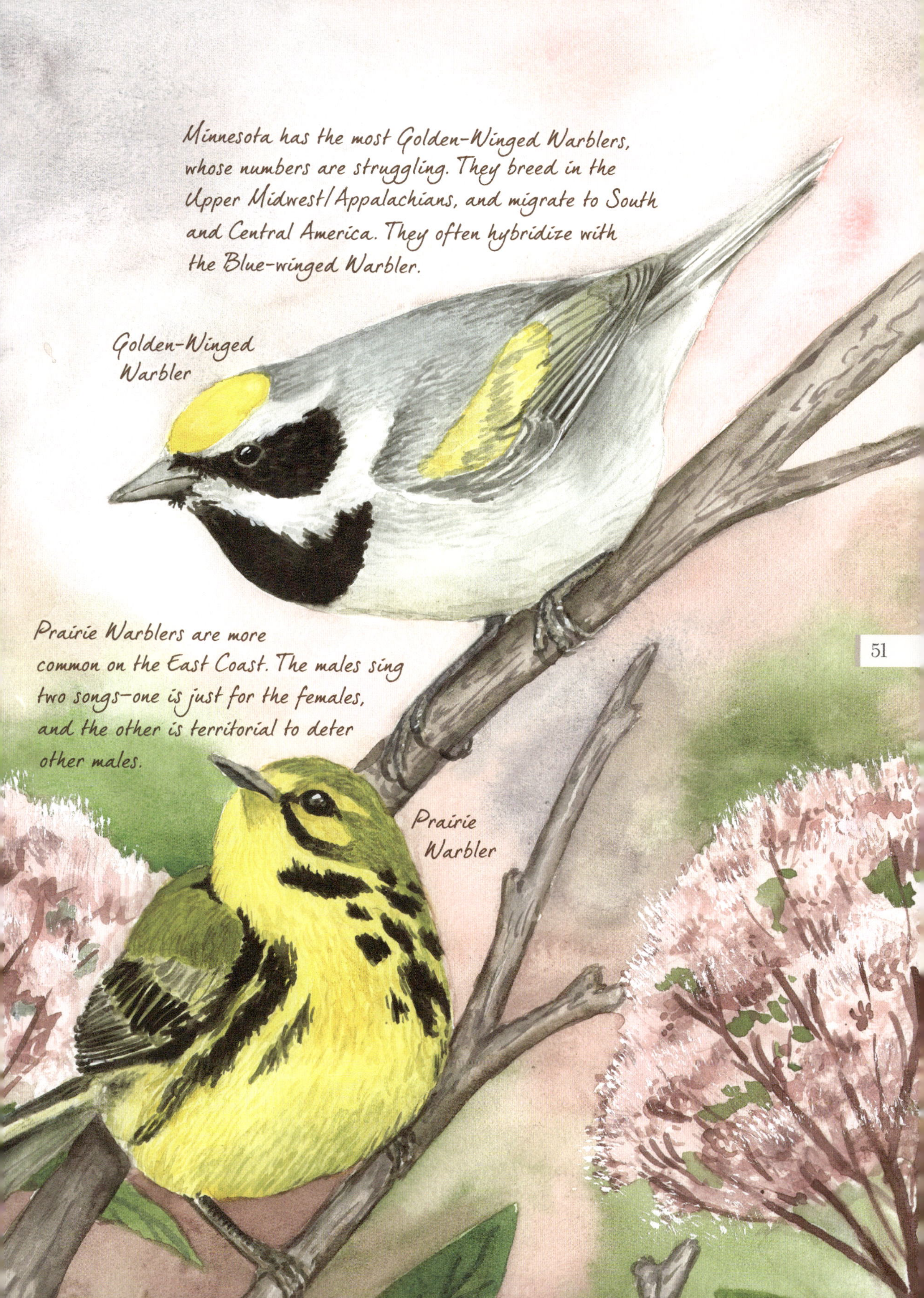
Minnesota has the most Golden-Winged Warblers, whose numbers are struggling. They breed in the Upper Midwest/Appalachians, and migrate to South and Central America. They often hybridize with the Blue-winged Warbler.
Golden-Winged Warbler
Prairie Warblers are more common on the East Coast. The males sing two songs–one is just for the females, and the other is territorial to deter other males.
Prairie Warbler

Carolina Wren

Small, quick, and cheerful birds with a loud "teakettle, teakettle, teakettle" song—you will usually hear them before you see them! They love brushy cover to feel safe. They are small but fierce to claim a nest, even harassing larger birds. They have been known to "plant" spider egg sacs in their nests to counter mite problems.

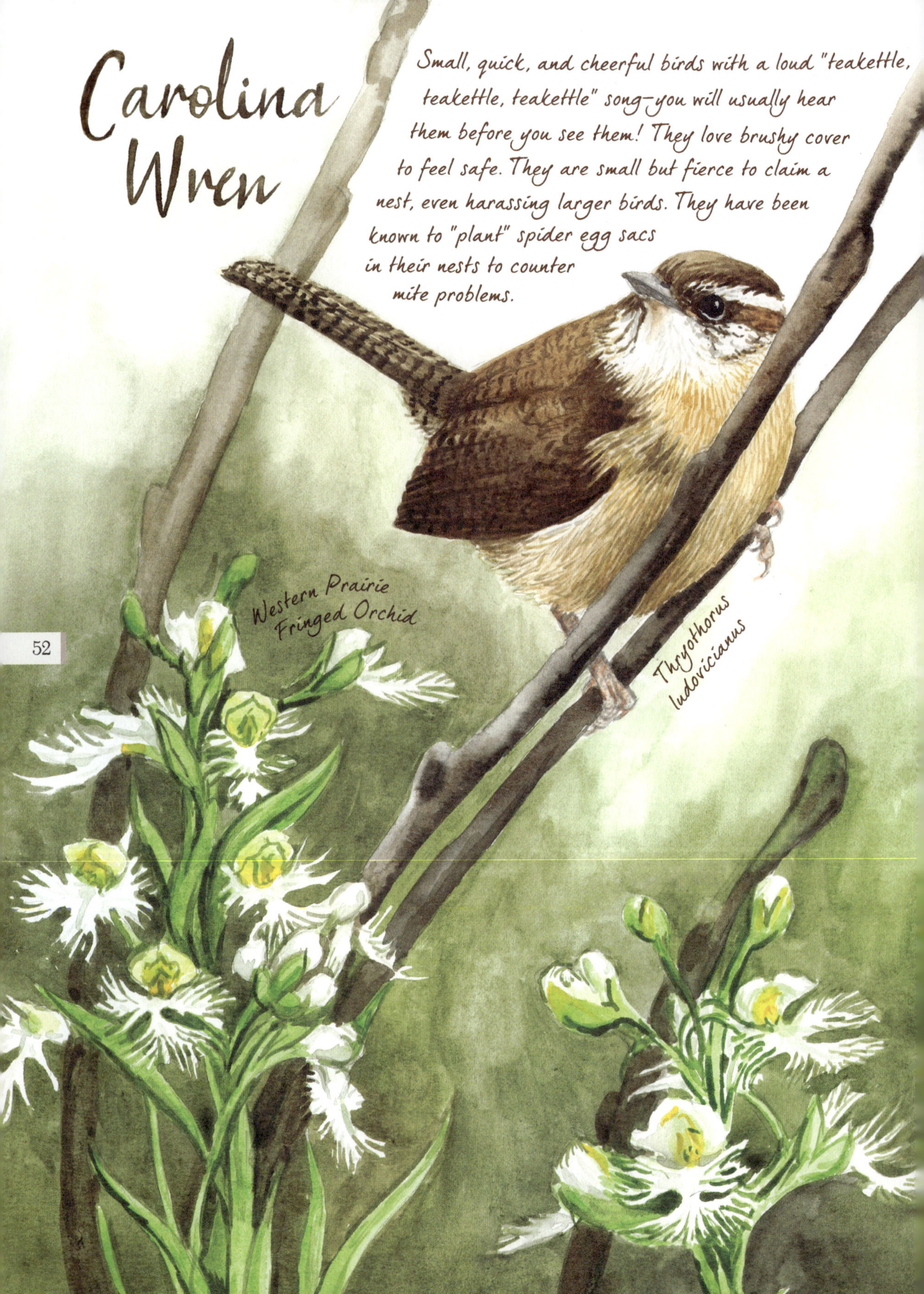

Purple Martin

Progne subis

The largest member of the swallow family, they perform spectacular aerial acrobatics when catching insects. They even eat and drink in flight (skimming the water's surface for a drink).

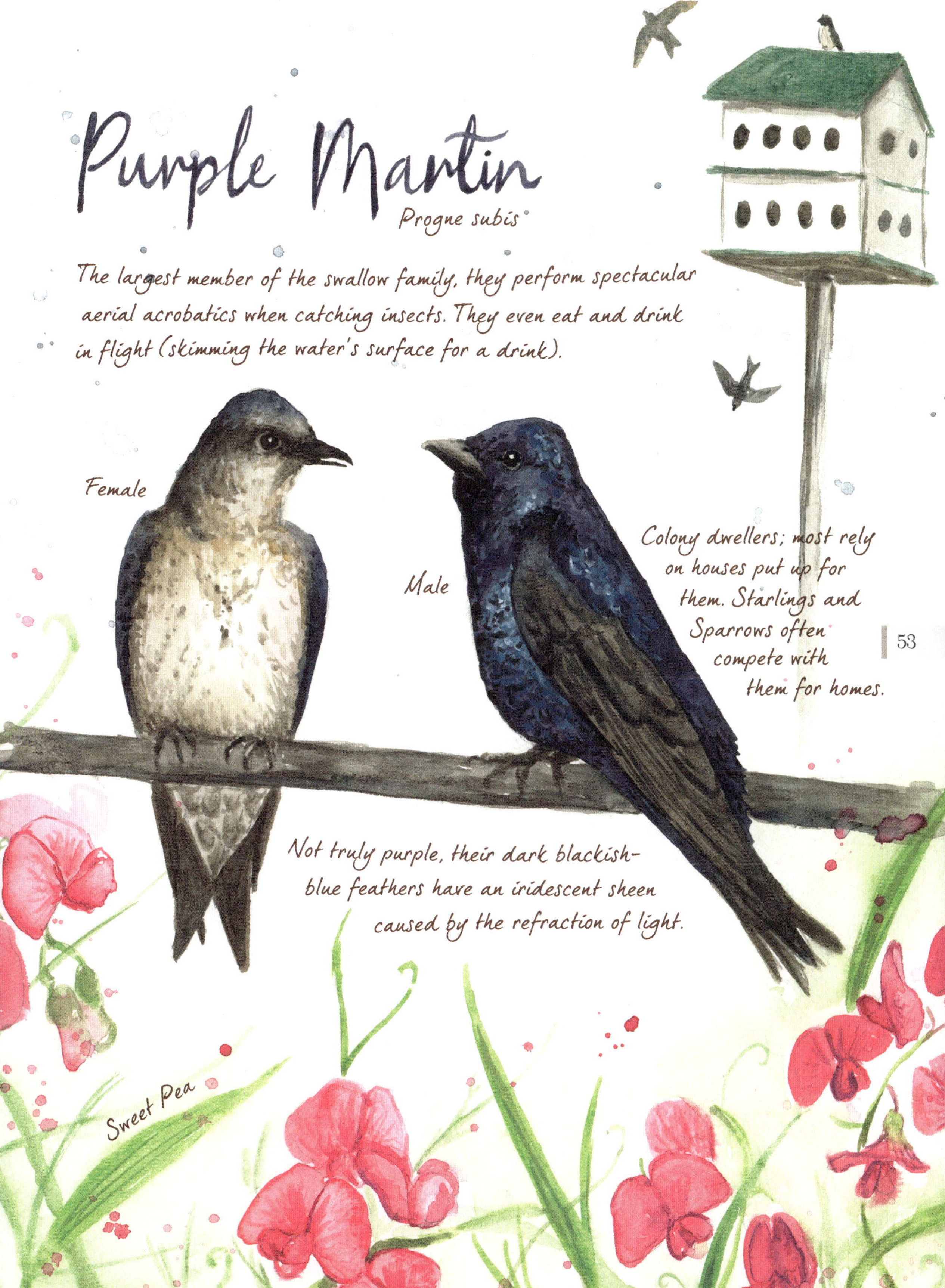

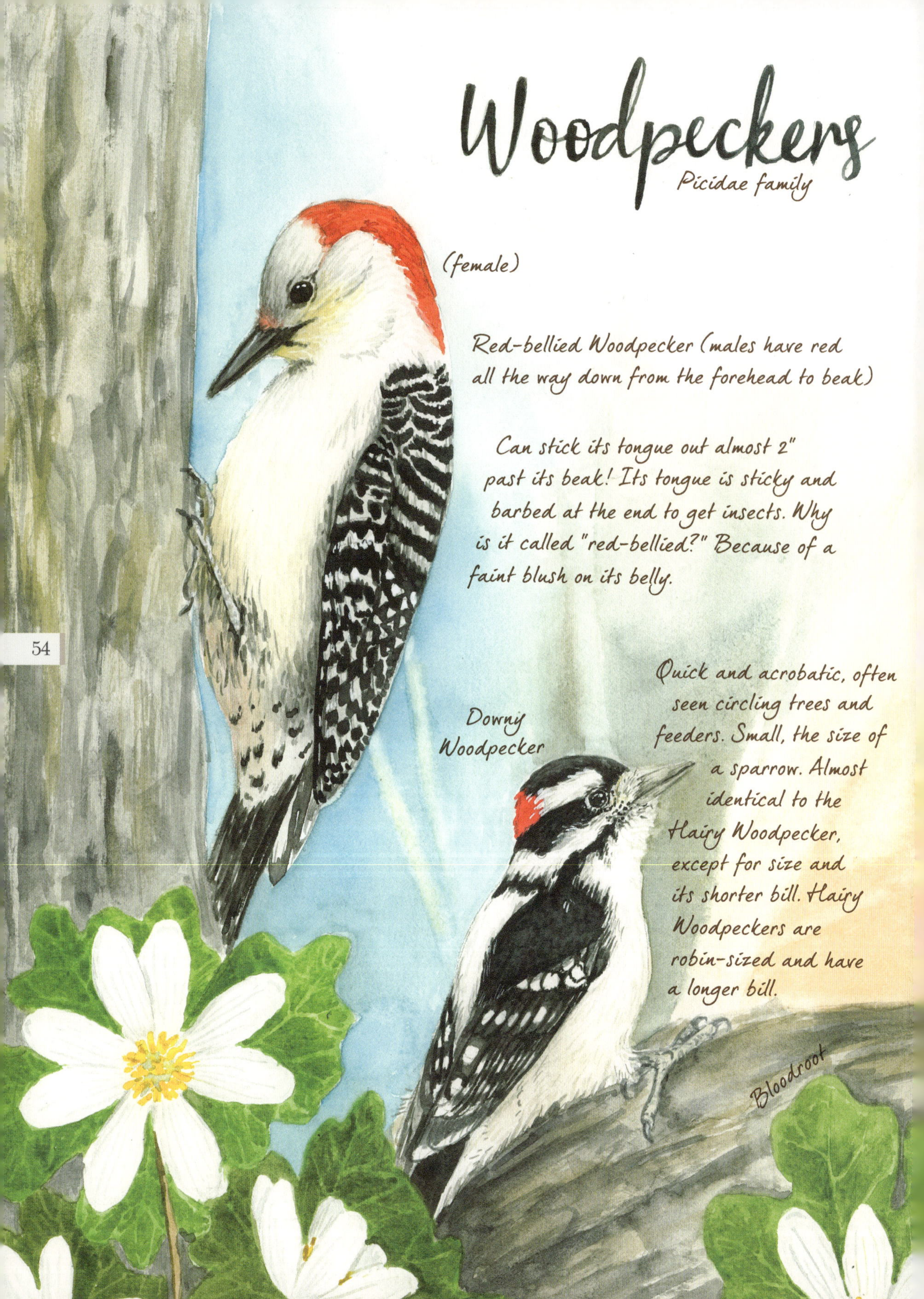
Woodpeckers
Picidae family
(female)
Red-bellied Woodpecker (males have red
all the way down from the forehead to beak)
Can stick its tongue out almost 2"
past its beak! Its tongue is sticky and
barbed at the end to get insects. Why
is it called "red-bellied?" Because of a
faint blush on its belly.
Downy
Woodpecker
Quick and acrobatic, often
seen circling trees and
feeders. Small, the size of
a sparrow. Almost
identical to the
Hairy Woodpecker,
except for size and
its shorter bill. Hairy
Woodpeckers are
robin-sized and have
a longer bill.
Bloodroot

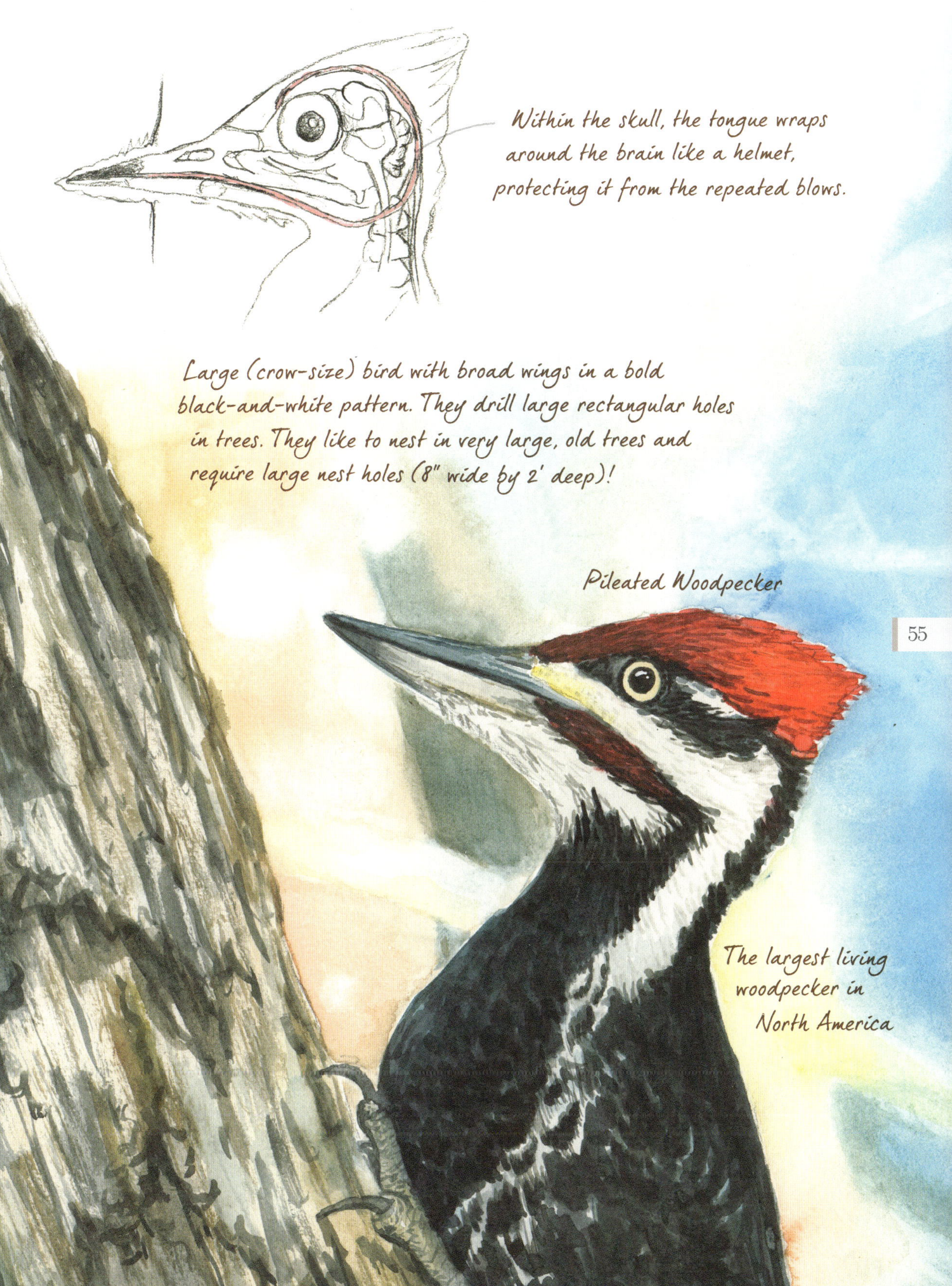
Within the skull, the tongue wraps
around the brain like a helmet,
protecting it from the repeated blows.
Large (crow-size) bird with broad wings in a bold
black-and-white pattern. They drill large rectangular holes
in trees. They like to nest in very large, old trees and
require large nest holes (8" wide by 2' deep)!
Pileated Woodpecker
The largest living
woodpecker in
North America

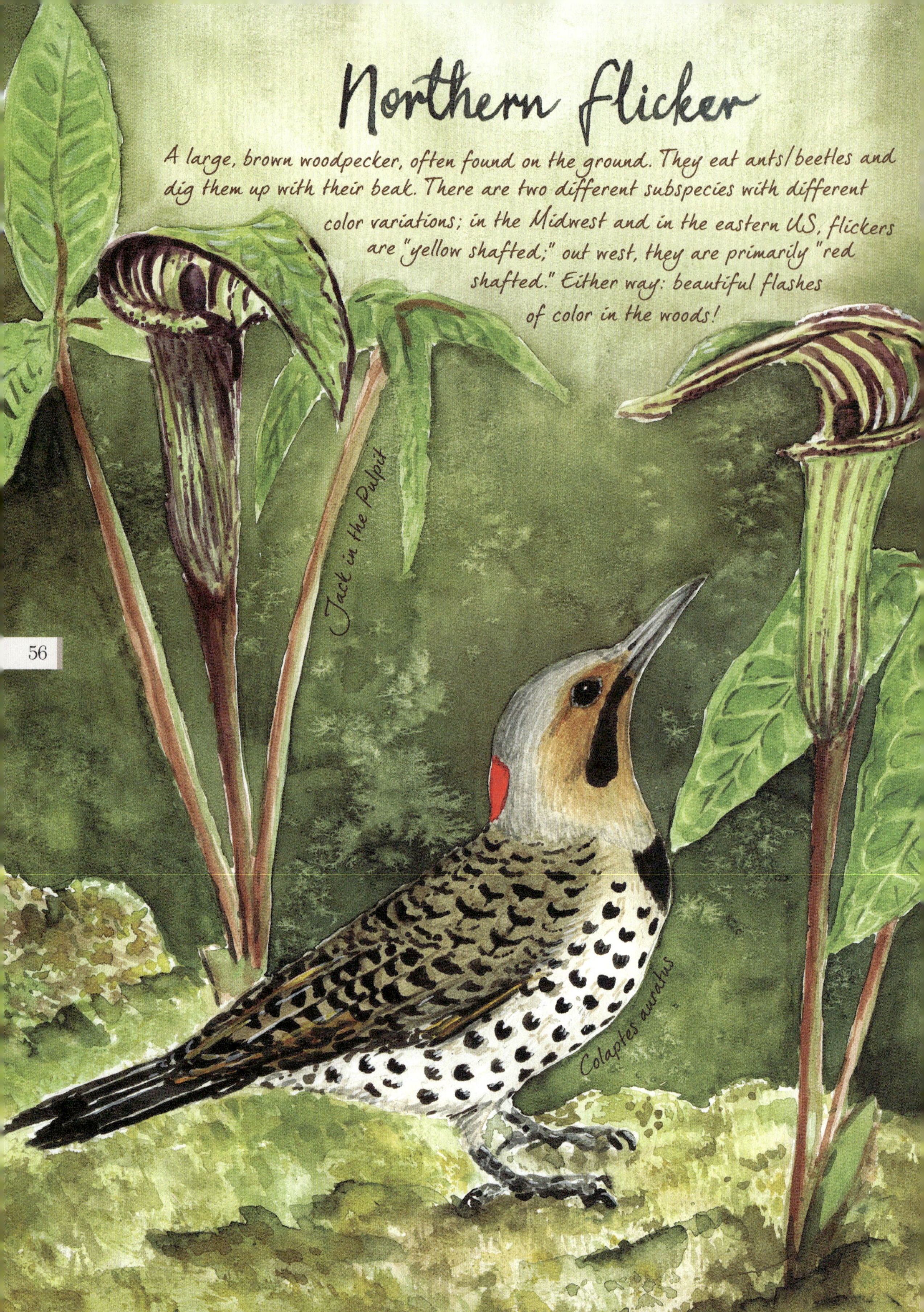
Northern flicker
A large, brown woodpecker, often found on the ground. They eat ants/beetles and dig them up with their beak. There are two different subspecies with different color variations; in the Midwest and in the eastern US, flickers are "yellow shafted;" out west, they are primarily "red shafted." Either way: beautiful flashes of color in the woods!
Jack in the Pulpit
Colaptes auratus

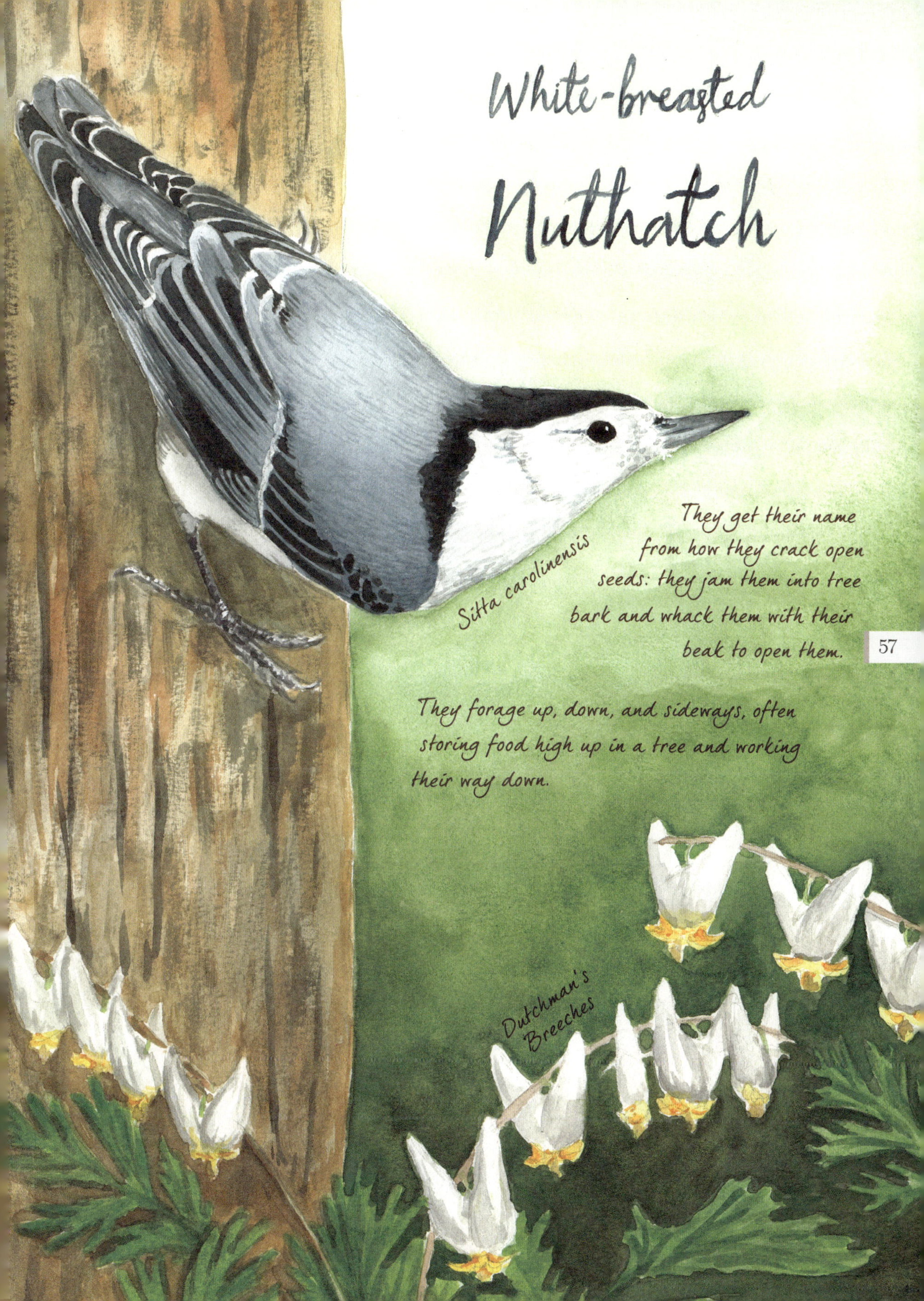
White-breasted
Nuthatch
Sitta carolinensis
They get their name from how they crack open seeds: they jam them into tree bark and whack them with their beak to open them.
They forage up, down, and sideways, often storing food high up in a tree and working their way down.
Dutchman's Breeches

American Robin

Turdus migratorius

A symbol of spring. They can have three successful broods in one year, though less than half of the nests successfully produce young.

They often gather in huge "roosts" and often stick around all winter.

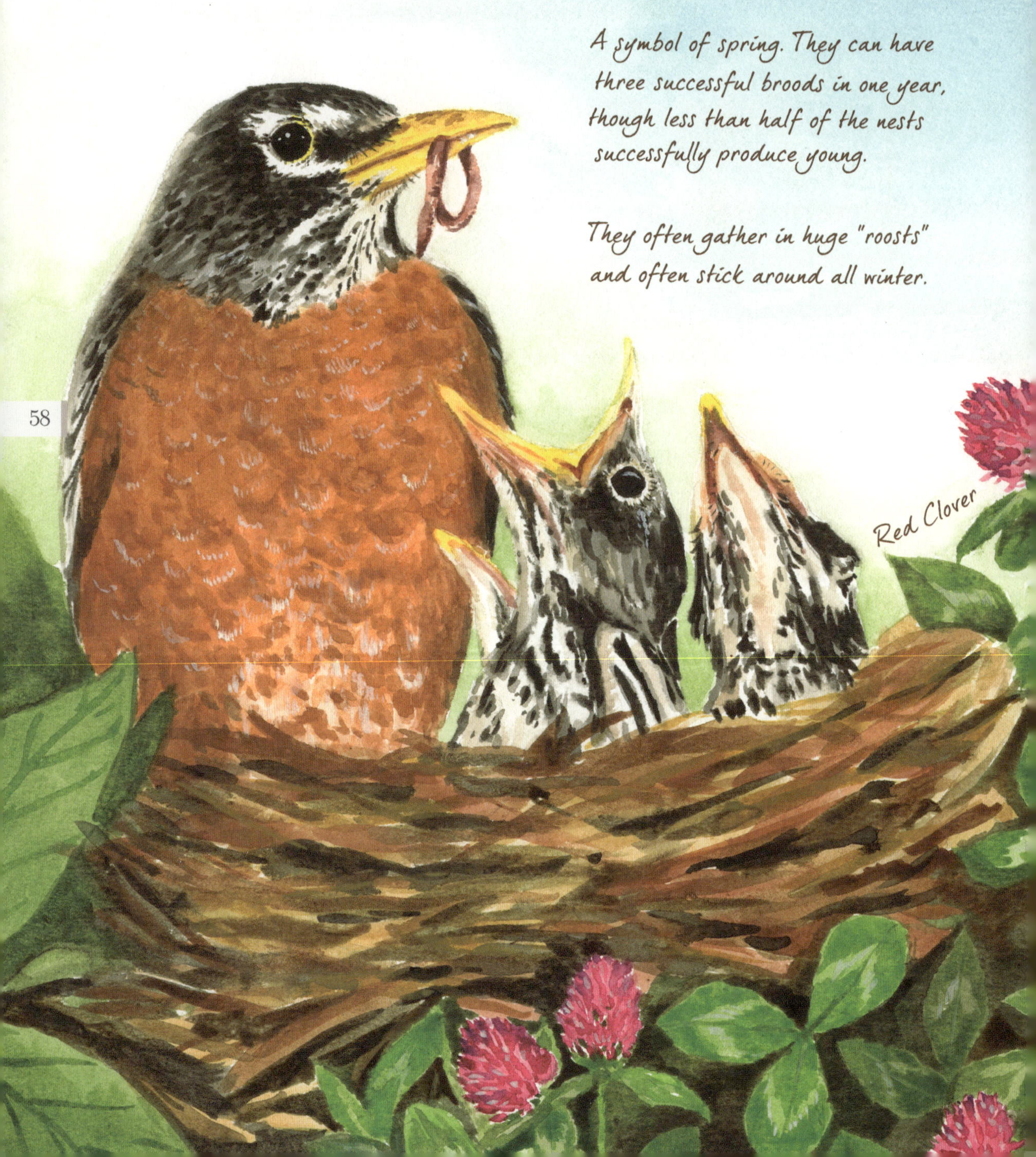

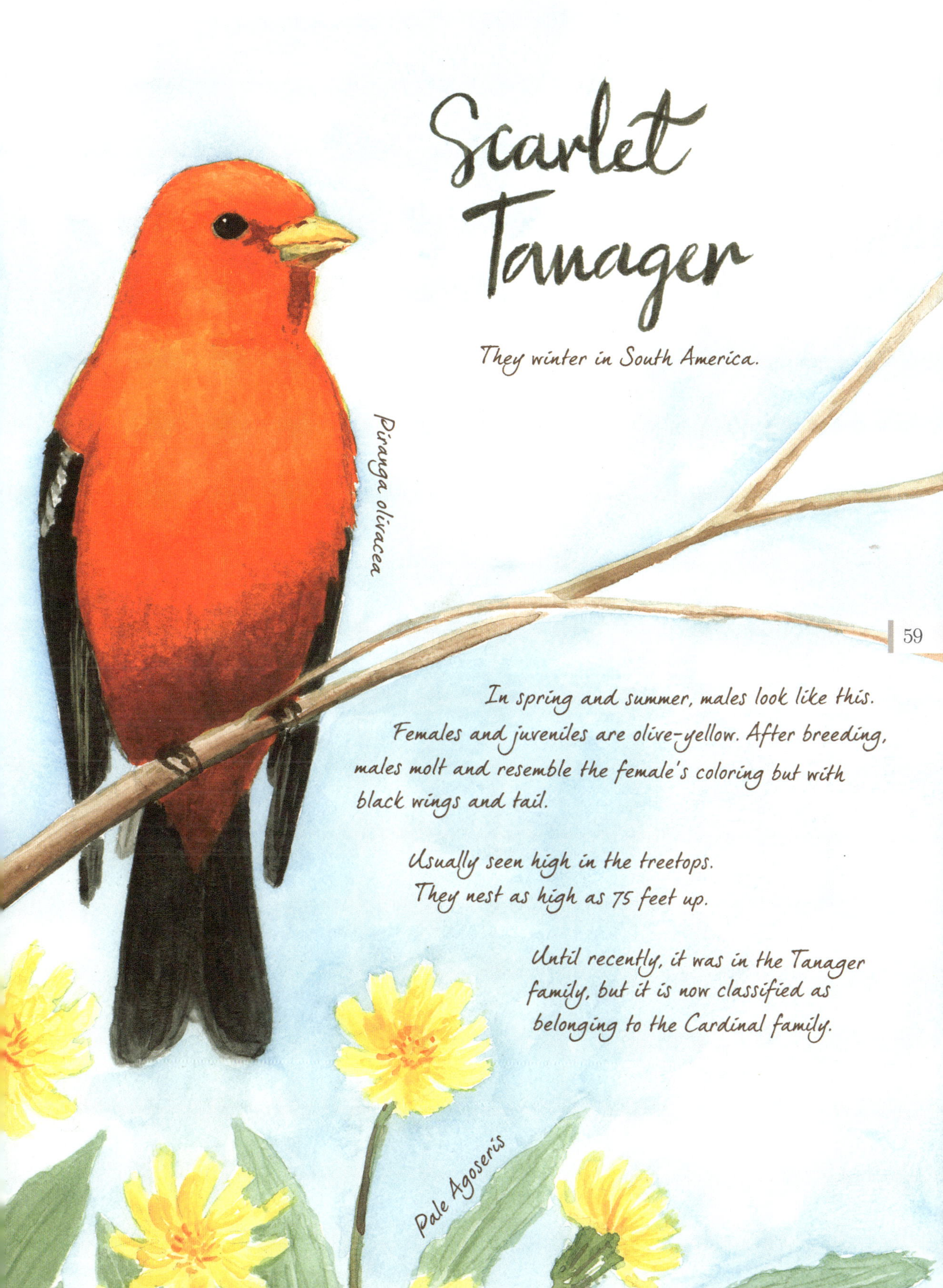

Scarlet Tanager

They winter in South America.

Piranga olivacea

In spring and summer, males look like this. Females and juveniles are olive-yellow. After breeding, males molt and resemble the female's coloring but with black wings and tail.

Usually seen high in the treetops. They nest as high as 75 feet up.

Until recently, it was in the Tanager family, but it is now classified as belonging to the Cardinal family.

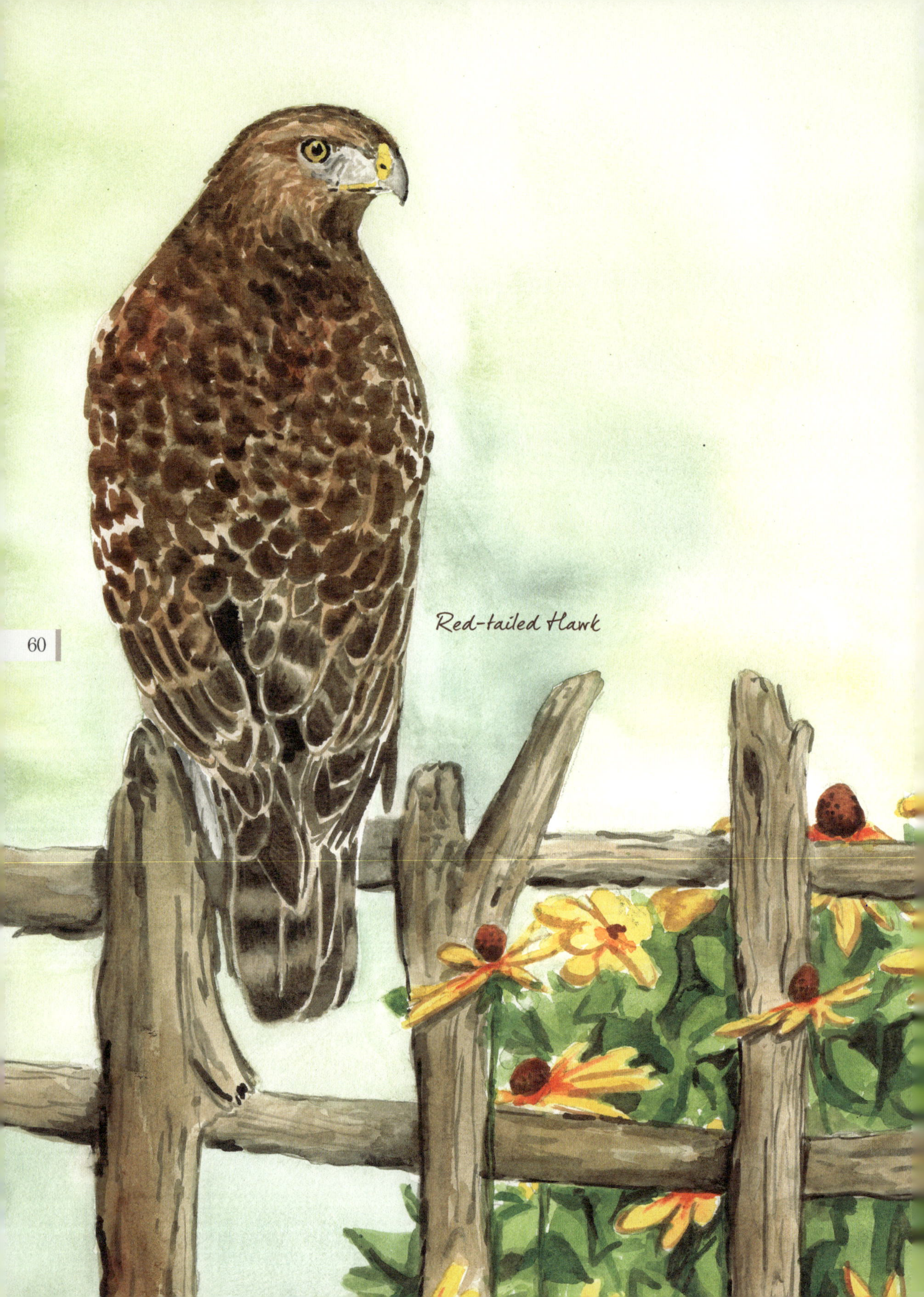
Red-tailed Hawk

Raptors

"Birds of Prey"

All raptors have a hooked beak, strong feet with sharp talons, keen eyesight, and a carnivorous diet. But each has its own special adaptations: falcons have a notchy tooth on their beak (tomial notch), while owls have a higher concentration of receptors (rods) in their eyes to see in low-light situations. All raptors have three eyelids to protect their eyes.

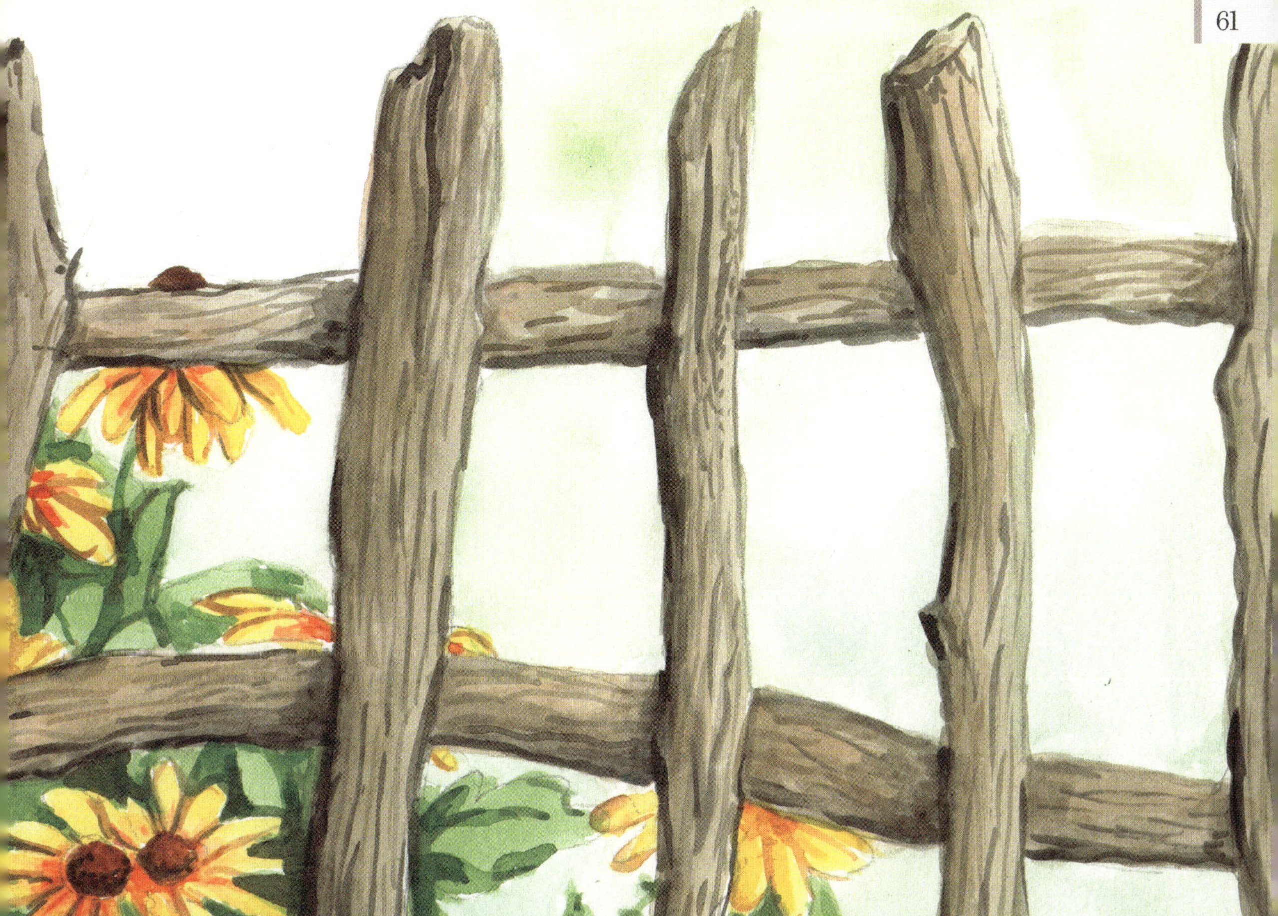

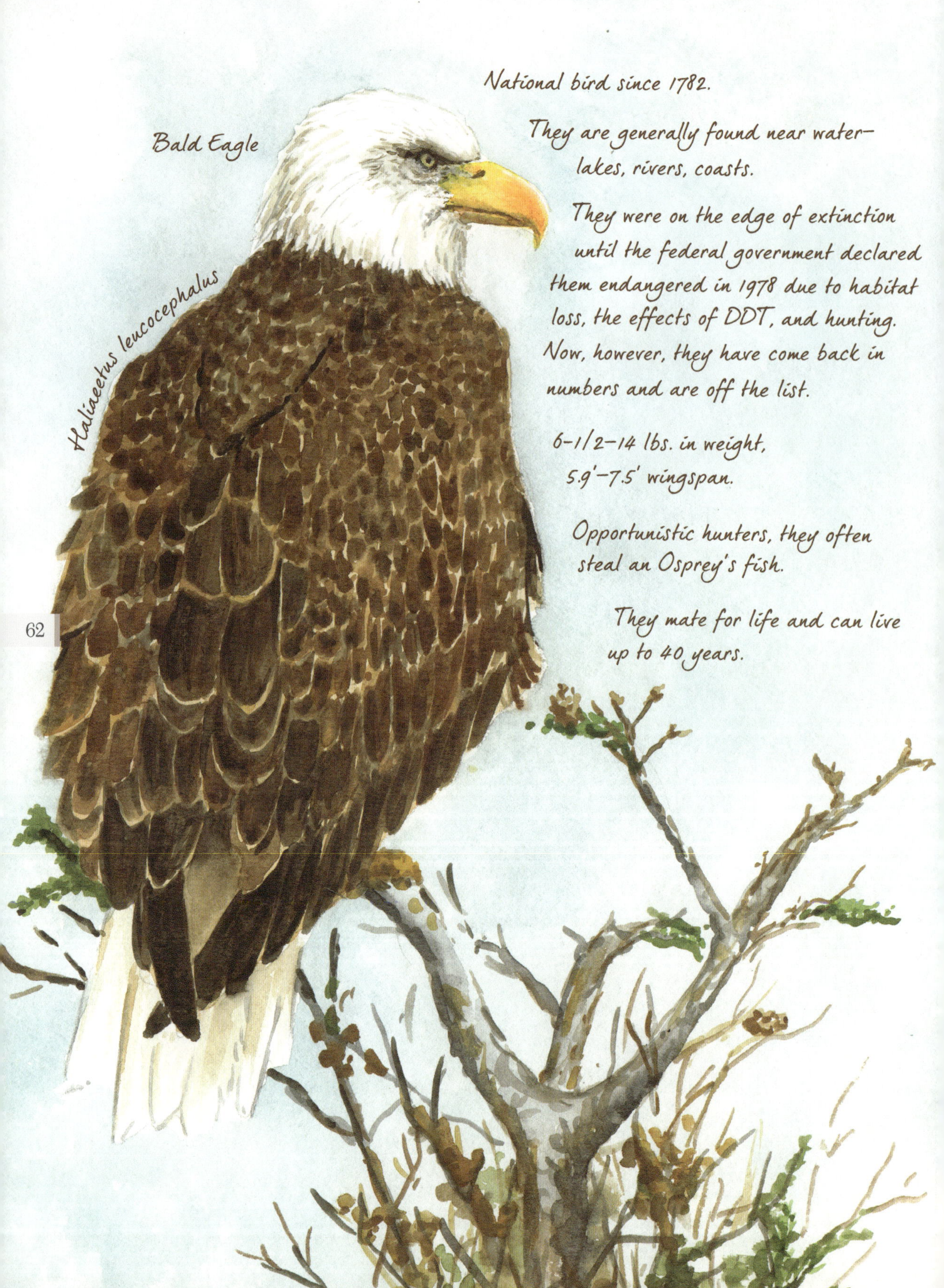
National bird since 1782.
Bald Eagle
Haliaeetus leucocephalus
They are generally found near water—lakes, rivers, coasts.
They were on the edge of extinction until the federal government declared them endangered in 1978 due to habitat loss, the effects of DDT, and hunting. Now, however, they have come back in numbers and are off the list.
6-1/2–14 lbs. in weight, 5.9'–7.5' wingspan.
Opportunistic hunters, they often steal an Osprey's fish.
They mate for life and can live up to 40 years.

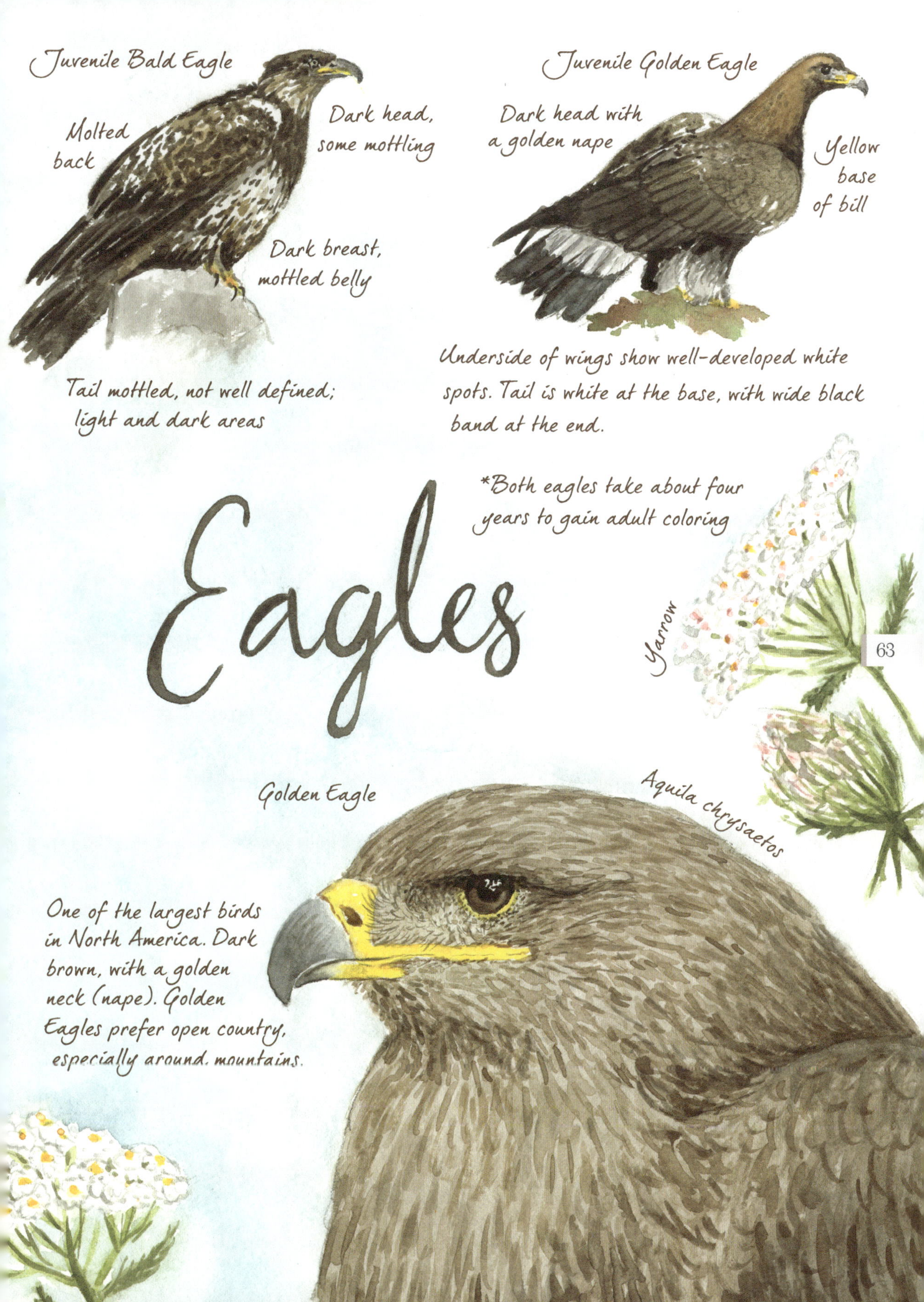
Juvenile Bald Eagle
Molted back
Dark head, some mottling
Dark breast, mottled belly
Tail mottled, not well defined; light and dark areas
Juvenile Golden Eagle
Dark head with a golden nape
Yellow base of bill
Underside of wings show well-developed white spots. Tail is white at the base, with wide black band at the end.
*Both eagles take about four years to gain adult coloring
Eagles
Yarrow
63
Golden Eagle
Aquila chrysaetos
One of the largest birds in North America. Dark brown, with a golden neck (nape). Golden Eagles prefer open country, especially around mountains.

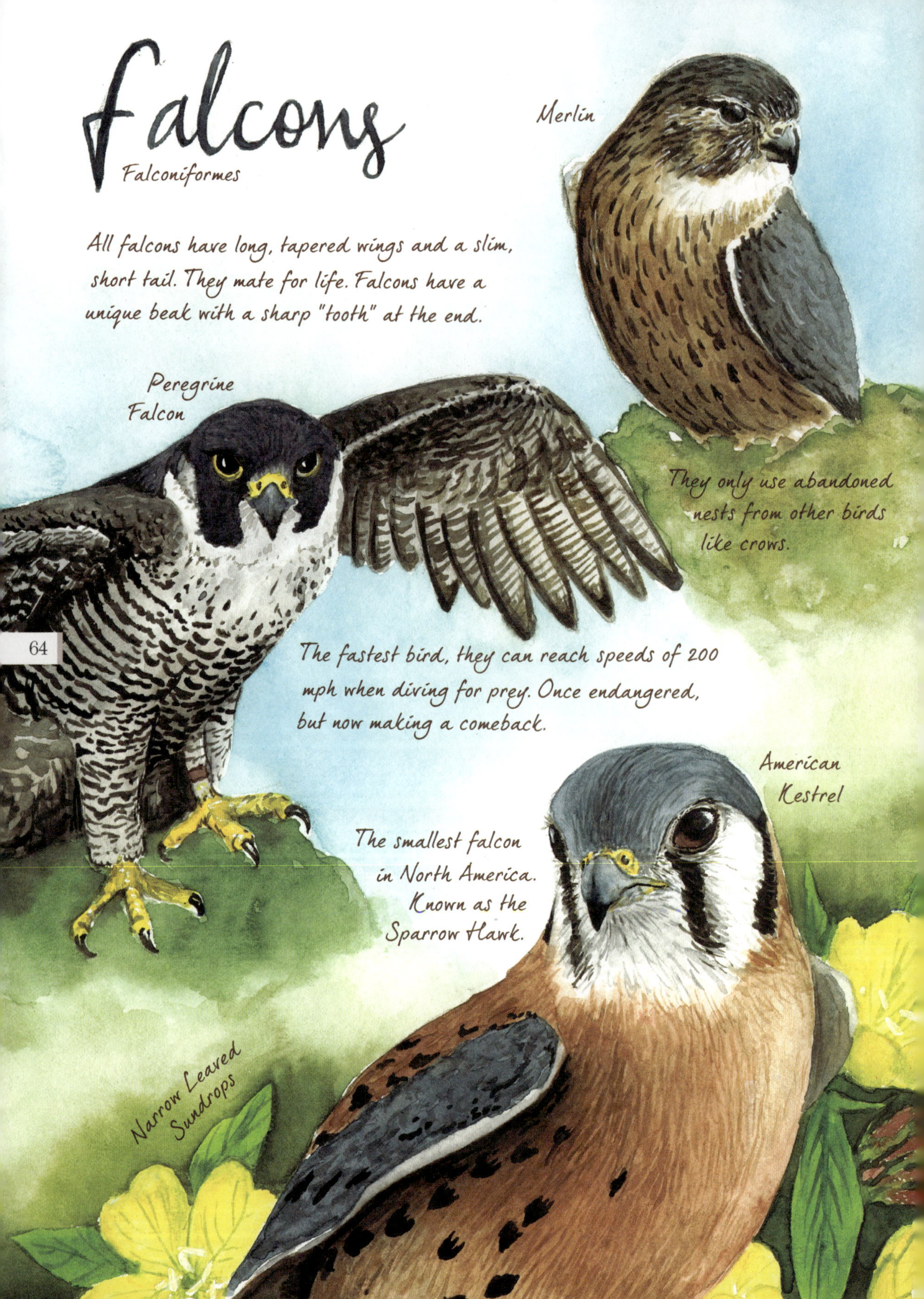
Falcons
Falconiformes
All falcons have long, tapered wings and a slim, short tail. They mate for life. Falcons have a unique beak with a sharp "tooth" at the end.
Merlin
Peregrine Falcon
They only use abandoned nests from other birds like crows.
The fastest bird, they can reach speeds of 200 mph when diving for prey. Once endangered, but now making a comeback.
American Kestrel
The smallest falcon in North America. Known as the Sparrow Hawk.
Narrow Leaved Sundrops

Nostrils have small tubercles to guide the air so they don't hurt their lungs while diving.

Beginning more than a half mile up in the air, they start their dive, known as a "stoop."

Tomial tooth-notch on their beak to snap the spinal cord of prey.

"Teardrop" shape-they tuck their wings in for lowest drag, and tuck their heads in to their wings.

Very large eye-to head ratio. A nictitating membrane protects the eye.

The peregrine falcon is like the Ferrari of the bird world. They have developed very specialized features that allow them to fly and hunt at great speeds. They can see at least 1 mile, and can track three moving objects at a time. Their eyes act like telephoto lenses. Besides the "third eyelid," they also have thick tears to keep their eyes from drying out.

They have an extra-large keel bone and an extra pair of vertebrae in their tails!

Long, sleek narrow wings cut through the air.

The "M shape"

They turn up slightly at the end of the dive, just short of their prey. While doing so, they withstand 25 Gs of force. They ball up their feet and punch their prey out of the air, which either kills it instantly, or knocks it out. They then land and finish it off. Only around 20% of their hunts are successful.

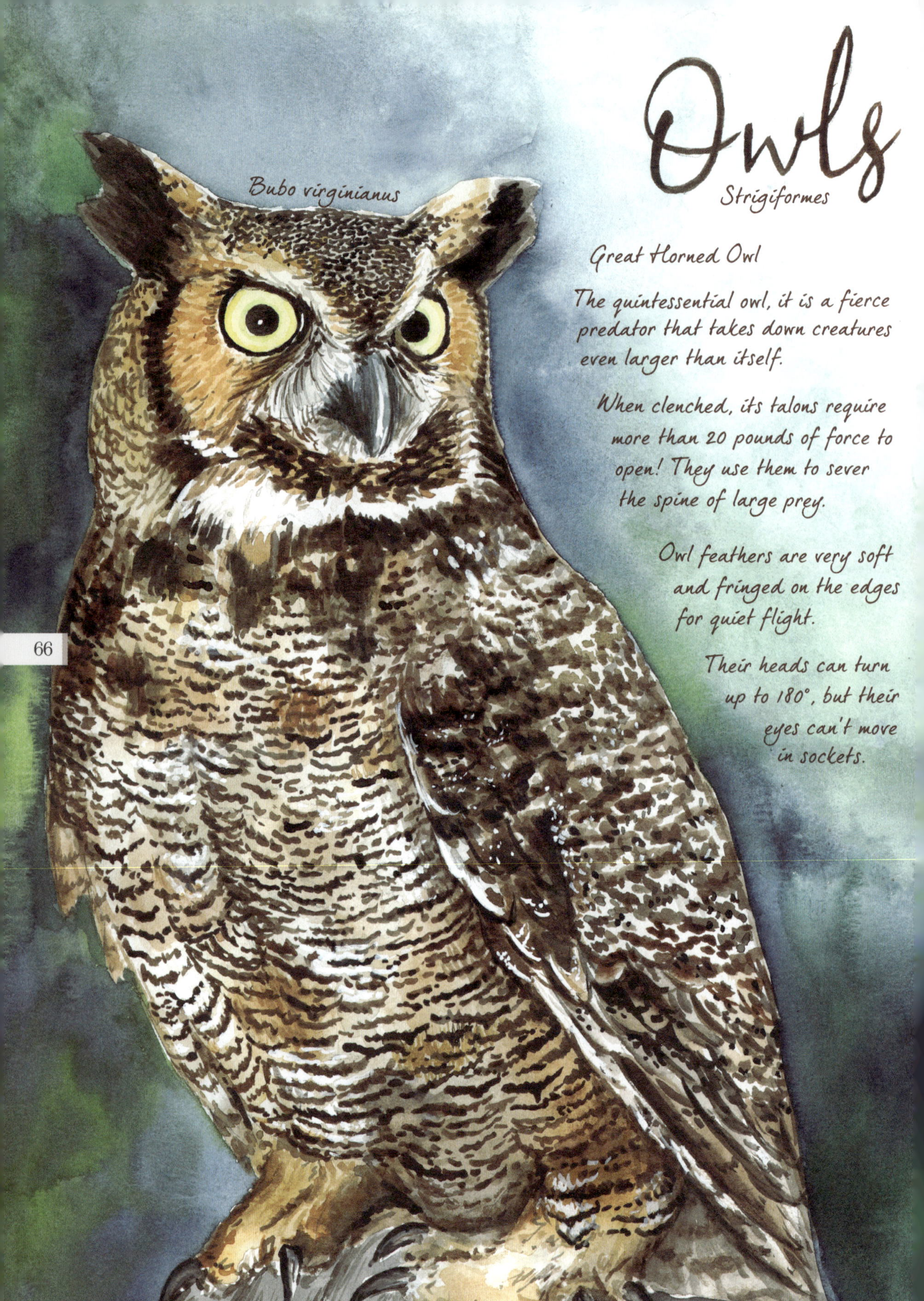
Owls
Strigiformes
Bubo virginianus
Great Horned Owl
The quintessential owl, it is a fierce predator that takes down creatures even larger than itself.
When clenched, its talons require more than 20 pounds of force to open! They use them to sever the spine of large prey.
Owl feathers are very soft and fringed on the edges for quiet flight.
Their heads can turn up to 180°, but their eyes can't move in sockets.

Short, stocky, and small (the size of a robin), the Screech Owl has a very complex marking pattern as camouflage against tree bark.

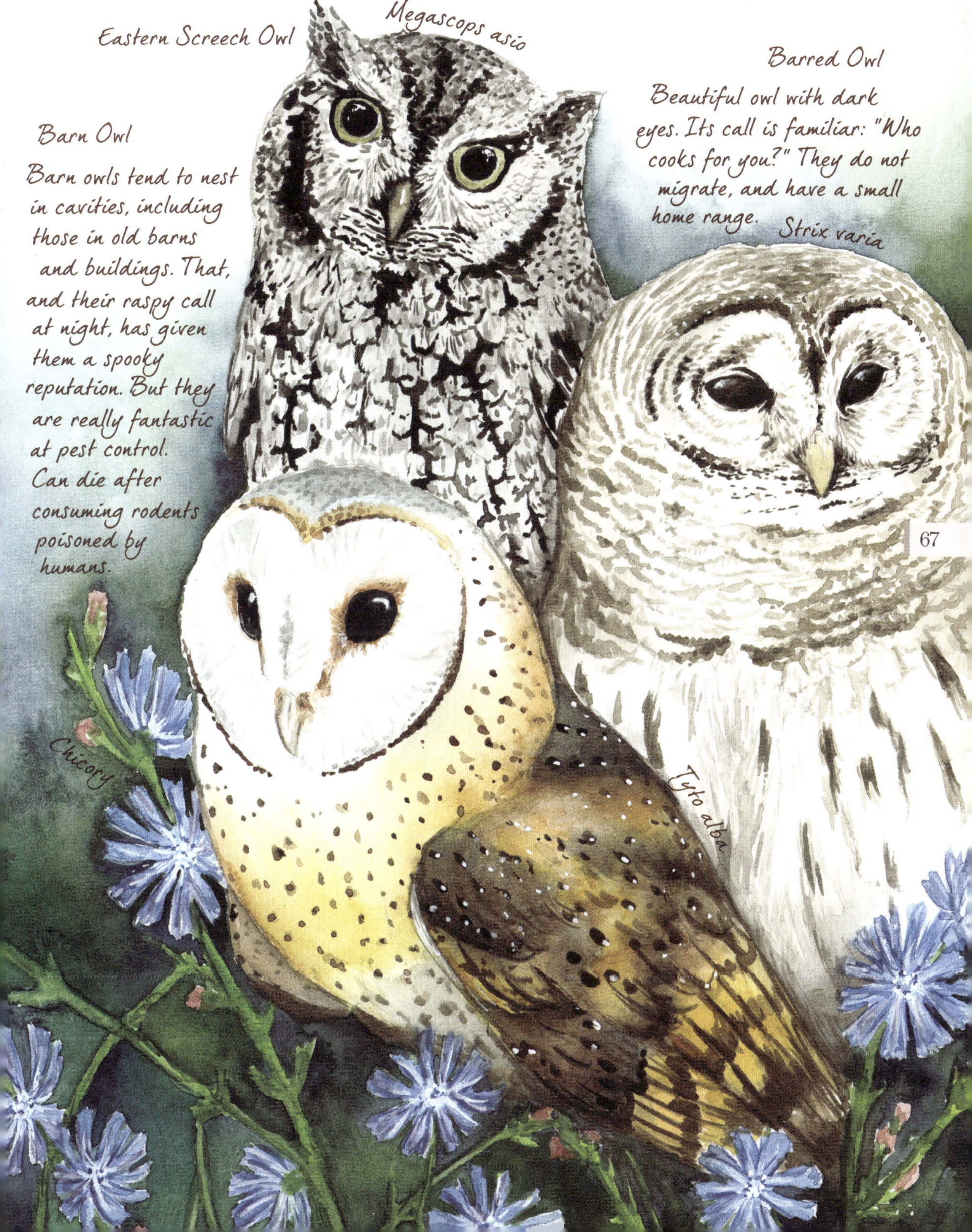

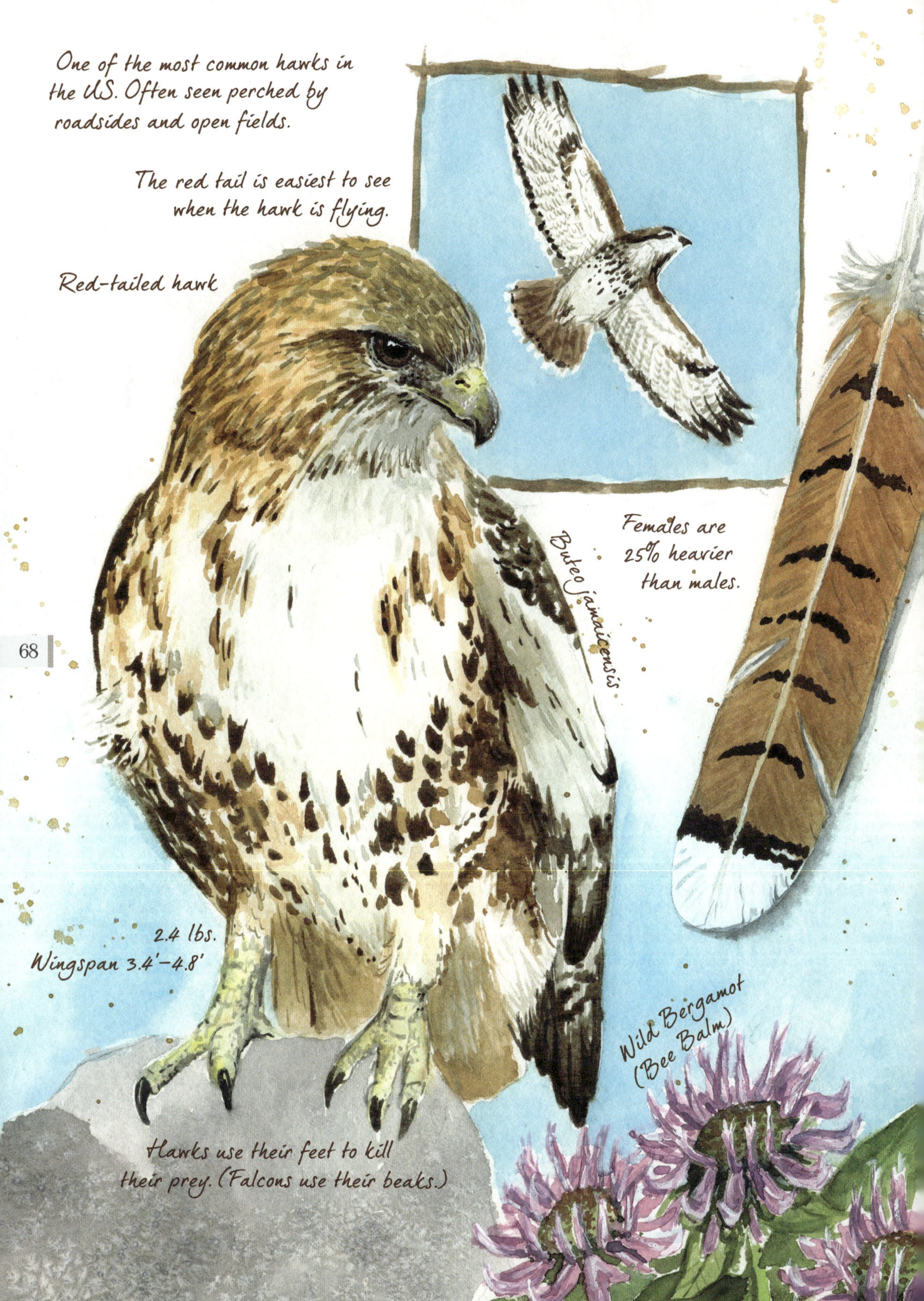
One of the most common hawks in the US. Often seen perched by roadsides and open fields.
The red tail is easiest to see when the hawk is flying.
Red-tailed hawk
Buteo jamaicensis
Females are 25% heavier than males.
2.4 lbs.
Wingspan 3.4'–4.8'
Wild Bergamot (Bee Balm)
Hawks use their feet to kill their prey. (Falcons use their beaks.)

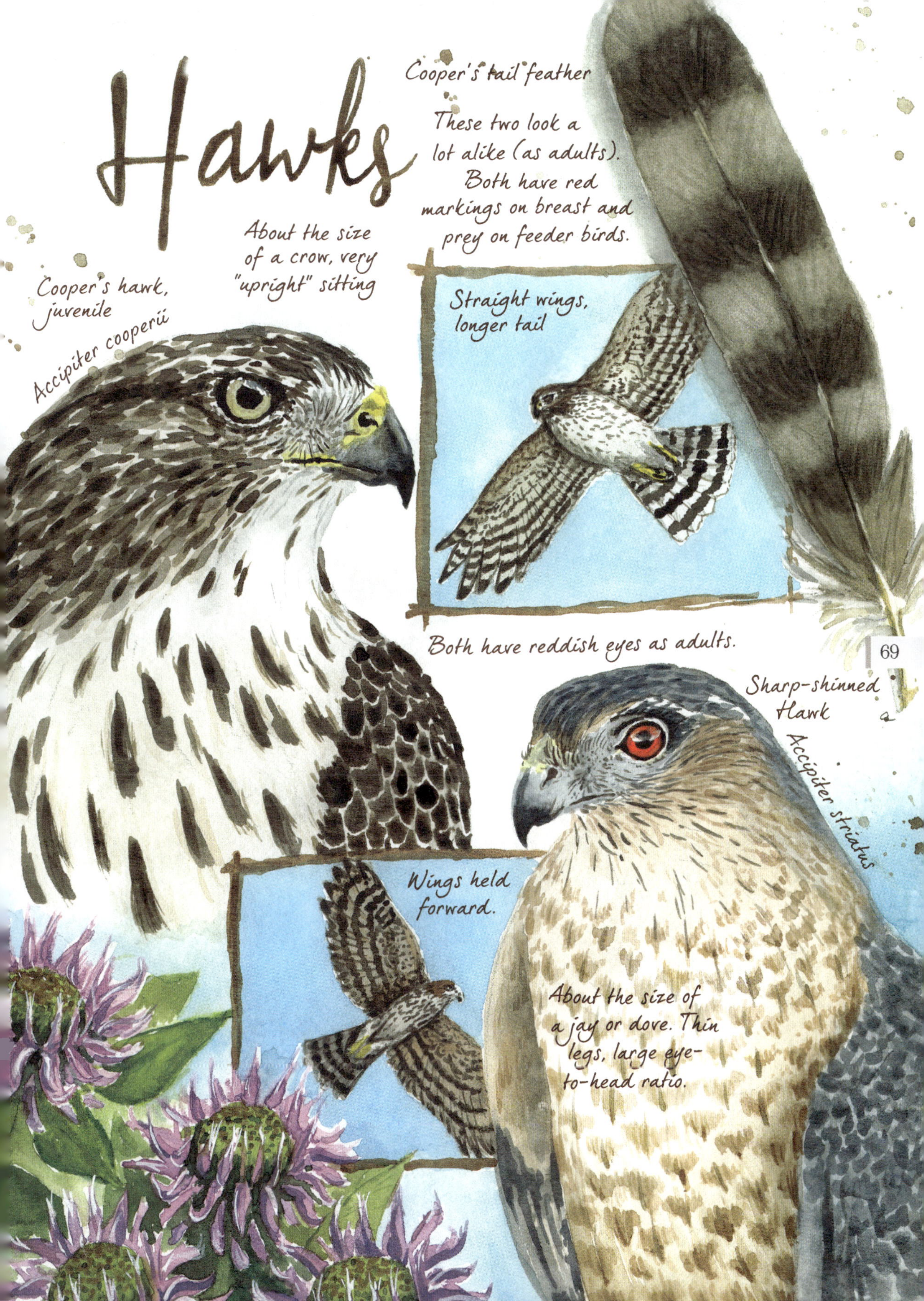
Hawks
Cooper's tail feather
These two look a lot alike (as adults). Both have red markings on breast and prey on feeder birds.
About the size of a crow, very "upright" sitting
Cooper's hawk, juvenile
Accipiter cooperii
Straight wings, longer tail
Both have reddish eyes as adults.
Sharp-shinned Hawk
Accipiter striatus
Wings held forward.
About the size of a jay or dove. Thin legs, large eye-to-head ratio.

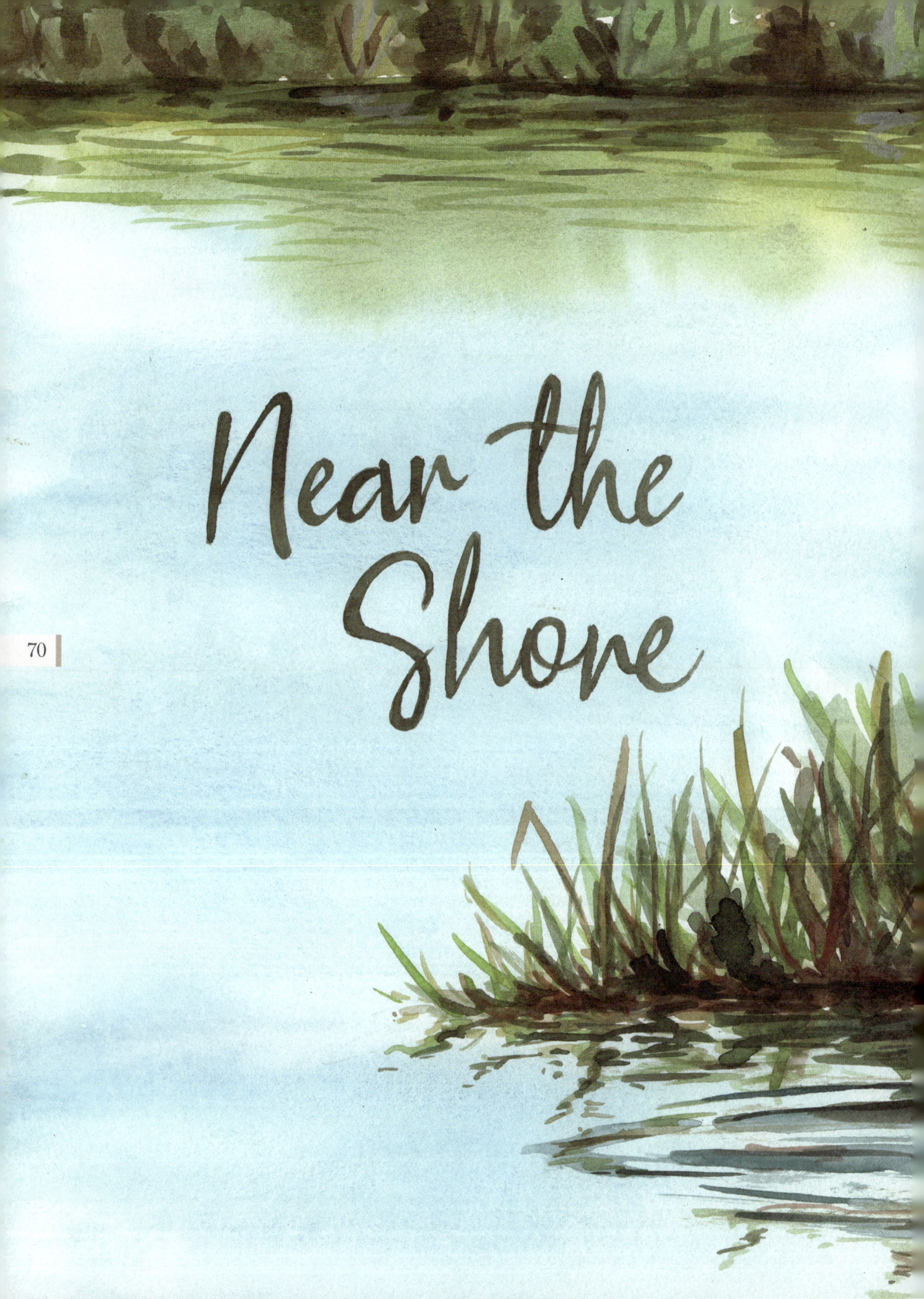

Near the Shore

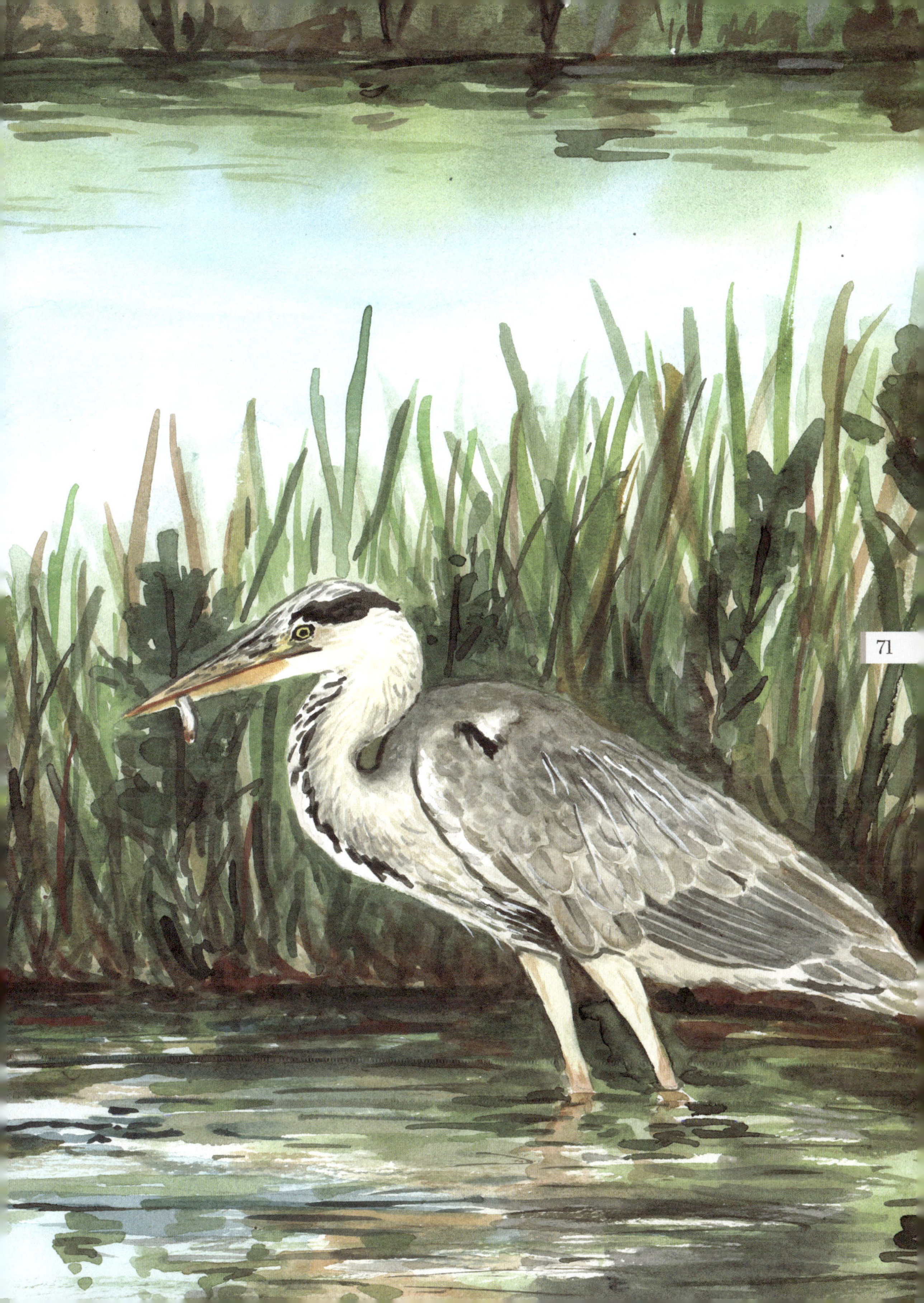

Ducks

Anas platyrhynchos

Mallards are the most common ducks, and mallard females are famous for their loud "quack."

"Dabbling ducks"

These kinds of ducks eat on the surface and as far underwater as they can reach.

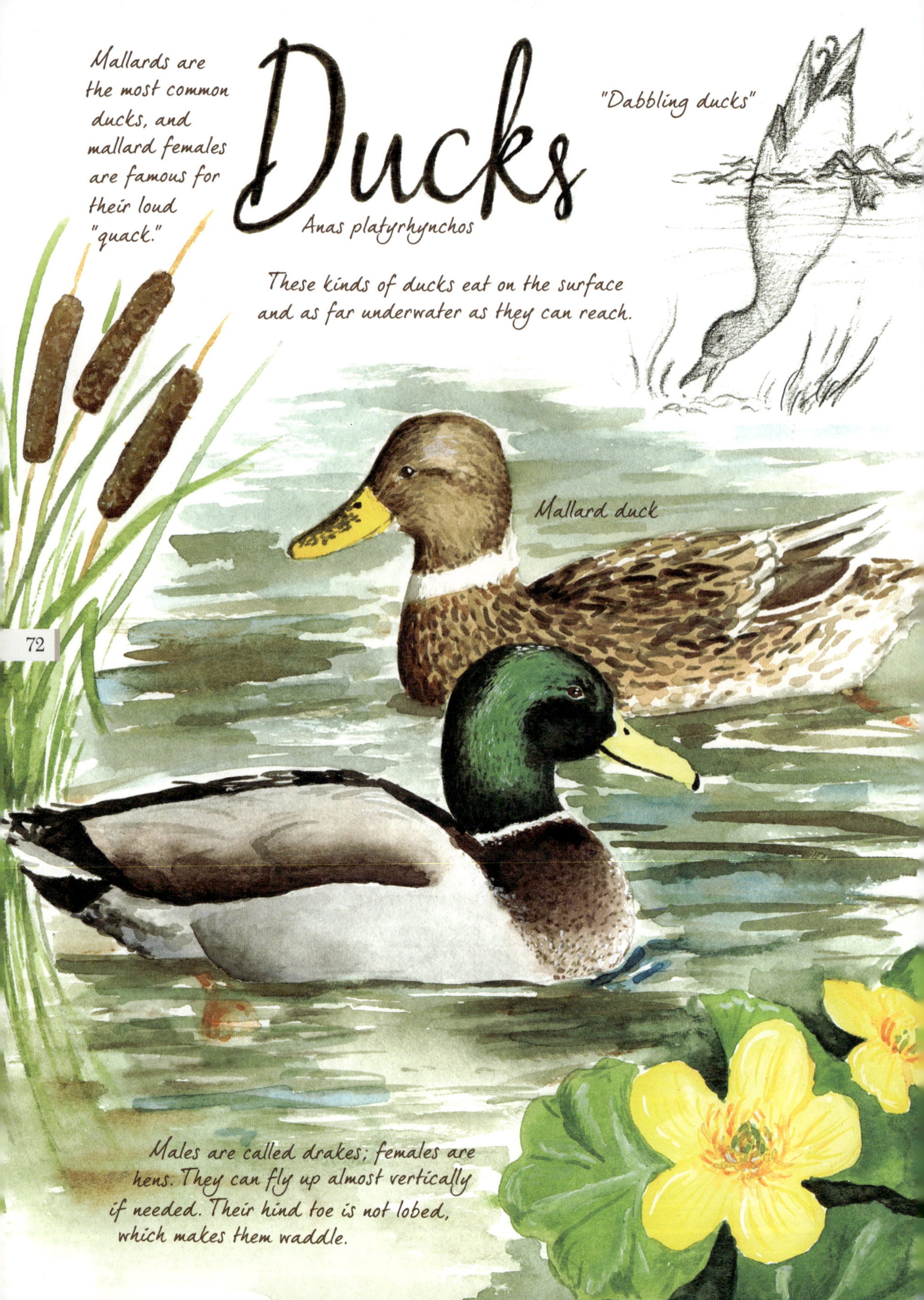

Males are called drakes; females are hens. They can fly up almost vertically if needed. Their hind toe is not lobed, which makes them waddle.

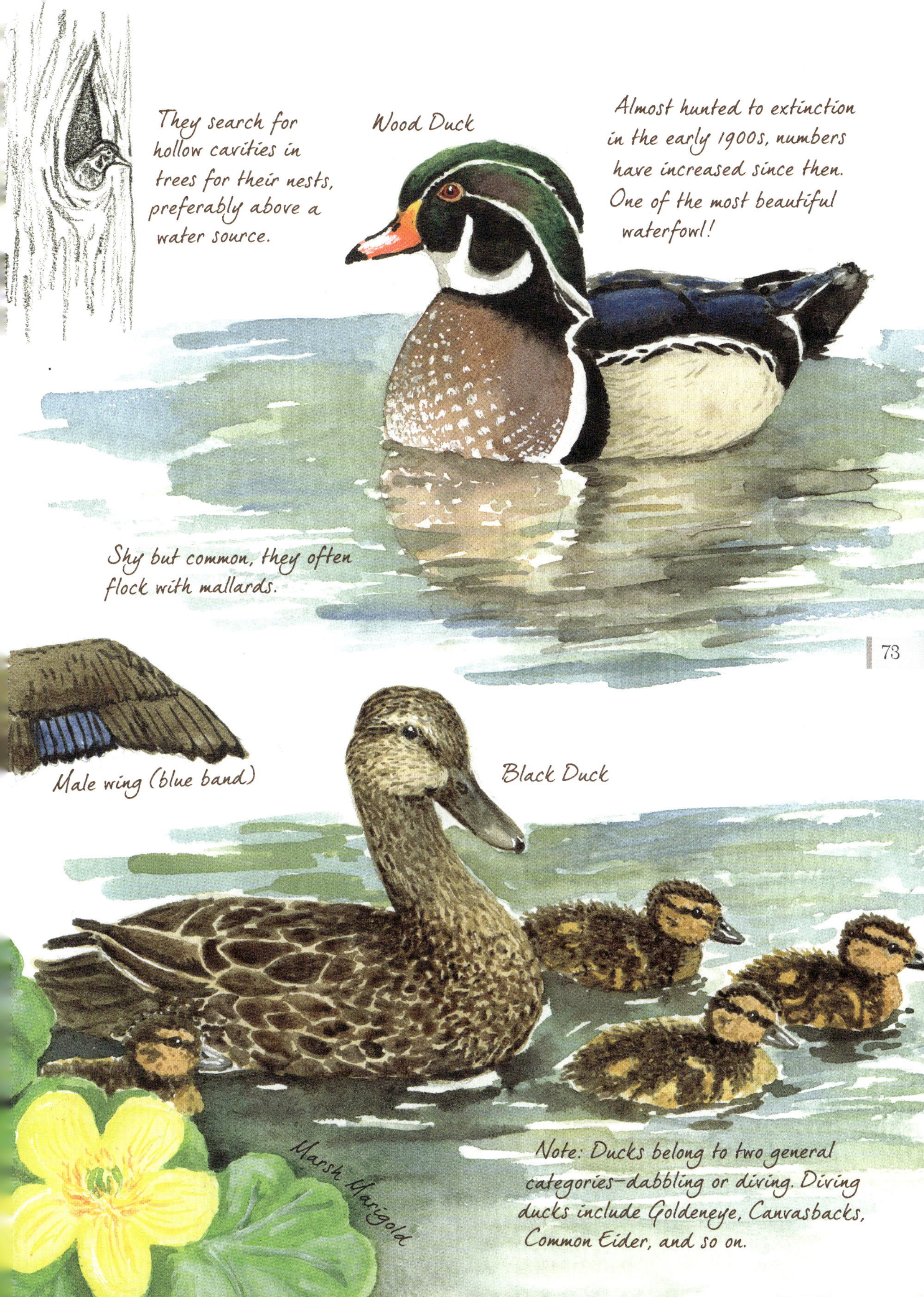
They search for hollow cavities in trees for their nests, preferably above a water source.
Wood Duck
Almost hunted to extinction in the early 1900s, numbers have increased since then. One of the most beautiful waterfowl!
Shy but common, they often flock with mallards.
Male wing (blue band)
Black Duck
Marsh Marigold
Note: Ducks belong to two general categories—dabbling or diving. Diving ducks include Goldeneye, Canvasbacks, Common Eider, and so on.

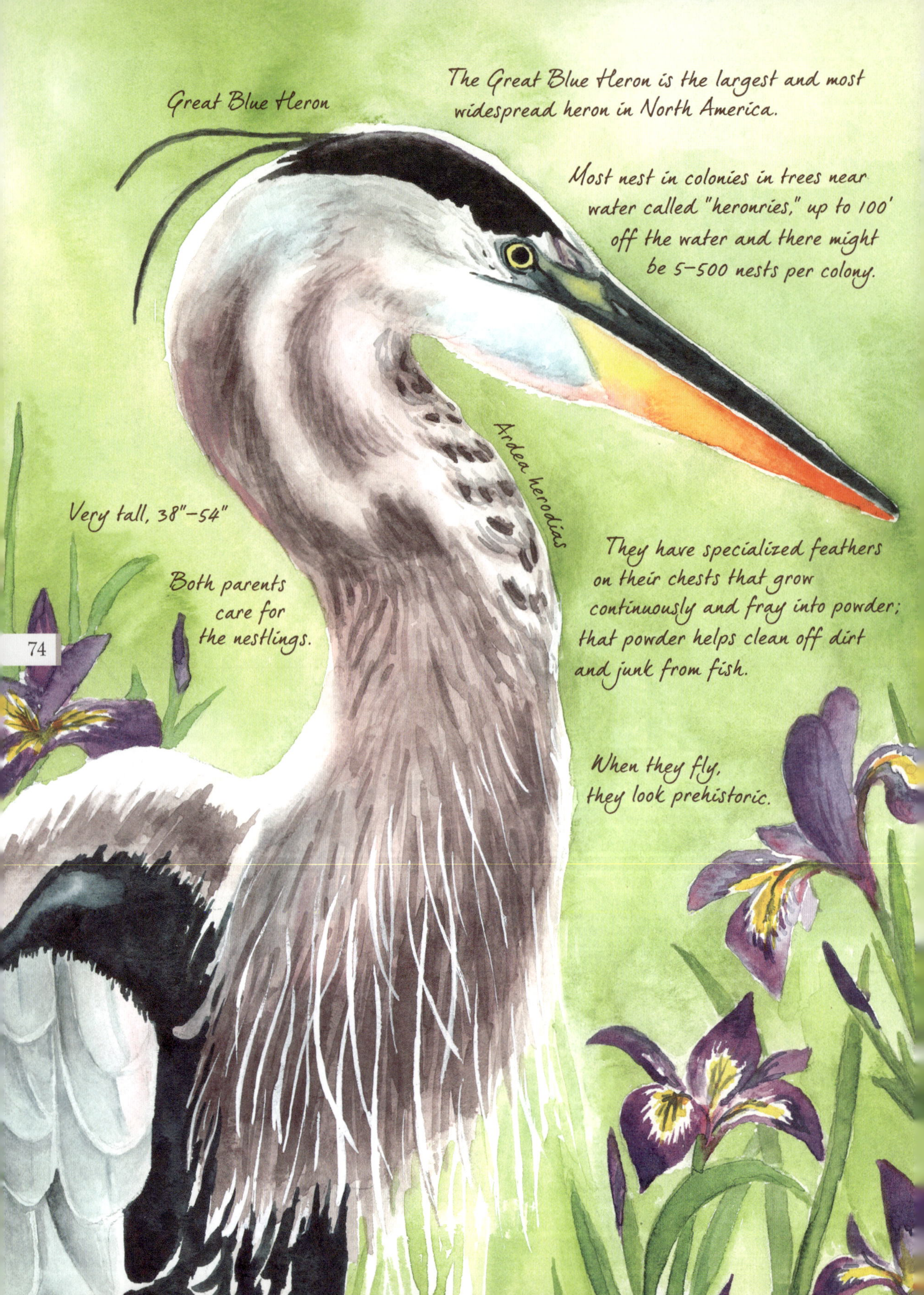
Great Blue Heron
The Great Blue Heron is the largest and most widespread heron in North America.
Most nest in colonies in trees near water called "heronries," up to 100' off the water and there might be 5–500 nests per colony.
Ardea herodias
Very tall, 38"–54"
Both parents care for the nestlings.
They have specialized feathers on their chests that grow continuously and fray into powder; that powder helps clean off dirt and junk from fish.
When they fly, they look prehistoric.

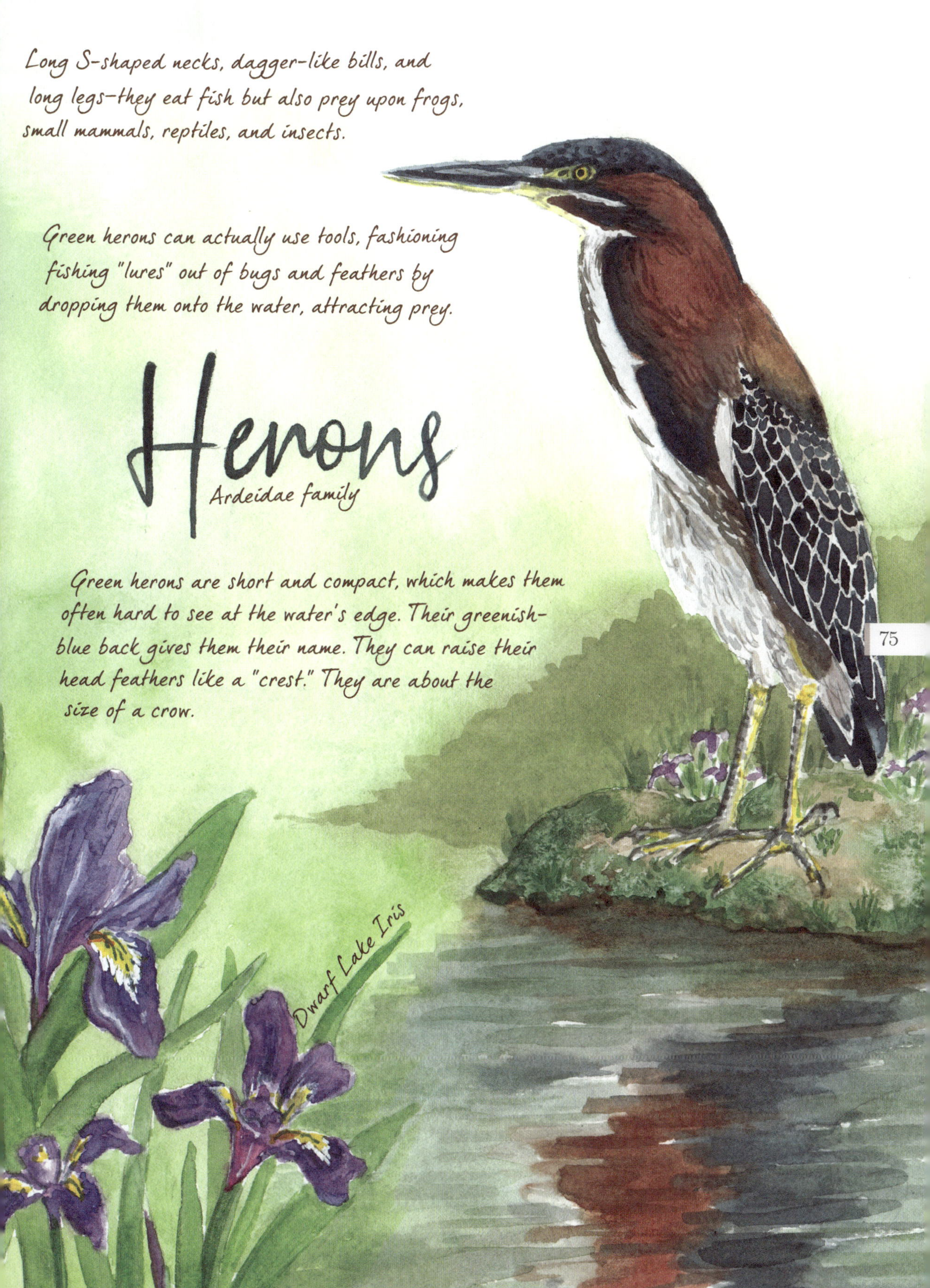
Long S-shaped necks, dagger-like bills, and long legs—they eat fish but also prey upon frogs, small mammals, reptiles, and insects.
Green herons can actually use tools, fashioning fishing "lures" out of bugs and feathers by dropping them onto the water, attracting prey.
Herons
Ardeidae family
Green herons are short and compact, which makes them often hard to see at the water's edge. Their greenish-blue back gives them their name. They can raise their head feathers like a "crest." They are about the size of a crow.
Dwarf Lake Iris

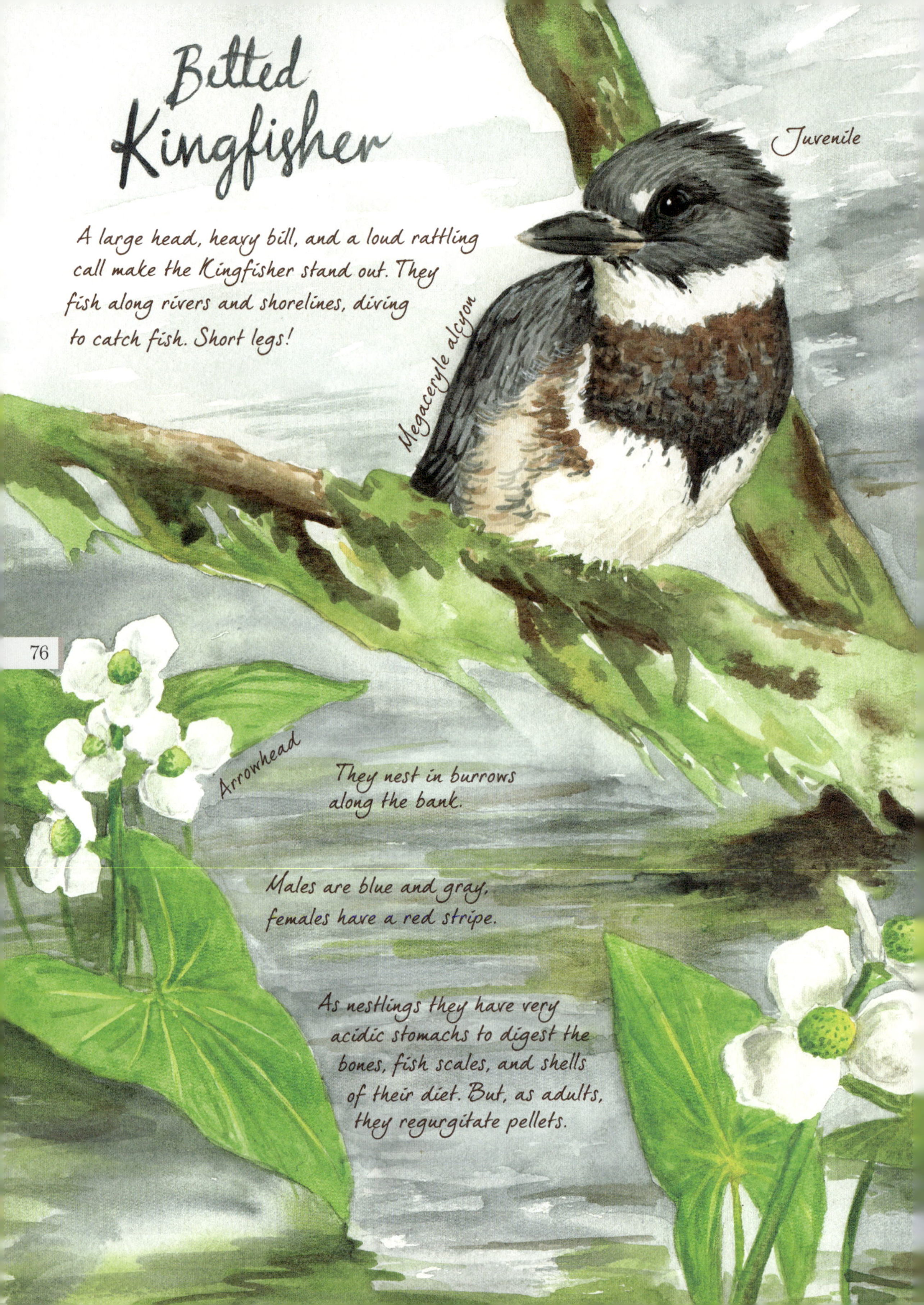
Belted Kingfisher
Juvenile
A large head, heavy bill, and a loud rattling call make the Kingfisher stand out. They fish along rivers and shorelines, diving to catch fish. Short legs!
Megaceryle alcyon
Arrowhead
They nest in burrows along the bank.
Males are blue and gray, females have a red stripe.
As nestlings they have very acidic stomachs to digest the bones, fish scales, and shells of their diet. But, as adults, they regurgitate pellets.

Red-winged Blackbird

Look for these in ditches along the roadside, in marshes, and in old fields.

They travel up to 800 miles south for the winter.

Very territorial! You might get "told off" if you get too close. A "cank-la-lee" call.

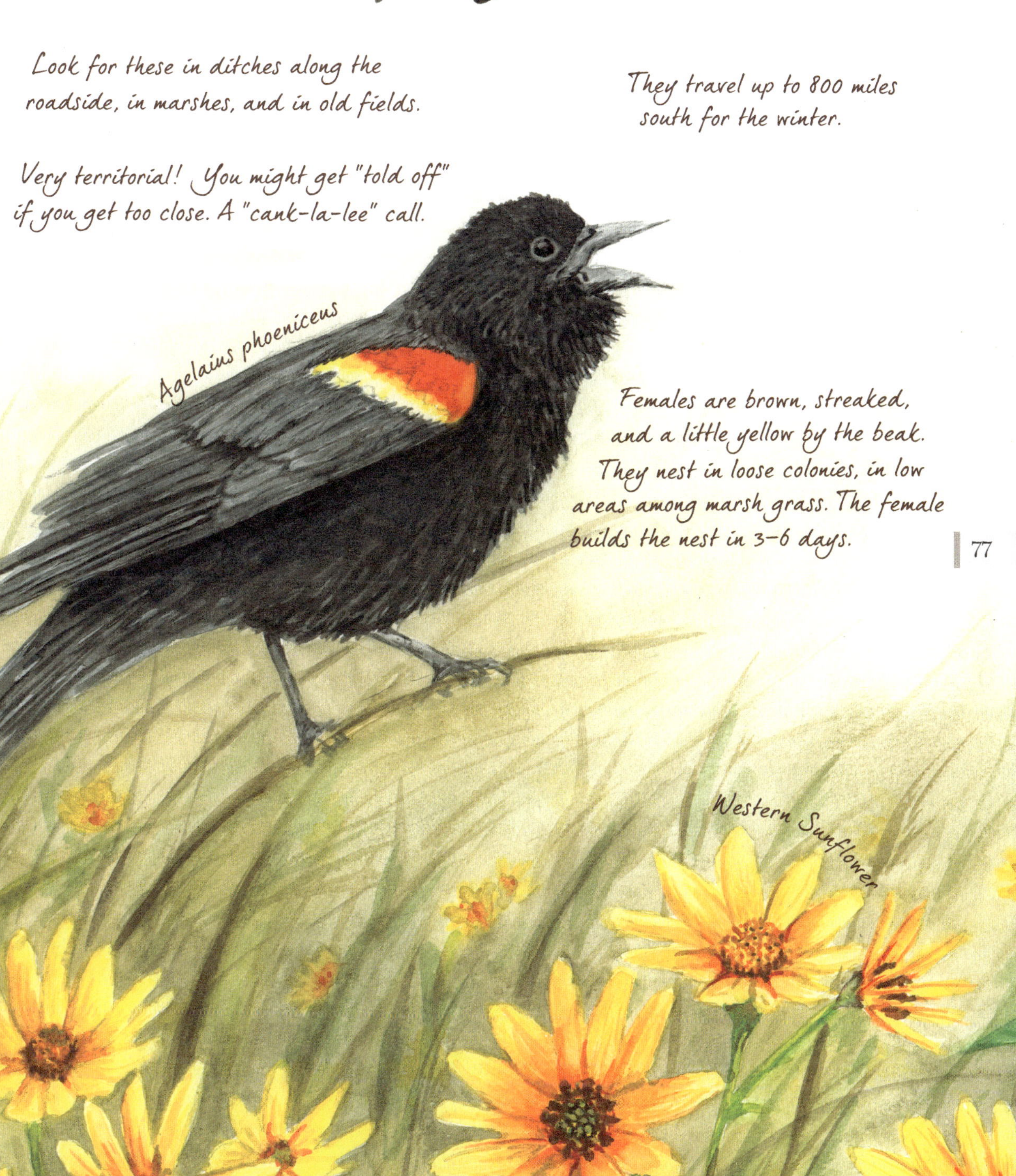

Females are brown, streaked, and a little yellow by the beak. They nest in loose colonies, in low areas among marsh grass. The female builds the nest in 3–6 days.

Piping Plover

Shorebirds—they blend in so well you won't see them until they run. They migrate far in the winter but return to close to the exact same spot to nest every year.

Endangered in the Great Lakes region. In 1986 only 17 pairs nested in Michigan. Numbers are rising, though!

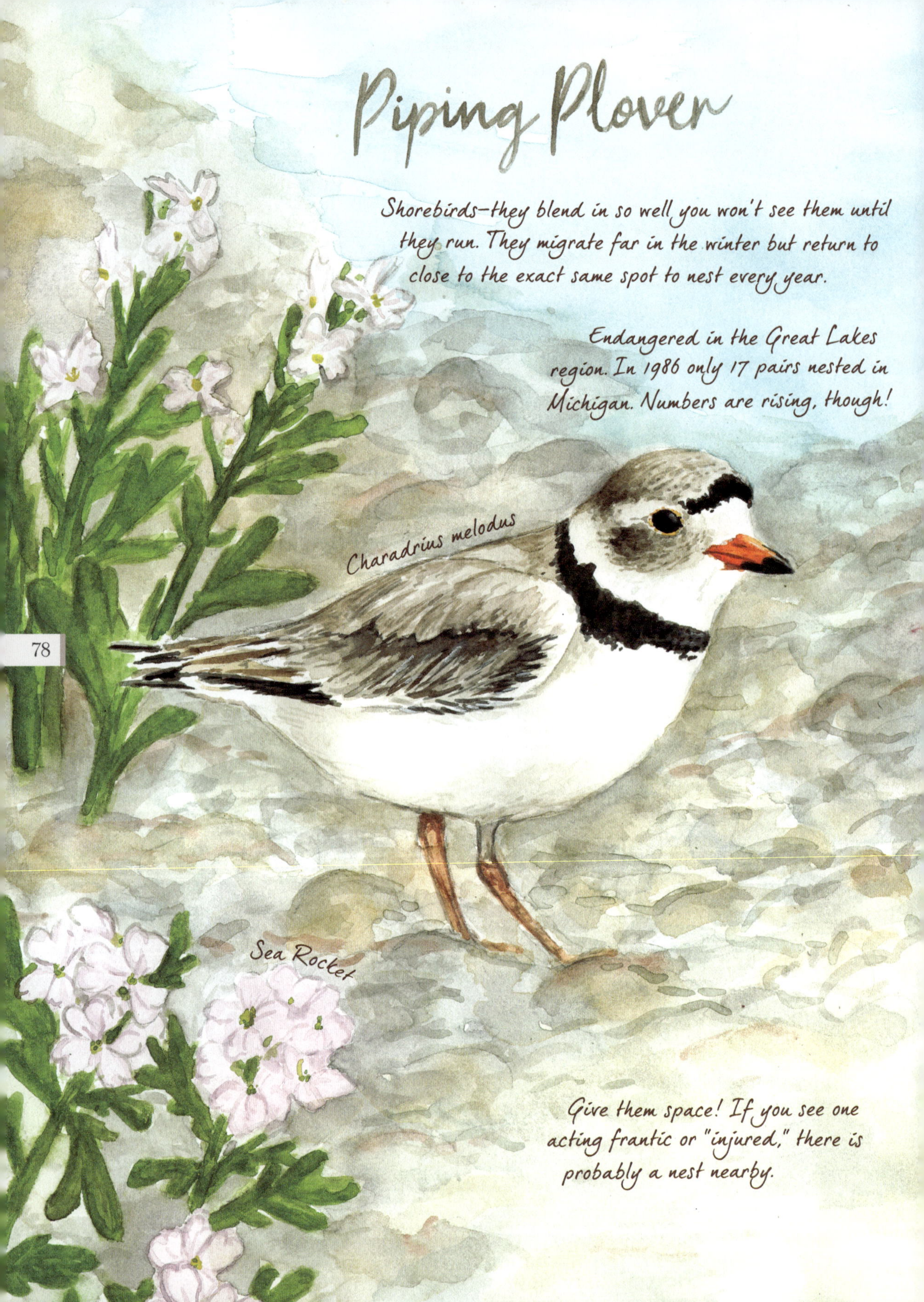

Give them space! If you see one acting frantic or "injured," there is probably a nest nearby.

Pied-billed Grebe

A small bird generally swimming in large ponds across North America. They like ponds with vegetation on the edges especially. Like loons, their feet are located near the back of their bodies, so they walk (and fly) awkwardly, but swim excellently! They can regulate how much air stays in their feathers, thus controlling their buoyancy (like filling and releasing airbags).

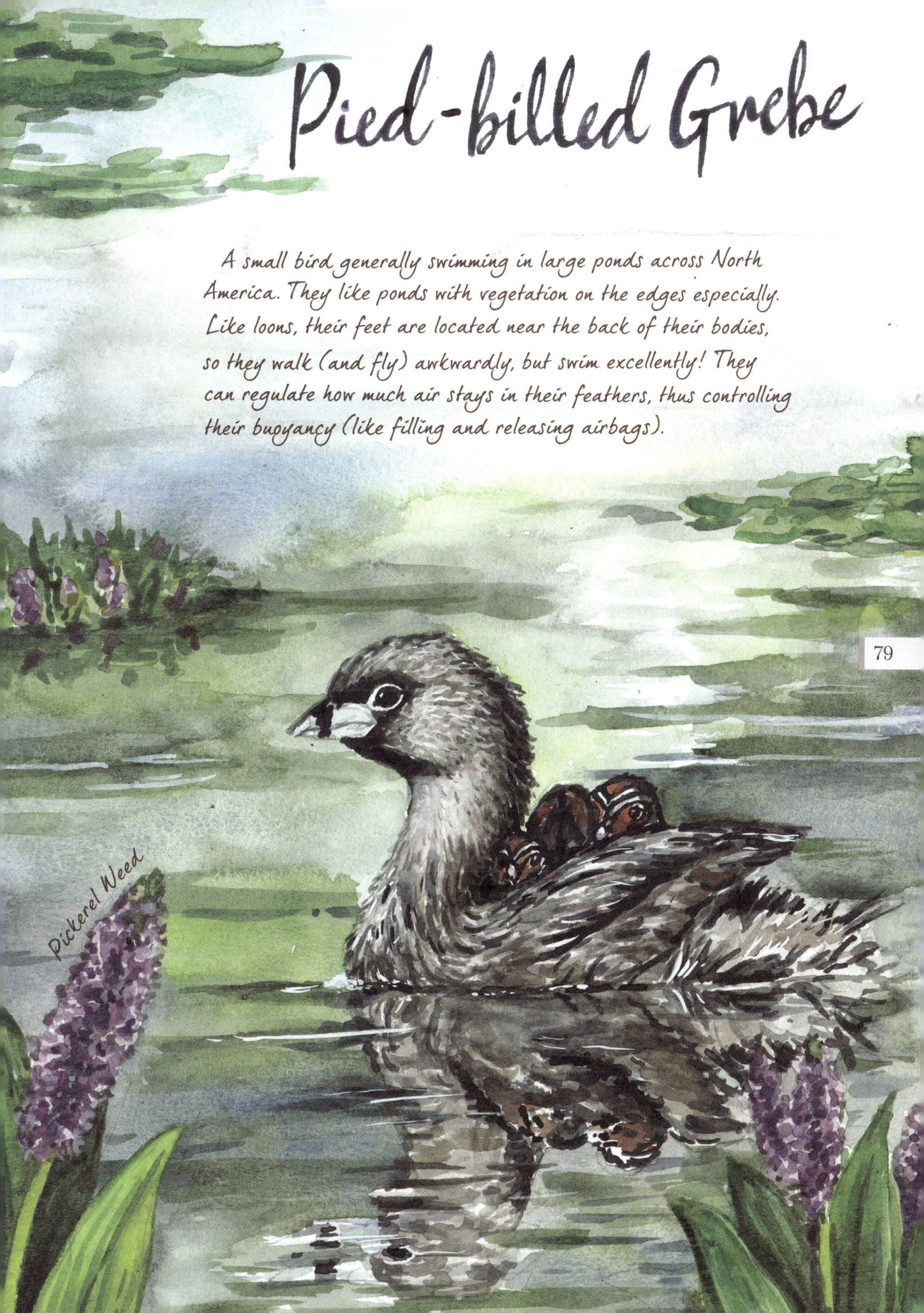

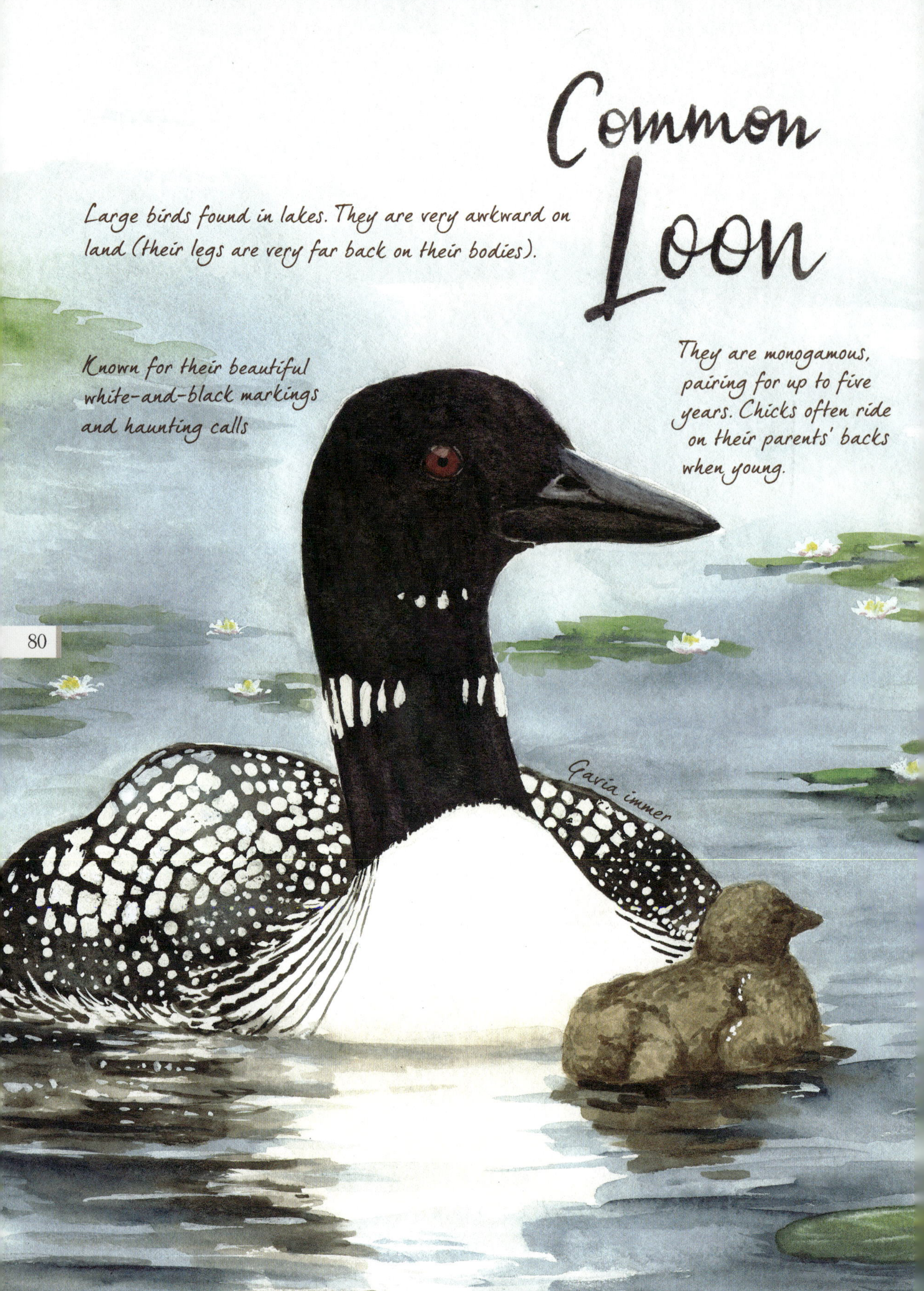
Common Loon
Large birds found in lakes. They are very awkward on land (their legs are very far back on their bodies).
Known for their beautiful white-and-black markings and haunting calls
They are monogamous, pairing for up to five years. Chicks often ride on their parents' backs when young.
Gavia immer

In winter, they turn gray. They have solid bones (unlike other birds), which allows them to dive better. Their heart even slows down to conserve oxygen underwater. Most dives last 8–60 seconds, but they can remain underwater for three minutes.

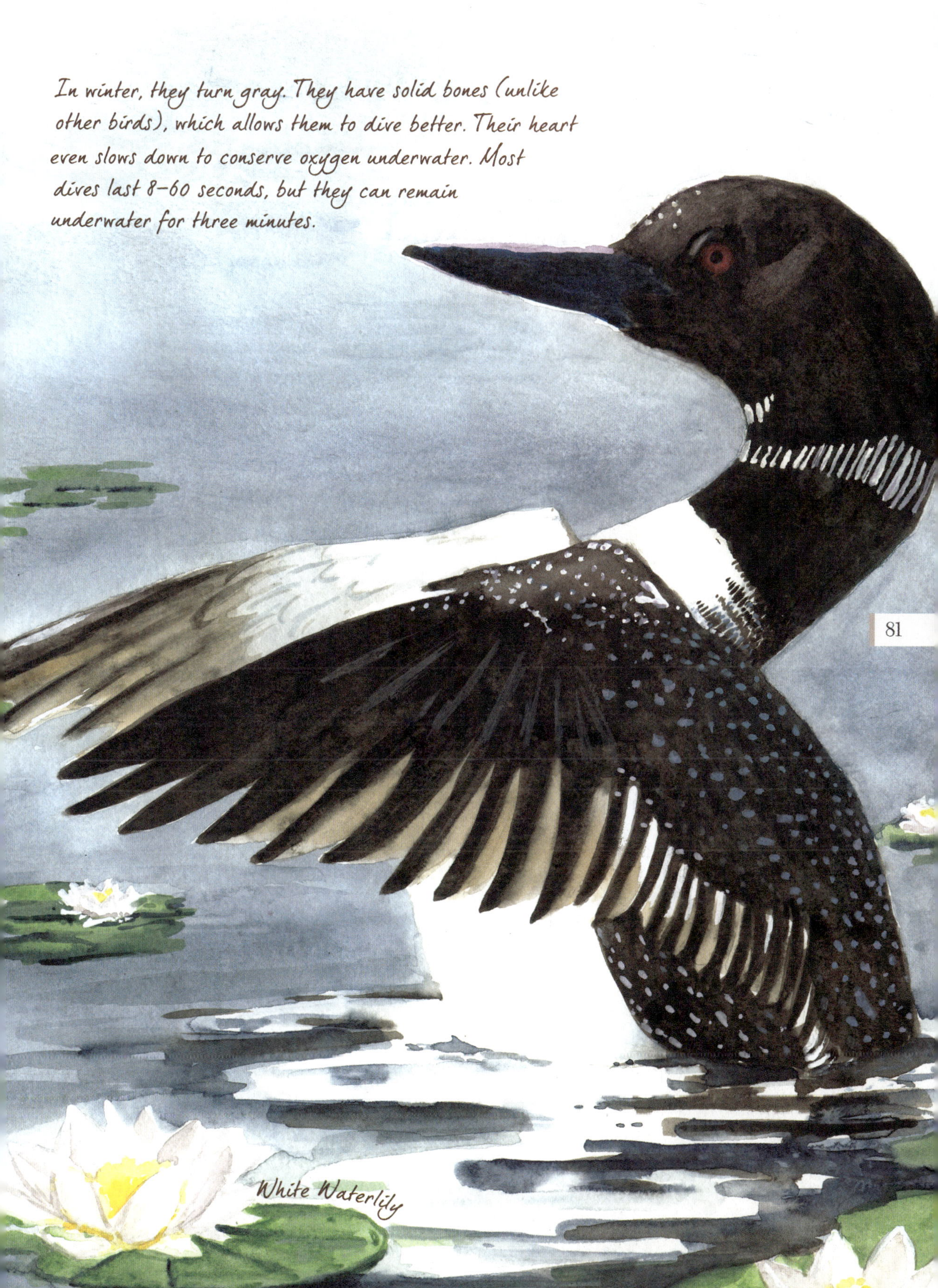

Prairie and Woods

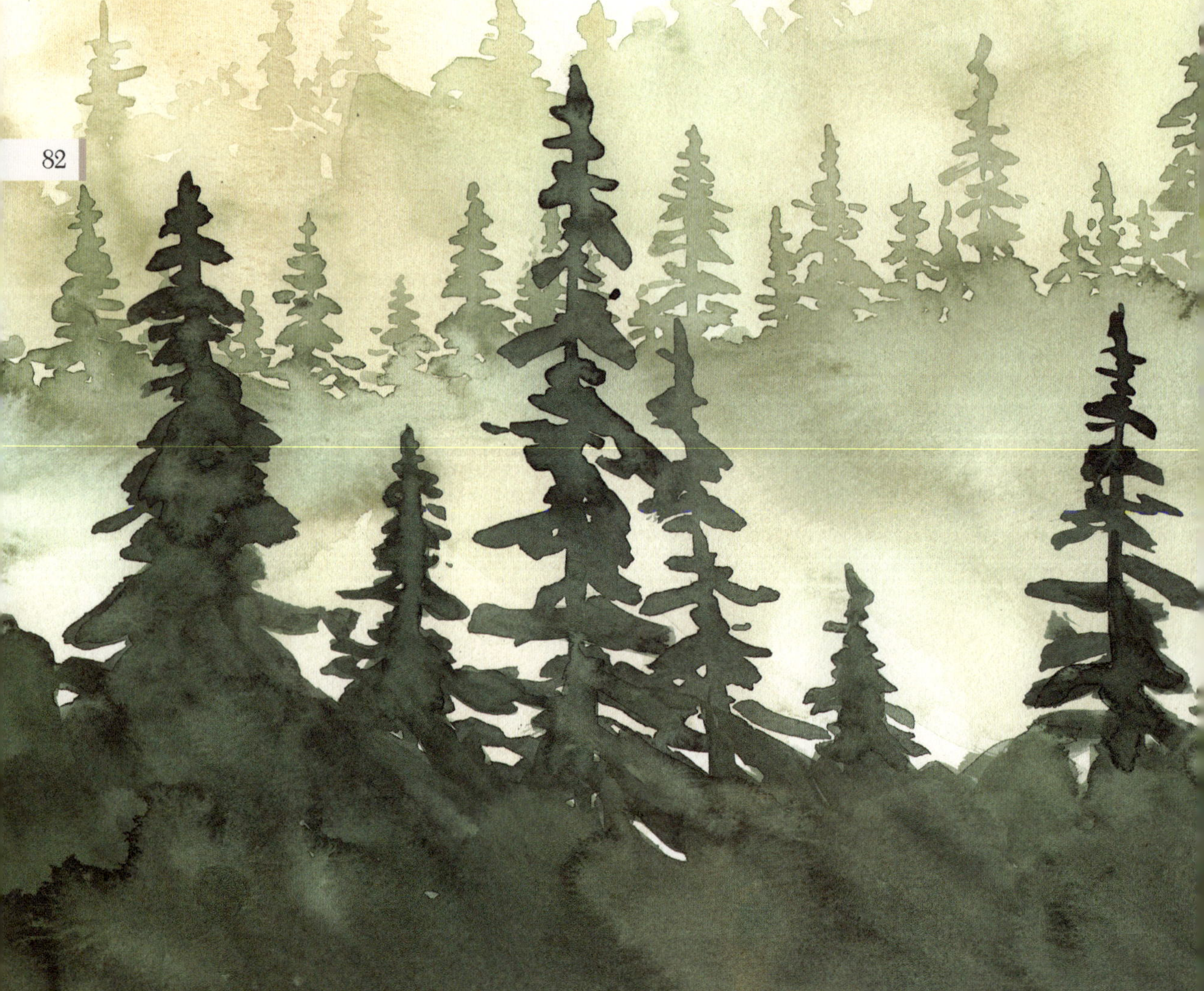

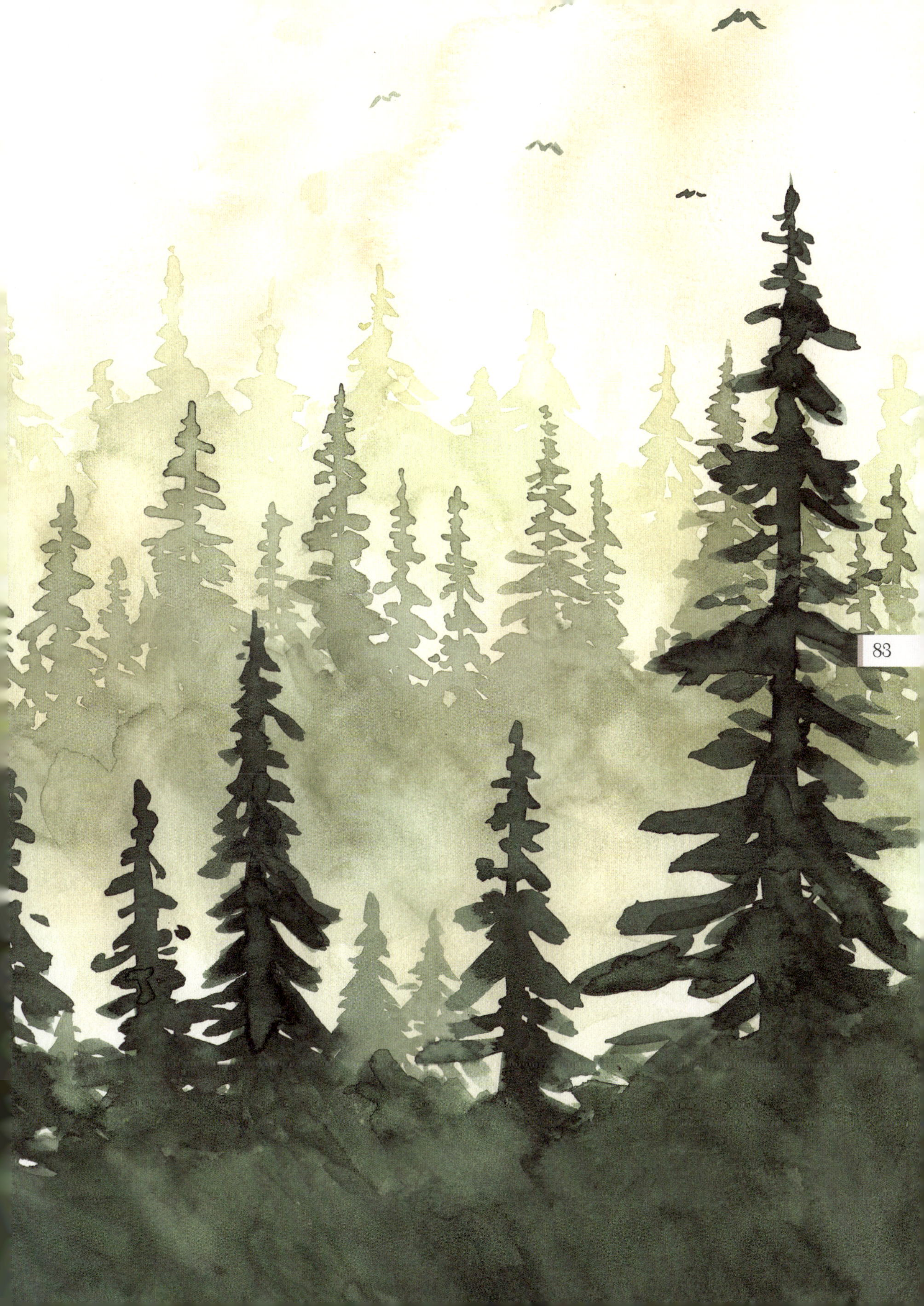

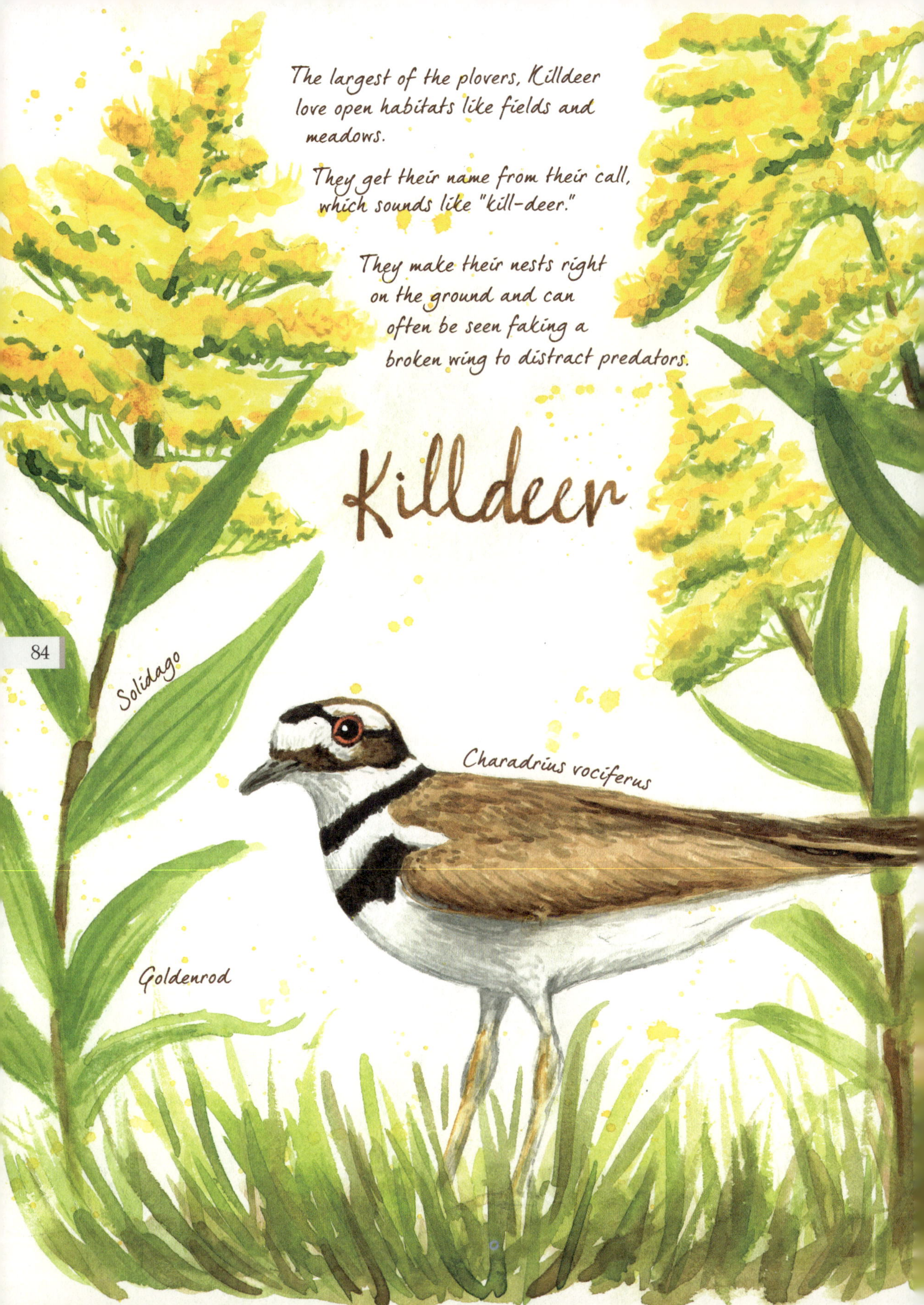
The largest of the plovers, Killdeer love open habitats like fields and meadows.
They get their name from their call, which sounds like "kill-deer."
They make their nests right on the ground and can often be seen faking a broken wing to distract predators.
Killdeer
Solidago
Charadrius vociferus
Goldenrod

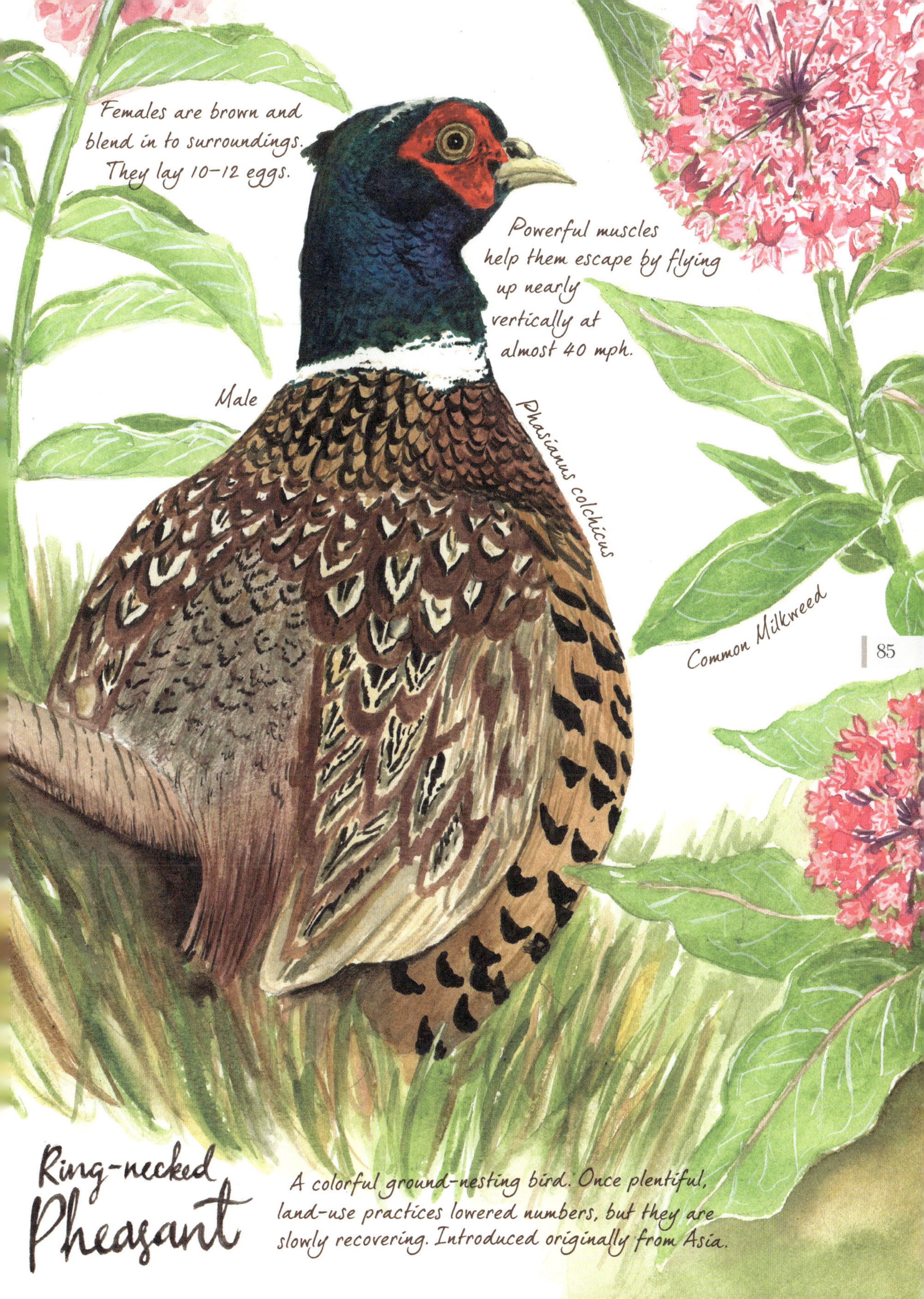

85

Ring-necked Pheasant

A colorful ground-nesting bird. Once plentiful, land-use practices lowered numbers, but they are slowly recovering. Introduced originally from Asia.

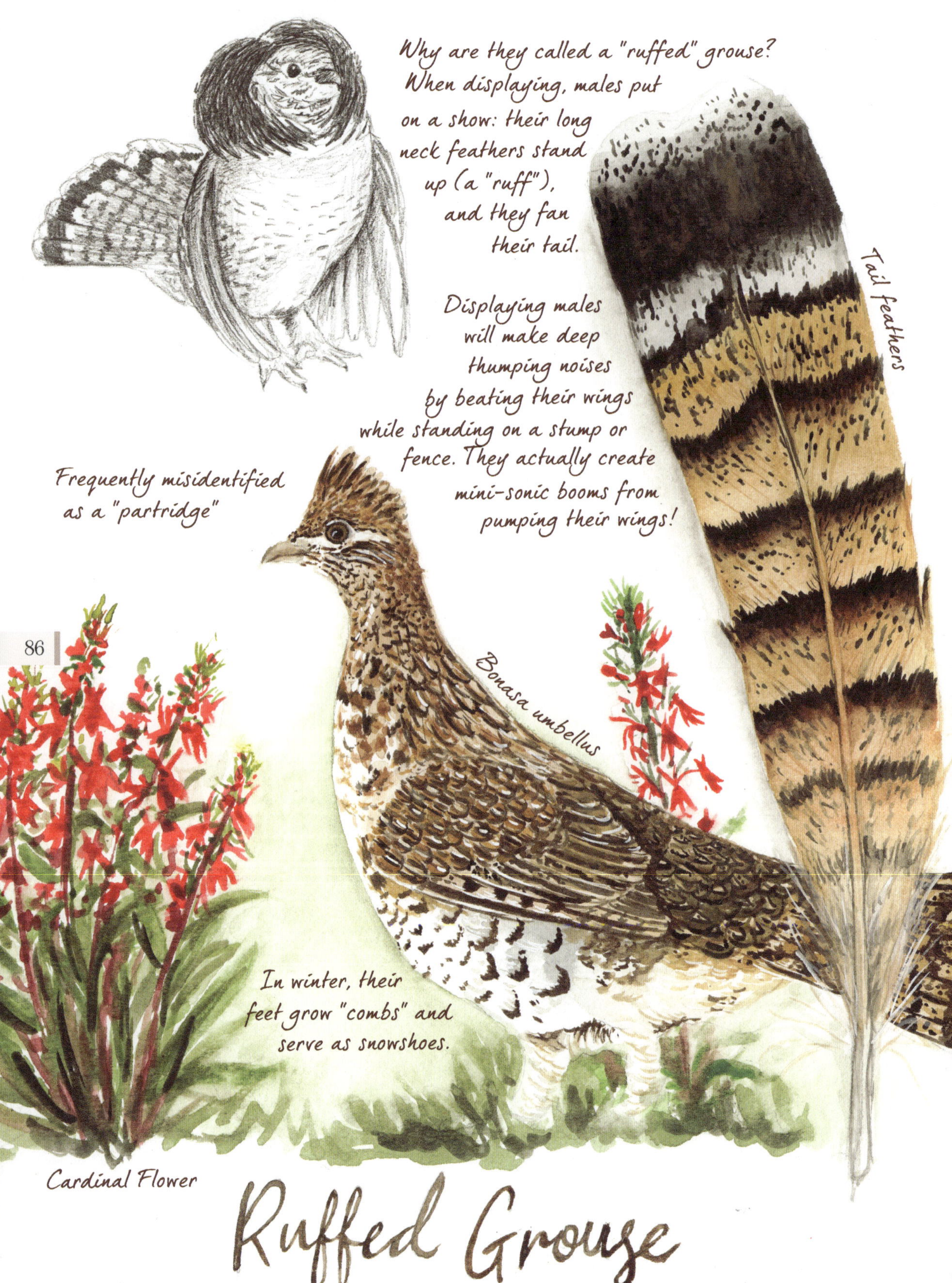
Why are they called a "ruffed" grouse? When displaying, males put on a show: their long neck feathers stand up (a "ruff"), and they fan their tail.
Displaying males will make deep thumping noises by beating their wings while standing on a stump or fence. They actually create mini-sonic booms from pumping their wings!
Tail feathers
Frequently misidentified as a "partridge"
Bonasa umbellus
In winter, their feet grow "combs" and serve as snowshoes.
Cardinal Flower
Ruffed Grouse

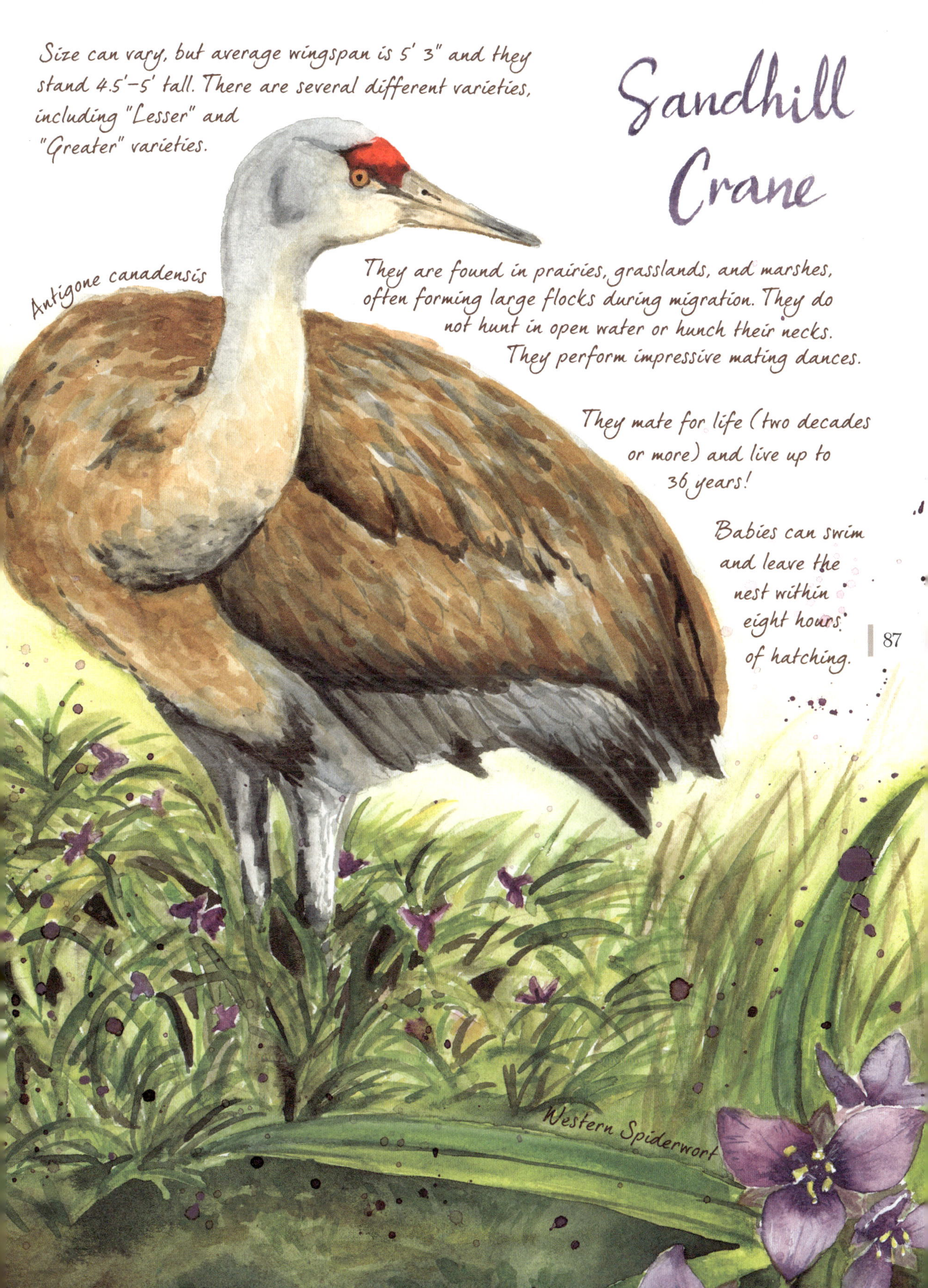
Size can vary, but average wingspan is 5' 3" and they stand 4.5'–5' tall. There are several different varieties, including "Lesser" and "Greater" varieties.
Sandhill Crane
Antigone canadensis
They are found in prairies, grasslands, and marshes, often forming large flocks during migration. They do not hunt in open water or hunch their necks. They perform impressive mating dances.
They mate for life (two decades or more) and live up to 36 years!
Babies can swim and leave the nest within eight hours of hatching.
Western Spiderwort

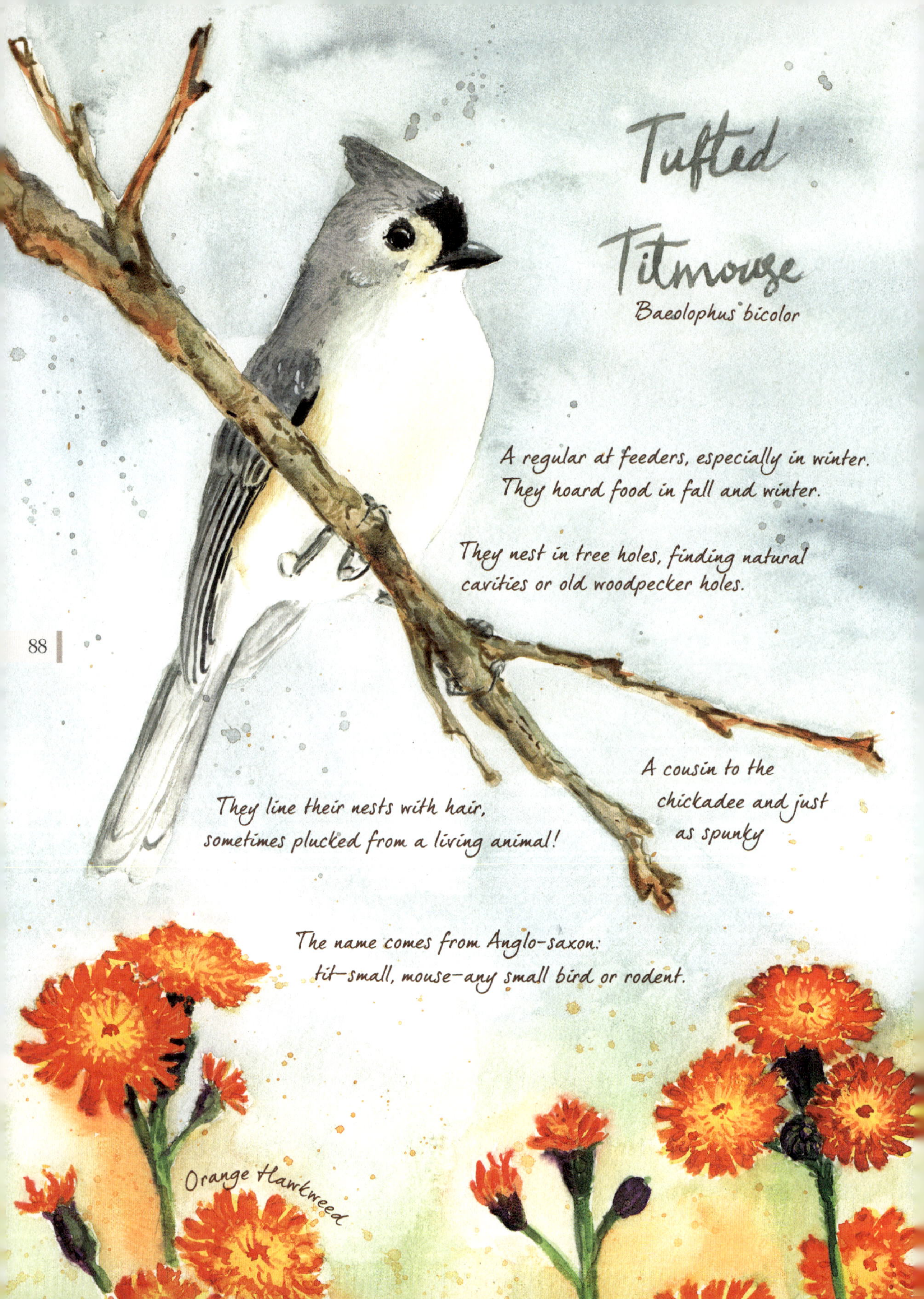
Tufted Titmouse
Baeolophus bicolor
A regular at feeders, especially in winter.
They hoard food in fall and winter.
They nest in tree holes, finding natural
cavities or old woodpecker holes.
They line their nests with hair,
sometimes plucked from a living animal!
A cousin to the
chickadee and just
as spunky
The name comes from Anglo-saxon:
tit—small, mouse—any small bird or rodent.
Orange Hawkweed

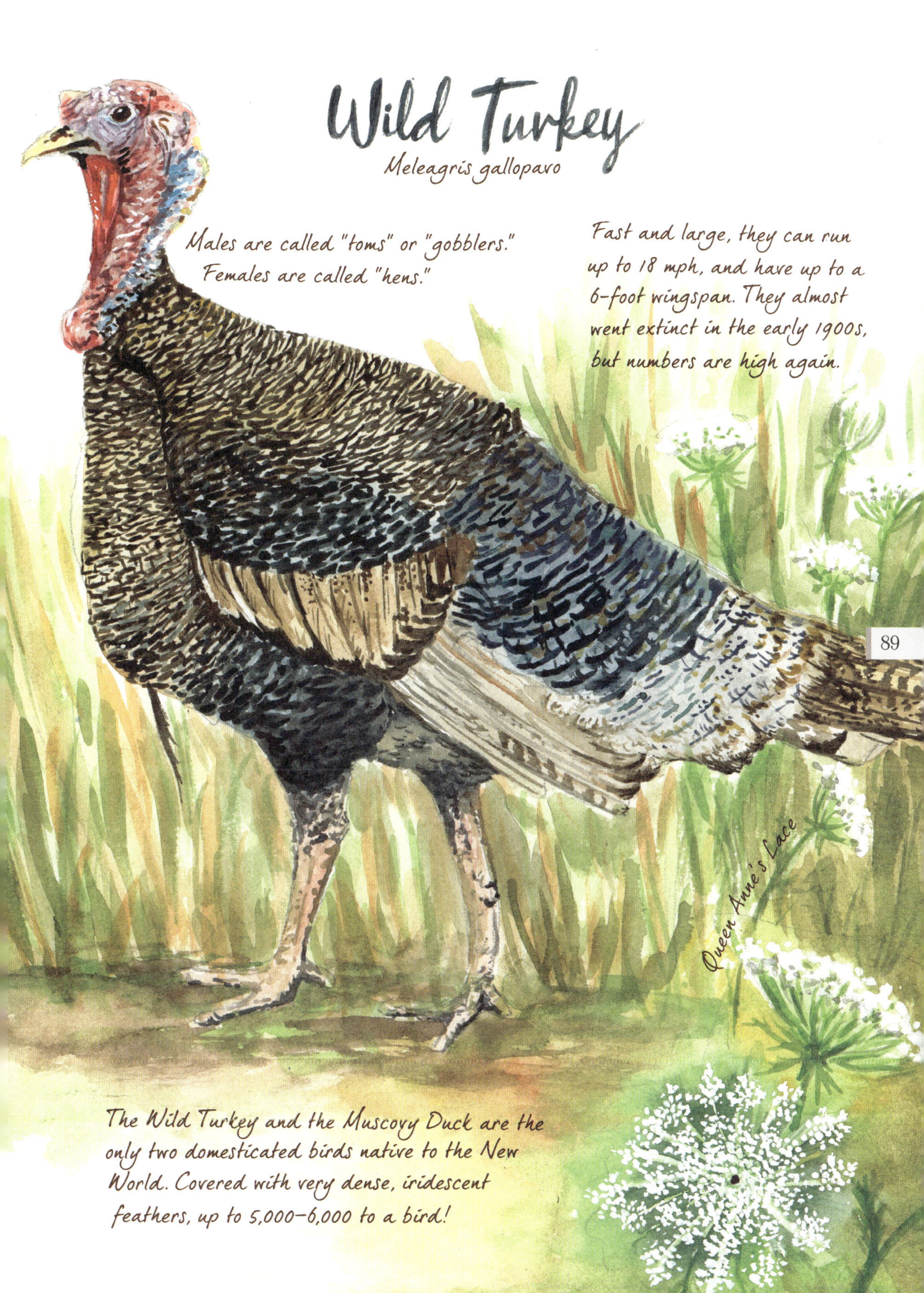
Wild Turkey
Meleagris gallopavo
Males are called "toms" or "gobblers." Females are called "hens."
Fast and large, they can run up to 18 mph, and have up to a 6-foot wingspan. They almost went extinct in the early 1900s, but numbers are high again.
Queen Anne's Lace
The Wild Turkey and the Muscovy Duck are the only two domesticated birds native to the New World. Covered with very dense, iridescent feathers, up to 5,000–6,000 to a bird!

The ovenbird gets its name from the oven-like appearance of its nests. They make a dome with a side entrance using sticks and leaves. Stay on trails to avoid stepping on one!

Ovenbird

In the warbler family

Generally found foraging on the forest floor, where they are very loud

A call of "teacher-teacher-teacher!"

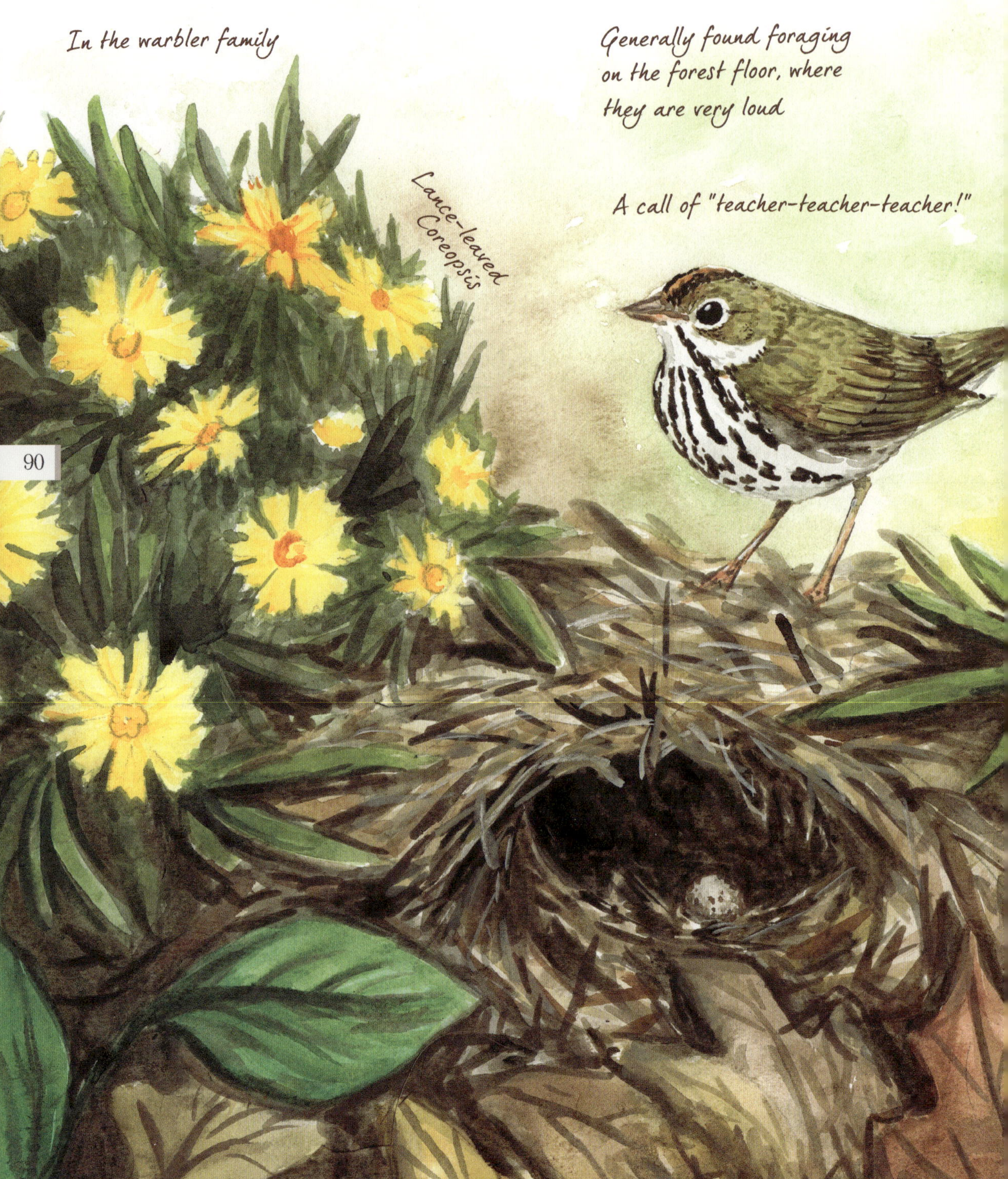

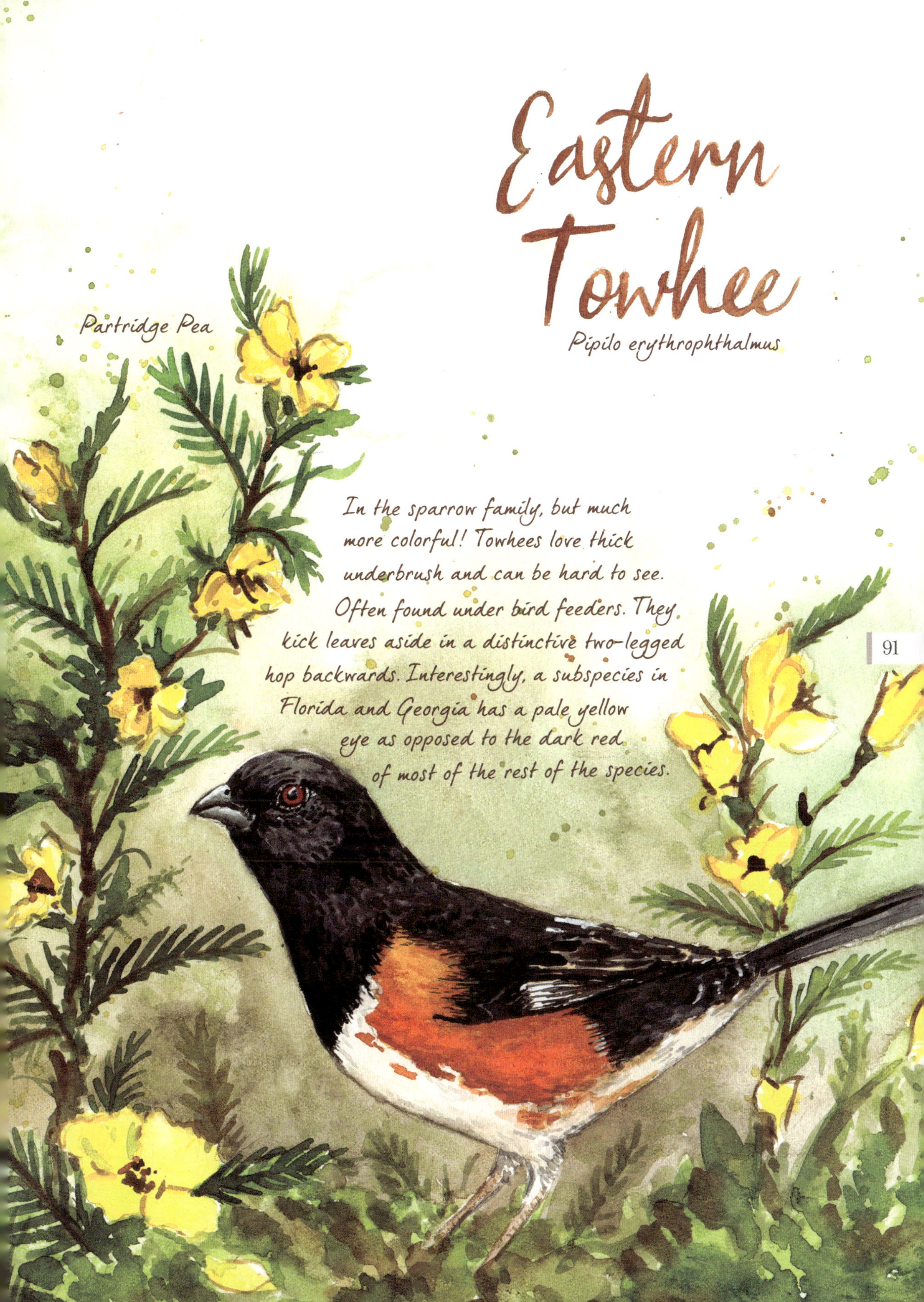

Eastern Towhee
Pipilo erythrophthalmus
Partridge Pea
In the sparrow family, but much more colorful! Towhees love thick underbrush and can be hard to see. Often found under bird feeders. They kick leaves aside in a distinctive two-legged hop backwards. Interestingly, a subspecies in Florida and Georgia has a pale yellow eye as opposed to the dark red of most of the rest of the species.

Invasive Species

A non-native species that negatively alters its new environment

One of the most widespread invasive species, starlings were released in New York in 1890 as part of an ill-conceived plan to introduce all of the birds mentioned in Shakespeare to the US. There are more starlings in the US than any other species.

European Starling

Mute Swan

Similar to a Mourning Dove but with a distinctive black "collar" and no black dots on its back. Populations spread quickly and compete with native species.

Instantly recognizable for its orange beak, black knob, and "S" shaped neck (native Trumpeter Swans have black beaks and "C" shaped necks). Introduced in 1919, these captive birds escaped. They are very aggressive and drive out native waterfowl; they also eat 4–8 lbs. of plants a day, which disrupts wetlands quickly.

Eurasian Collared Dove

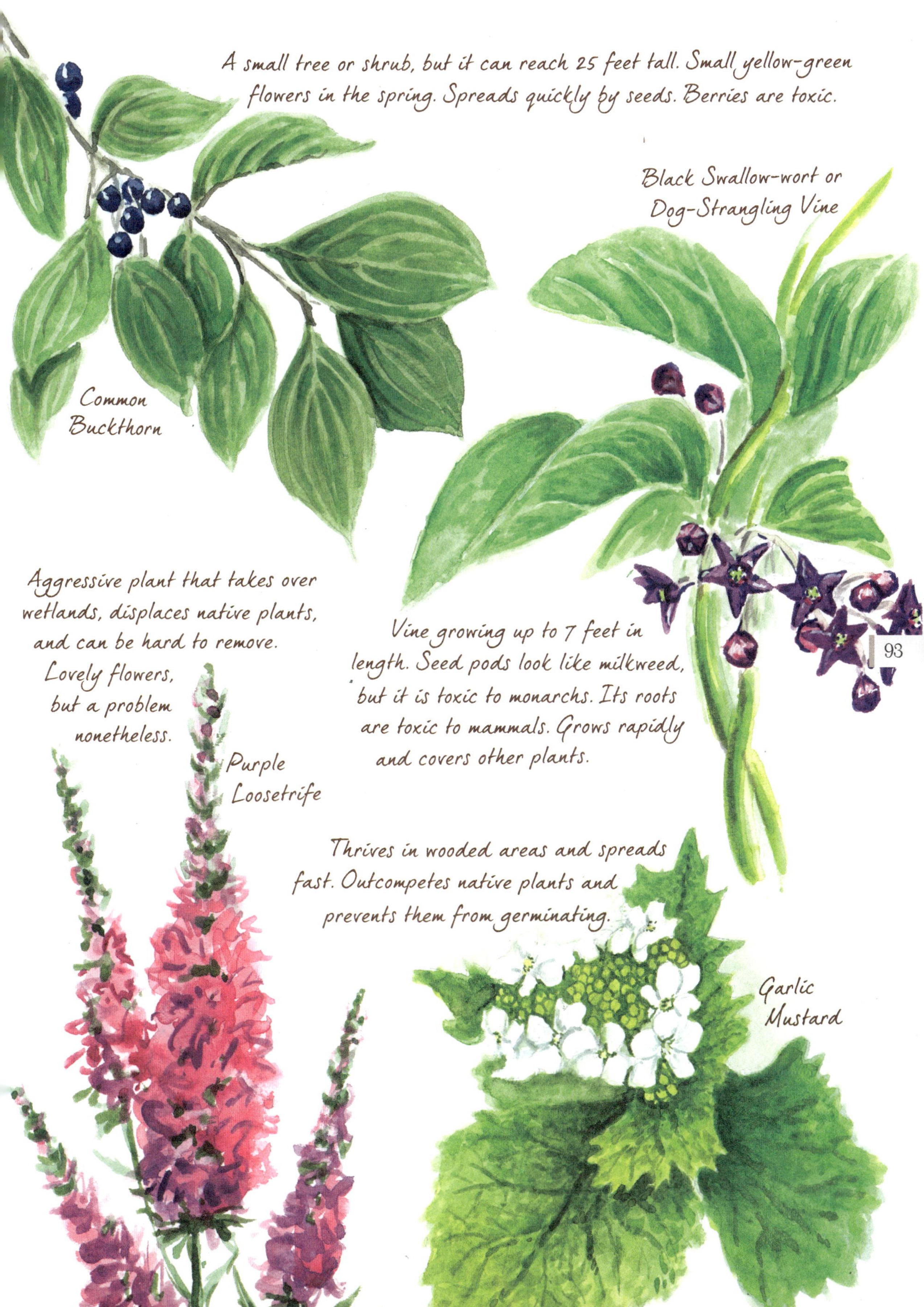
A small tree or shrub, but it can reach 25 feet tall. Small yellow-green flowers in the spring. Spreads quickly by seeds. Berries are toxic.
Common Buckthorn
Black Swallow-wort or Dog-Strangling Vine
Aggressive plant that takes over wetlands, displaces native plants, and can be hard to remove. Lovely flowers, but a problem nonetheless.
Vine growing up to 7 feet in length. Seed pods look like milkweed, but it is toxic to monarchs. Its roots are toxic to mammals. Grows rapidly and covers other plants.
Purple Loosetrife
Thrives in wooded areas and spreads fast. Outcompetes native plants and prevents them from germinating.
Garlic Mustard

How to be a Naturalist

1) Notice

What makes you stop and look closer? Take a walk around your backyard or a park. What are you drawn to? Take your time.

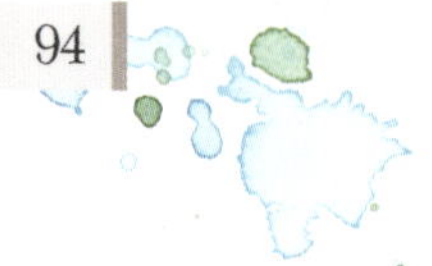

2) Take some notes

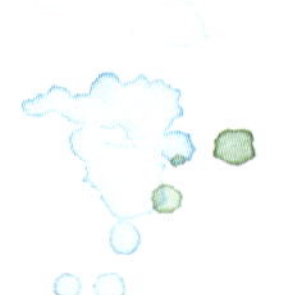

What do you see? Where?

When? What season or time of day?

How often? Notice variations.

Keep a notebook or sketchbook.

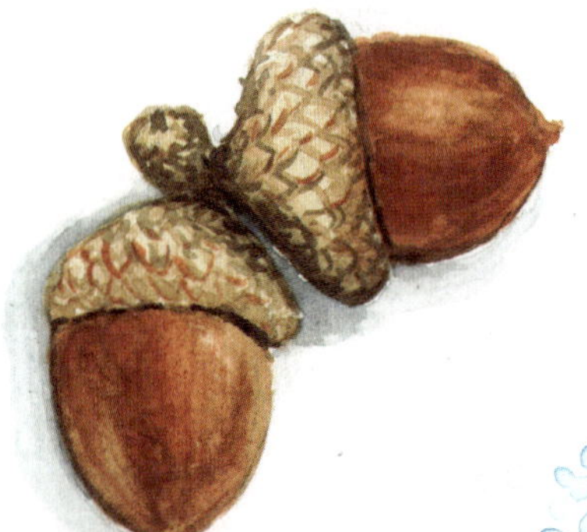

Naturalist–def. Noun. "A person who studies nature, especially by direct observation of animals and plants."

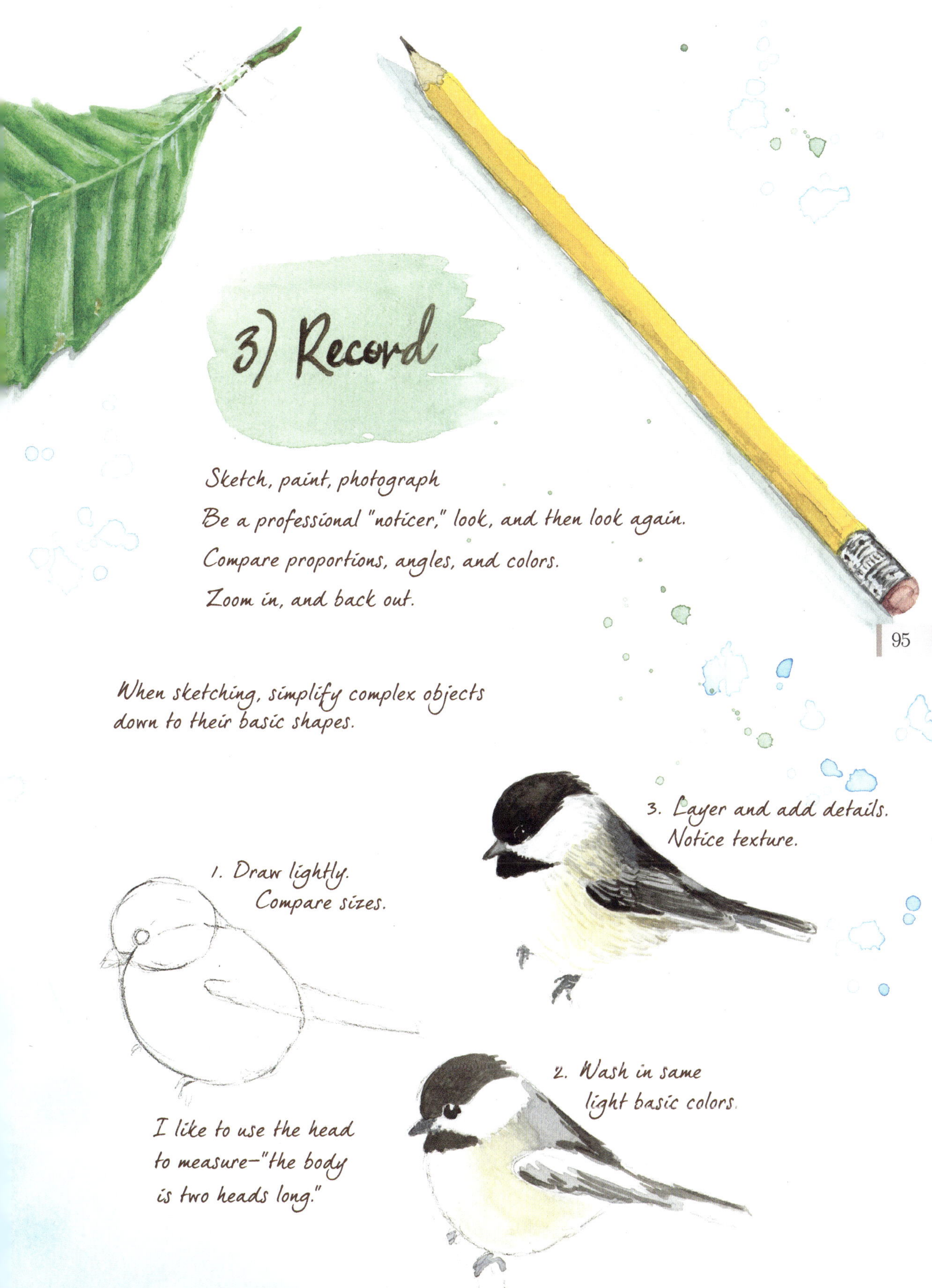

3) Record

Sketch, paint, photograph

Be a professional "noticer," look, and then look again.

Compare proportions, angles, and colors.

Zoom in, and back out.

When sketching, simplify complex objects down to their basic shapes.

I like to use the head to measure—"the body is two heads long."

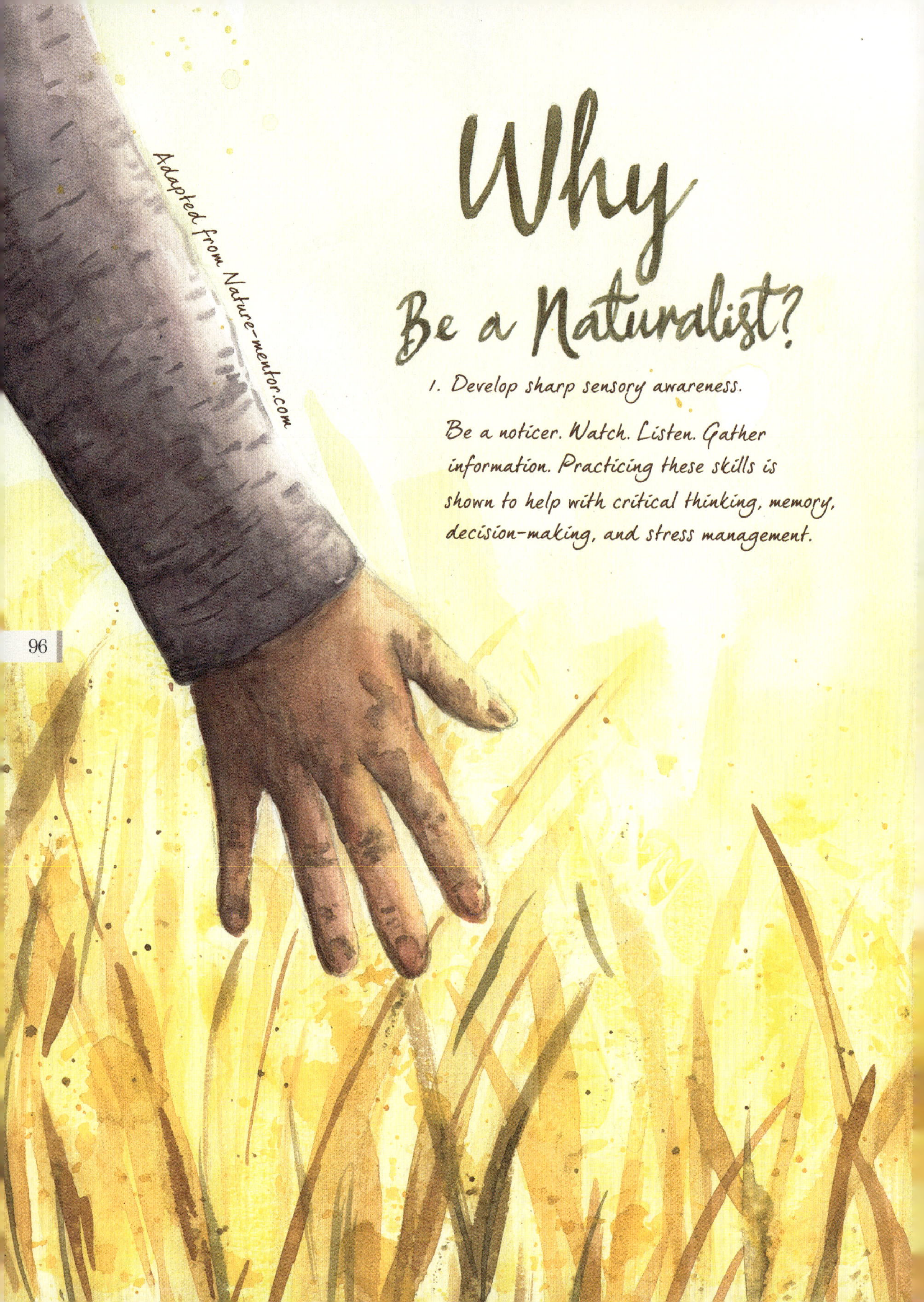

Why Be a Naturalist?

1. Develop sharp sensory awareness.

Be a noticer. Watch. Listen. Gather information. Practicing these skills is shown to help with critical thinking, memory, decision-making, and stress management.

2. Develop common sense.

Paying attention to your surroundings—and being aware of the world around you—is a very useful skill. It teaches long-term thinking and patience, rather than instant gratification.

3. Care for our world.

John Muir wrote: "When we try to pick out anything by itself, we find it hitched to everything else in the universe."

Noticing the relationships and patterns in nature helps us understand the past, present, and future of our environments.

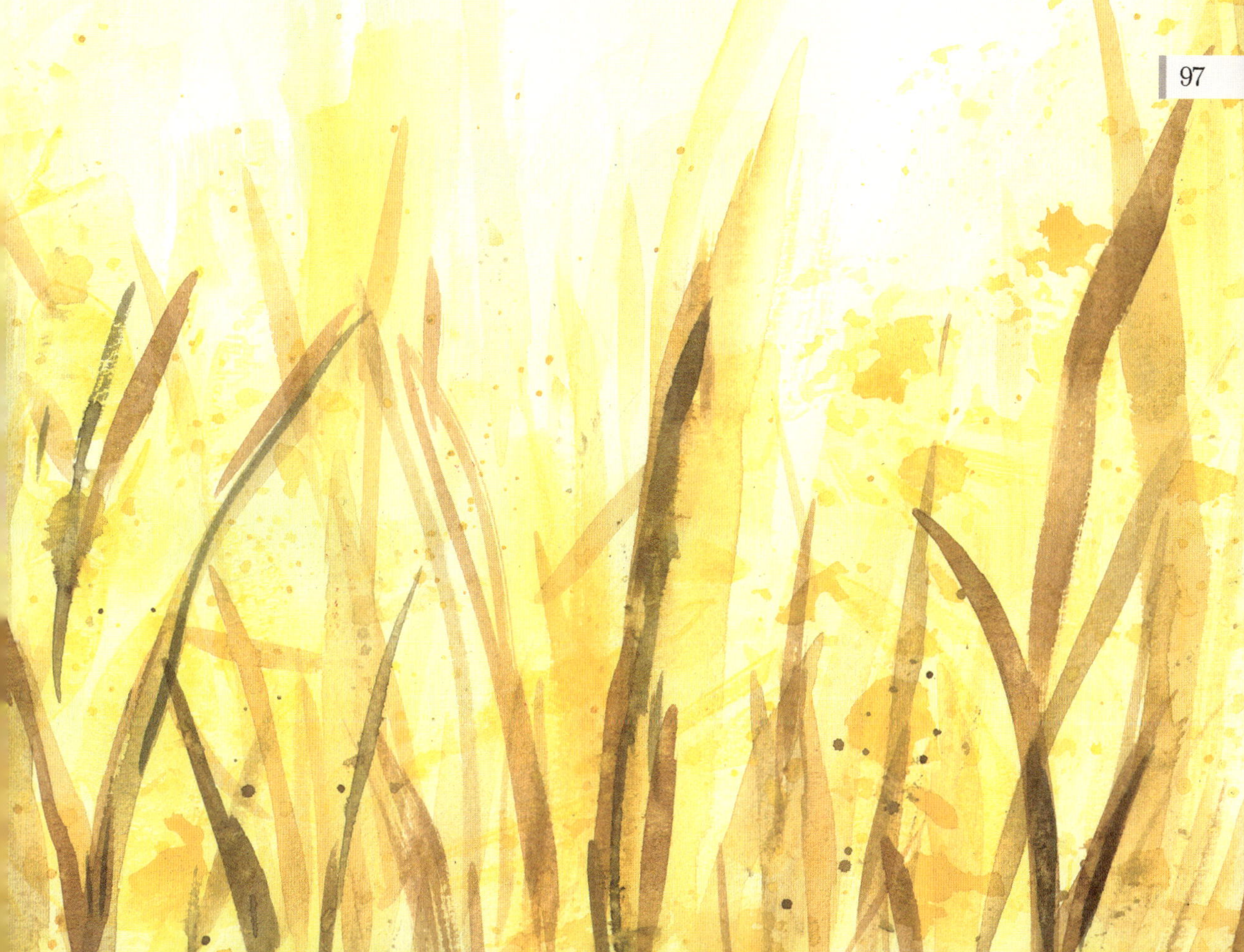

Helpful Items

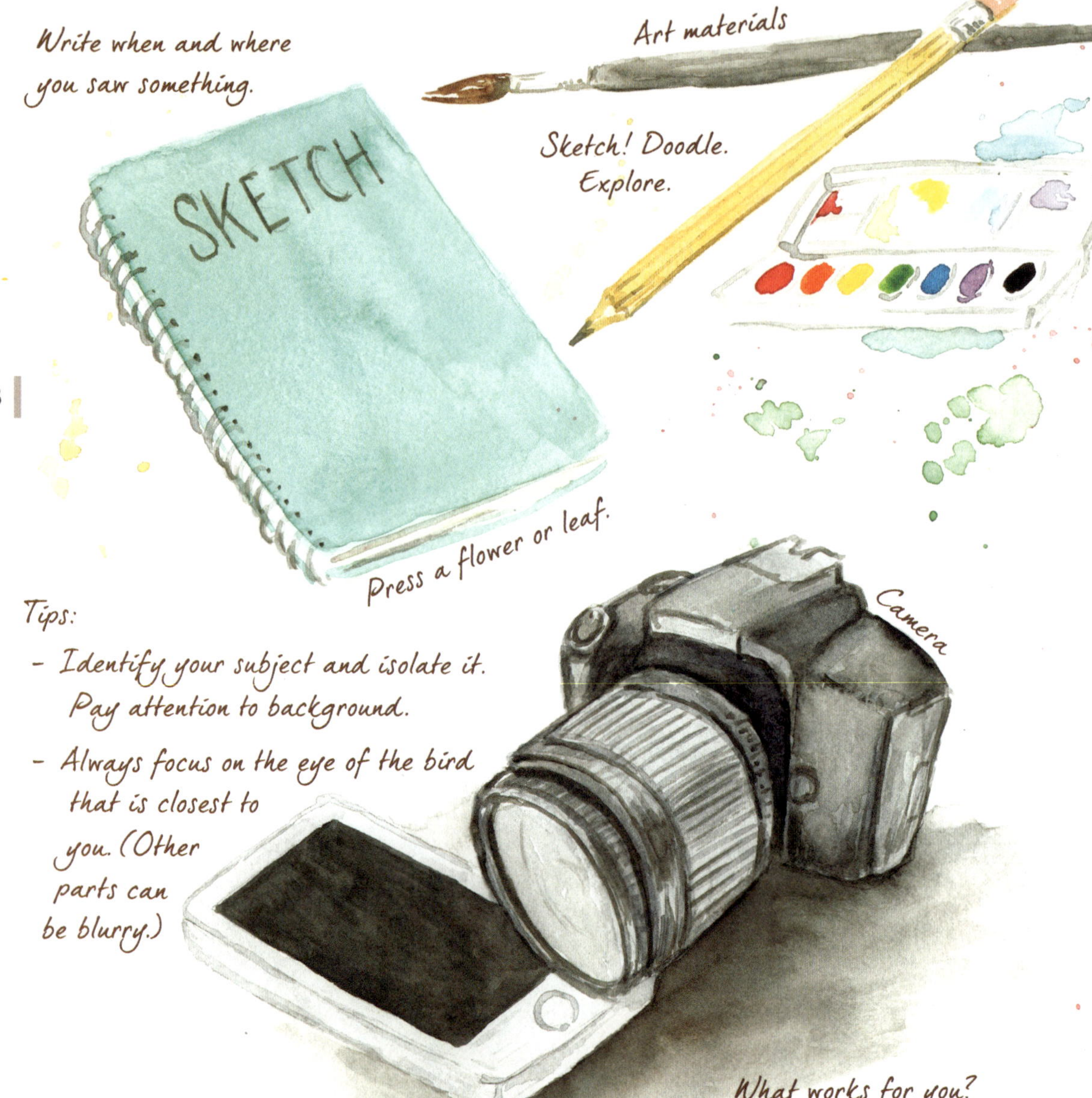

Tips:

- Identify your subject and isolate it. Pay attention to background.
- Always focus on the eye of the bird that is closest to you. (Other parts can be blurry.)

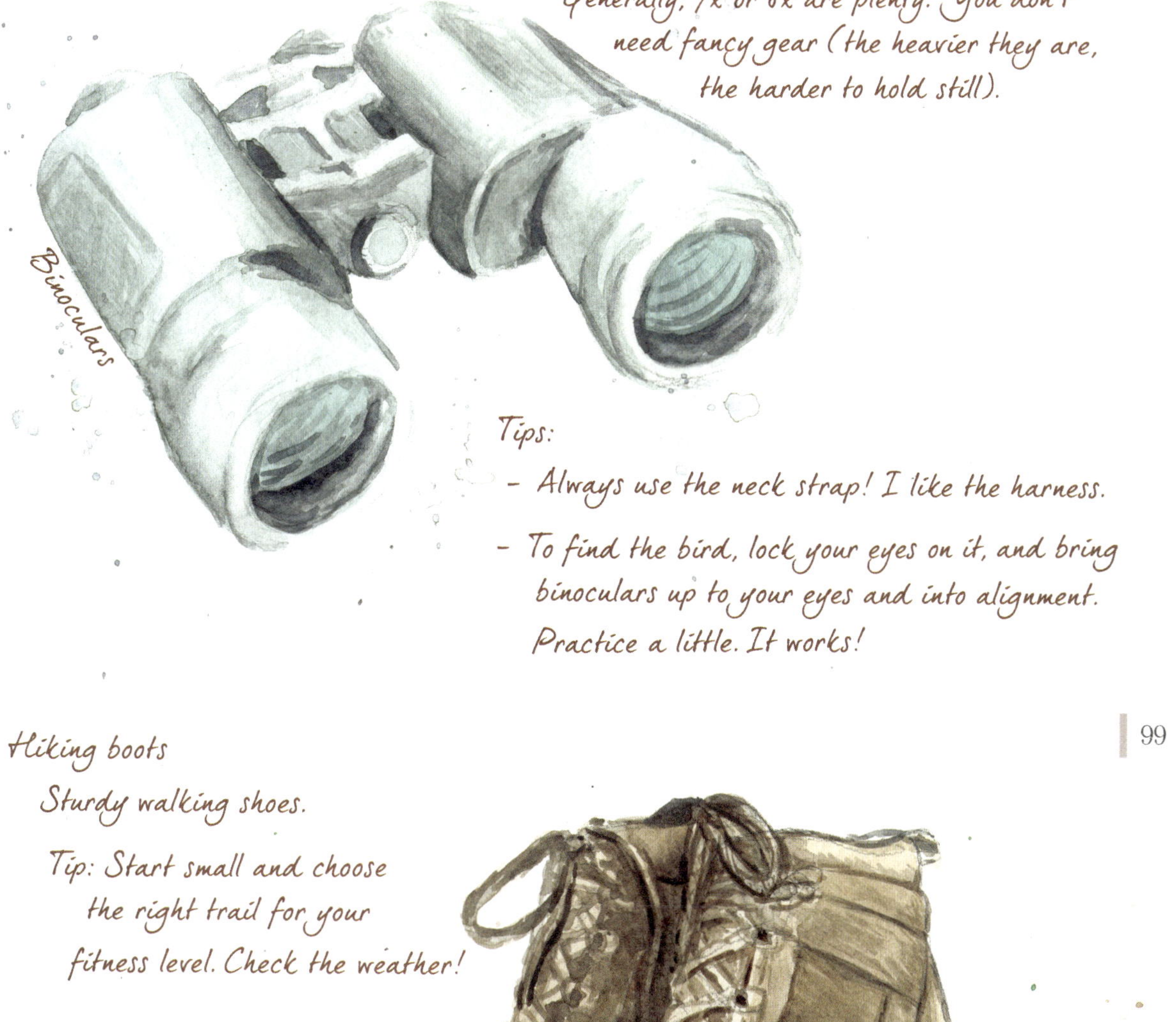

Generally, 7x or 8x are plenty. You don't need fancy gear (the heavier they are, the harder to hold still).

Tips:

- Always use the neck strap! I like the harness.
- To find the bird, lock your eyes on it, and bring binoculars up to your eyes and into alignment. Practice a little. It works!

Hiking boots

Sturdy walking shoes.

Tip: Start small and choose the right trail for your fitness level. Check the weather!

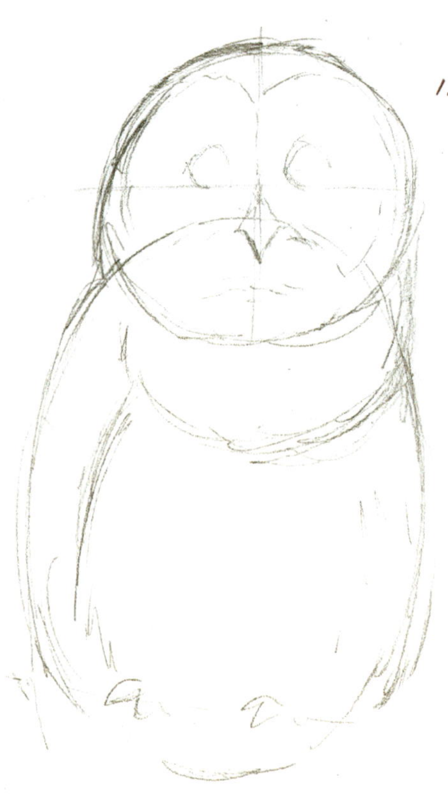

1. Start with the basic shapes—this Barred Owl is a circle on an oval. Keep your pencil lines light. Measure. His body is about 2 heads long.

Draw light until you know it's right!

2. Erase your extra lines. Look for details around eyes, beak, feet, and feather groups. If you plan on painting, don't shade anything in!

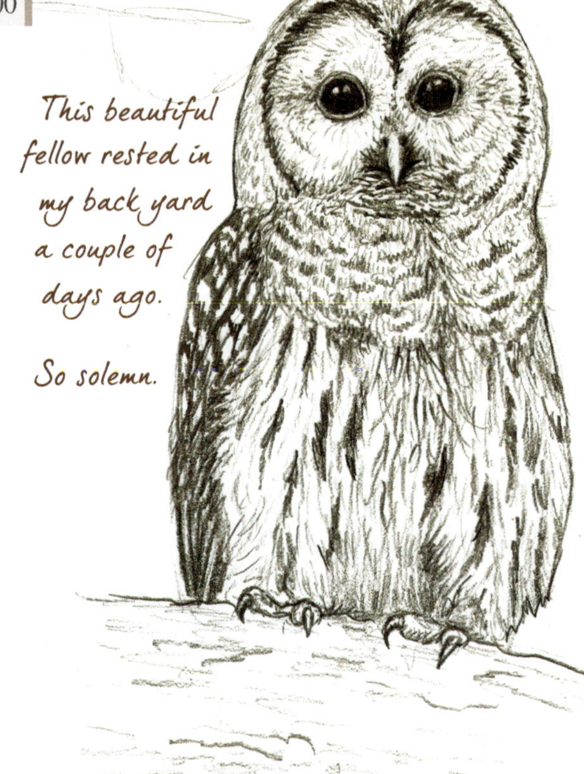

This beautiful fellow rested in my back yard a couple of days ago.

So solemn.

3. Add shading (a range of value) or color. Pay attention to the direction the feathers (or fur) grow in.

Push for more contrast, the darkest darks, the lightest lights.

Try it!

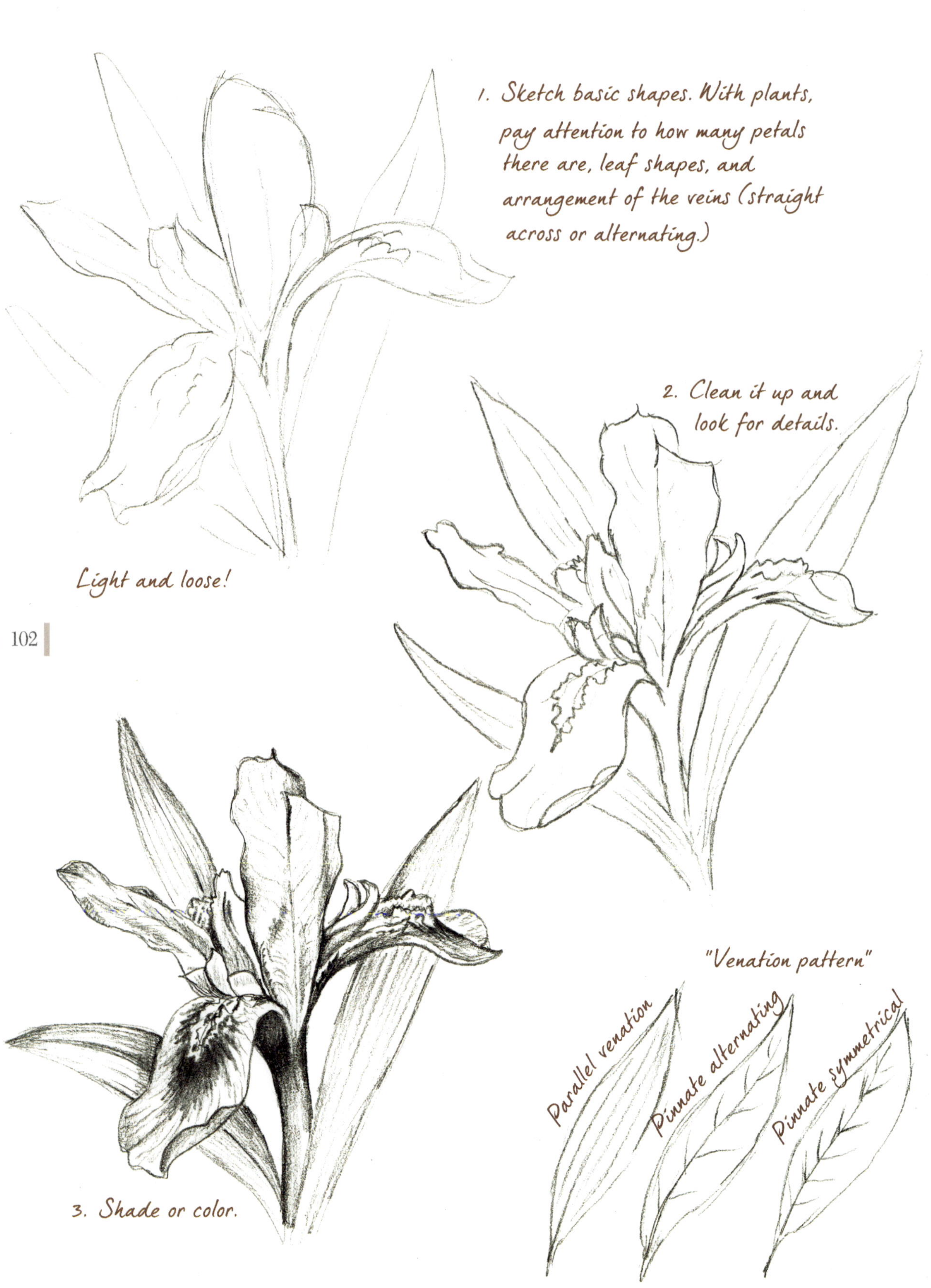
1. Sketch basic shapes. With plants, pay attention to how many petals there are, leaf shapes, and arrangement of the veins (straight across or alternating.)
Light and loose!
2. Clean it up and look for details.
3. Shade or color.
"Venation pattern"
Parallel venation
Pinnate alternating
Pinnate symmetrical

Try it!

Ink & Watercolor

a "loose" style

a more detailed, controlled style
– "scientific illustration"

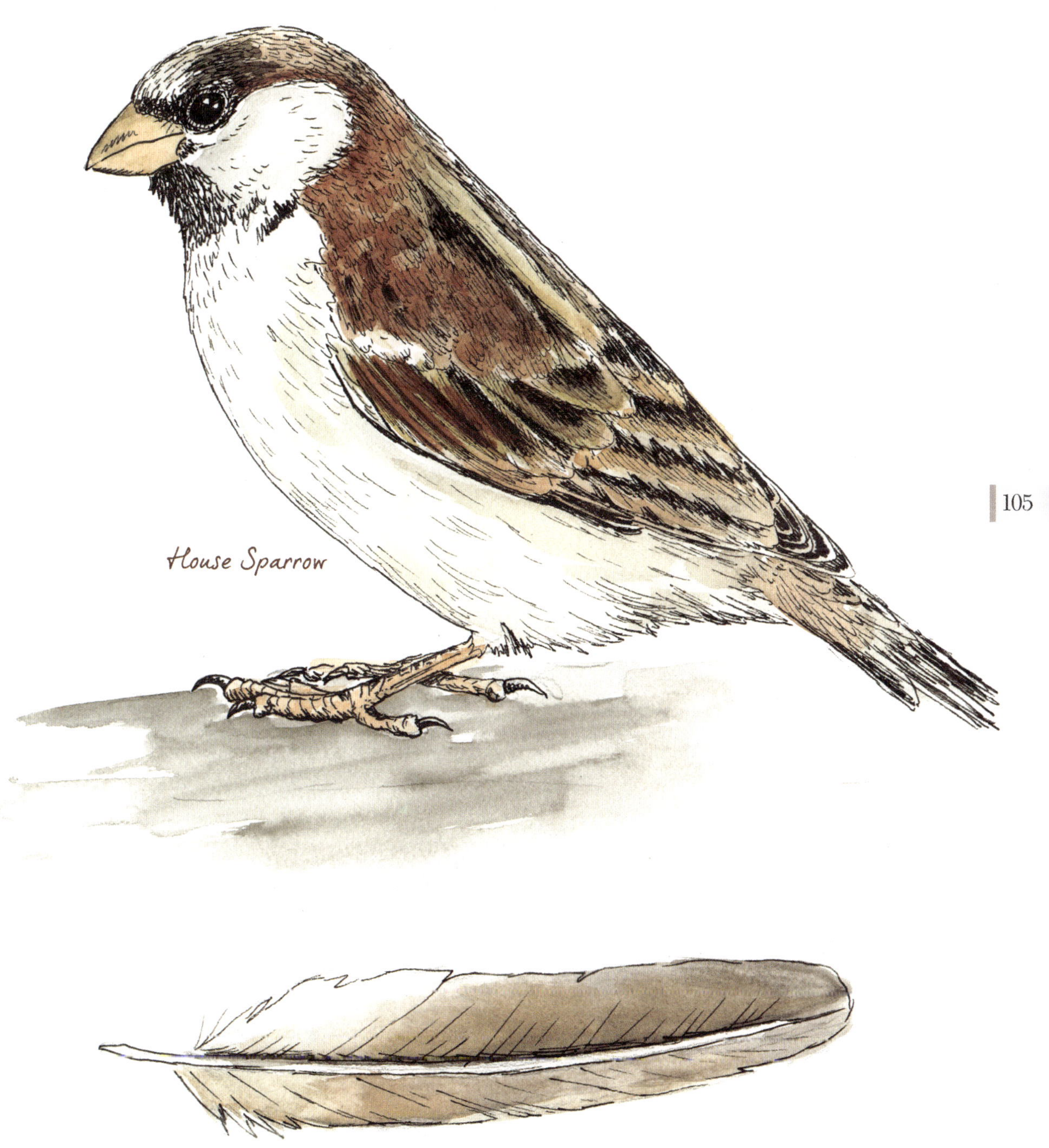

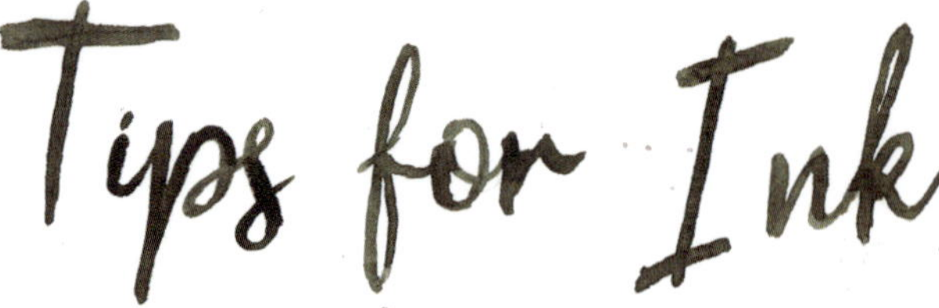

Tips for Ink

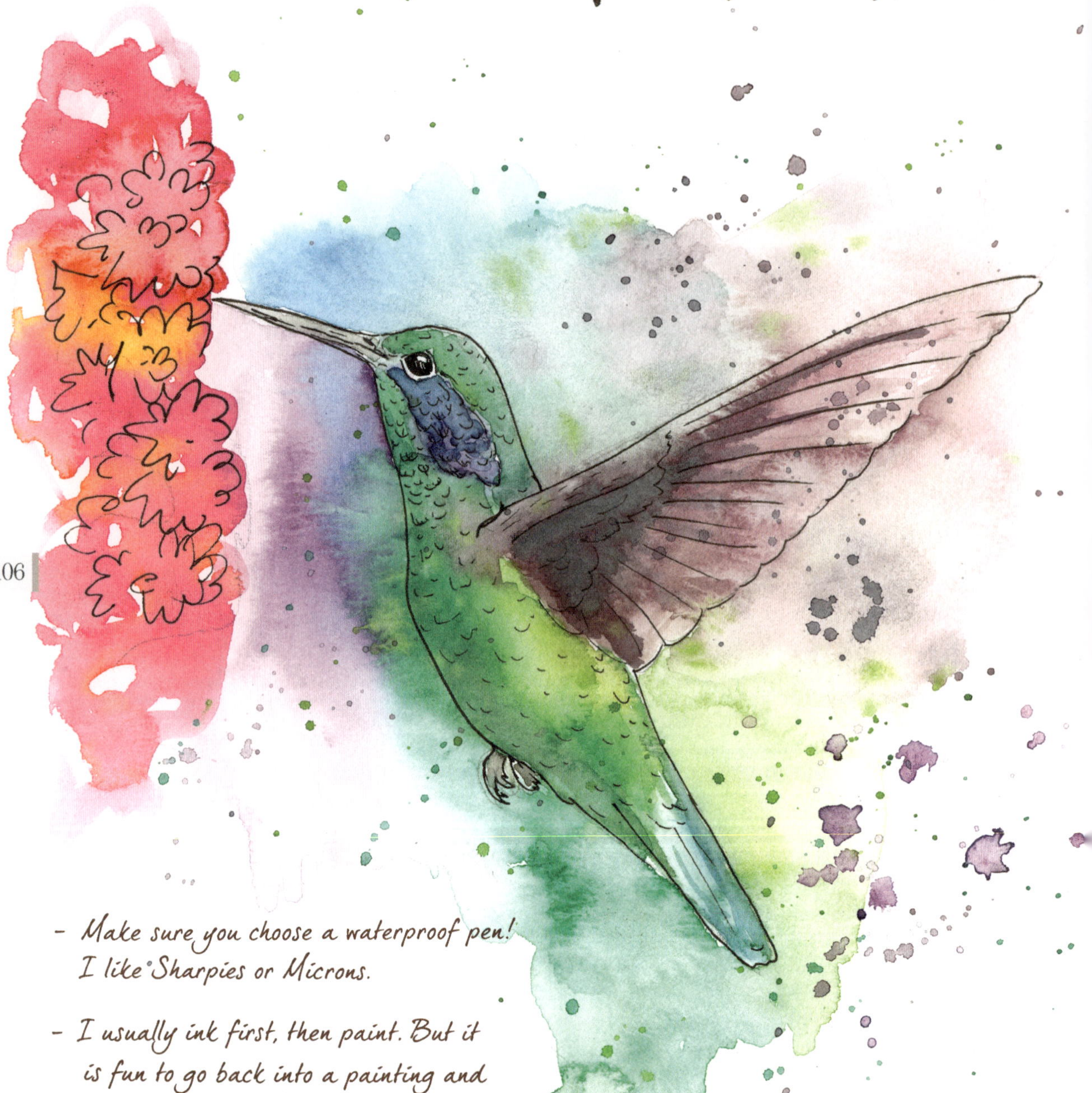

- Make sure you choose a waterproof pen! I like Sharpies or Microns.

- I usually ink first, then paint. But it is fun to go back into a painting and add more ink later!

- Painting "loose" usually means not following the lines very closely—purposely letting the paint "blend" together. But be careful of complementary colors touching (colors across from each other on the color wheel). Those can look "muddy."

and Watercolor (or Ink and Wash)

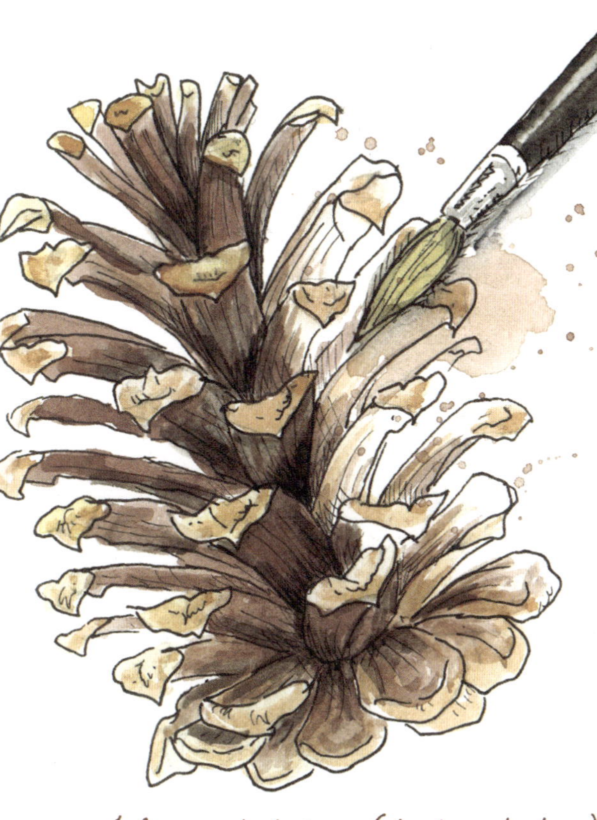

A few pen techniques (shade or texture)

Hatching	Cross hatching	Stipple	Stumble/ scribble

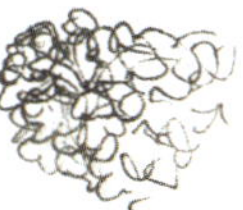

Pen Sizes

.05 mm
.1 mm
.2 mm
.3 mm
.4 mm
.5 mm
.6 mm
.8 mm
Brush

Welcoming Birds to your Yard

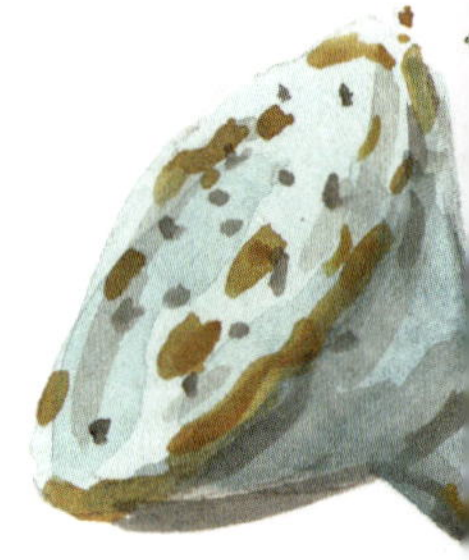

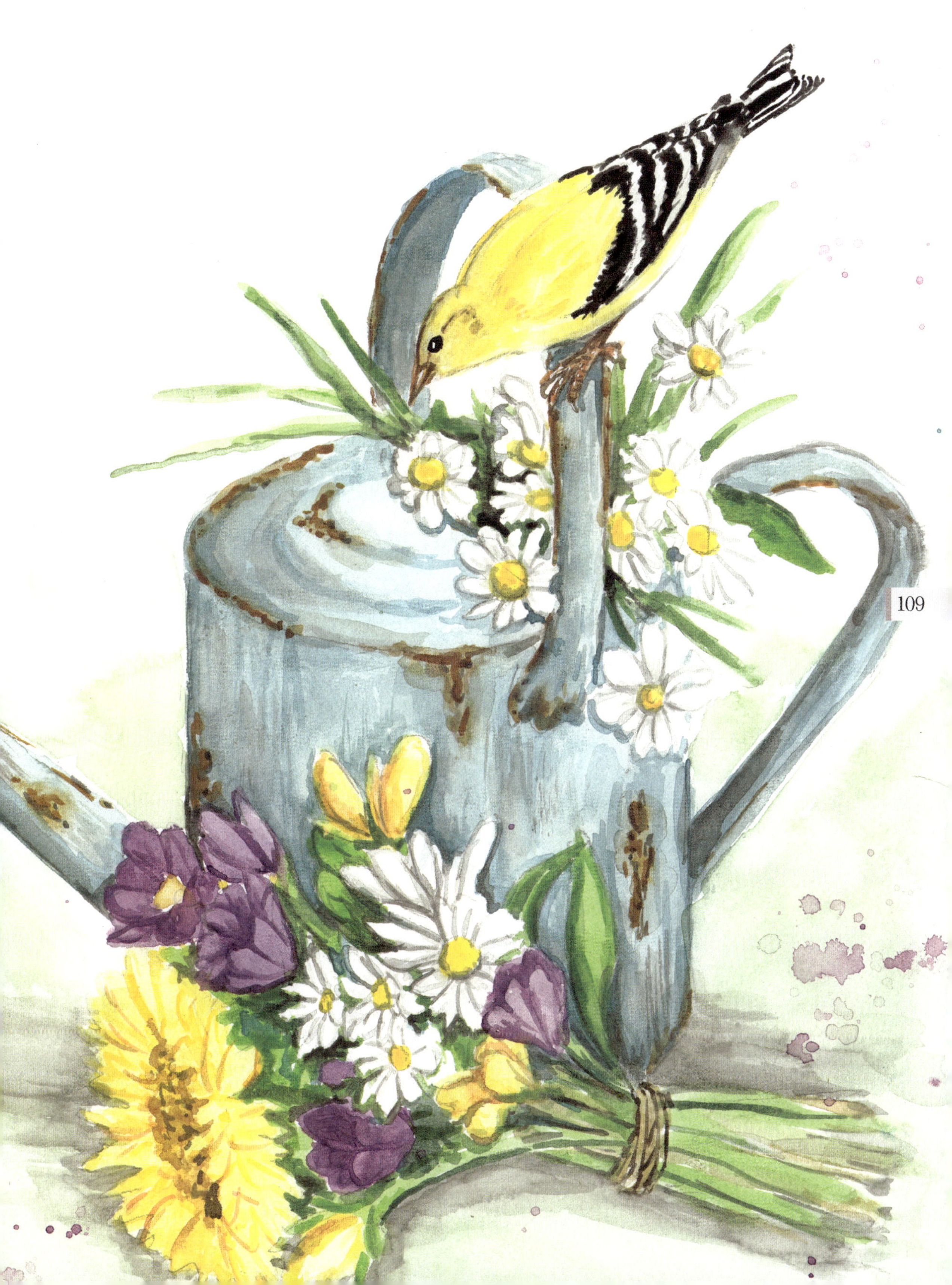

109

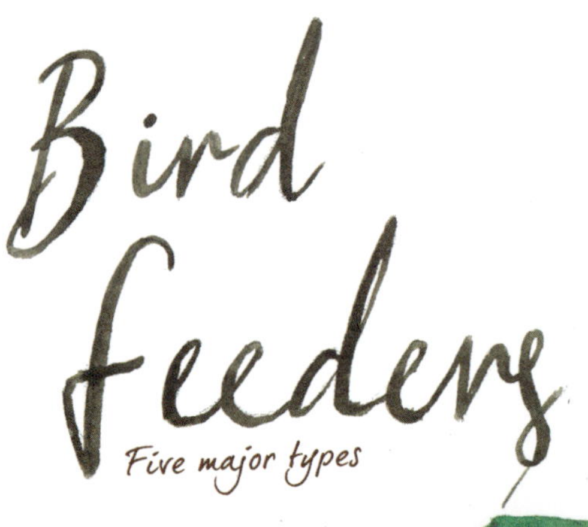

Five major types

Hopper

Best overall! The hopper appeals to a wide variety of birds and handles most seeds.

Platform/tray

Wide appeal to birds and gives the larger birds more room to move. Fruit (oranges) and grape jelly may attract orioles, tanagers, mockingbirds, thrashers, and so on.

Tube feeder (plus sock feeder)

Great for smaller birds, including goldfinches, chickadees, finches, etc. Nyjer "sock" feeders are made only for Nyjer seed.

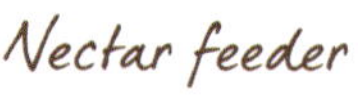

Usually intended for hummingbirds, but can attract orioles too! Clean often; nectar goes bad. Note: Sugar water does not need to be red. Simply mix four parts water, one part sugar.

Suet feeder

Provides healthy fats and proteins that birds need for energy. Especially during winter months!

Boneset

food

Sunflower Seeds

Best overall feeder seed!

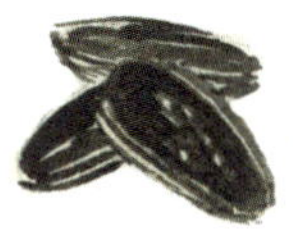

Two kinds:

- Black oil–thin shell, high oil content. Good for winter feeders.
- Striped–might help deter sparrows and blackbirds because the shell is harder to open. Very attractive to squirrels though!

Safflower

Thick shell, but a favorite with cardinals. Good for tray and hopper feeders.

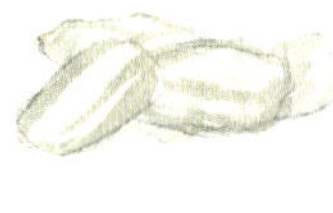

Nyjer Seed

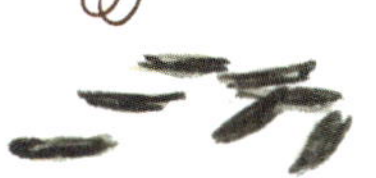

A favorite with the small finches! Some commonly sold thistle seeds can be invasive, so Nyjer (a similar seed) is a good alternative. Use a tube or sock feeder for these small, needle-like seeds.

Millet

Loved by birds that feed on the ground. It is often scattered on the ground. Can be a favorite with some undesirable birds like cowbirds and sparrows.

Corn

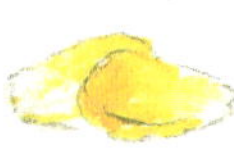

Eaten by many larger birds (cardinals, jays, doves, ducks,). Also can bring undesirable birds and backyard visitors (raccoons, bears!). Be careful: wet corn can have aflatoxins! Don't buy it in plastic bags, and clean up old corn. And only feed small amounts at a time.

Peanuts

Popular with jays, chickadees, woodpeckers, etc. Can also have aflatoxins, so only offer in small amounts. Works well in the shell on platforms, if your jays can get them before the squirrels.

Bird Houses

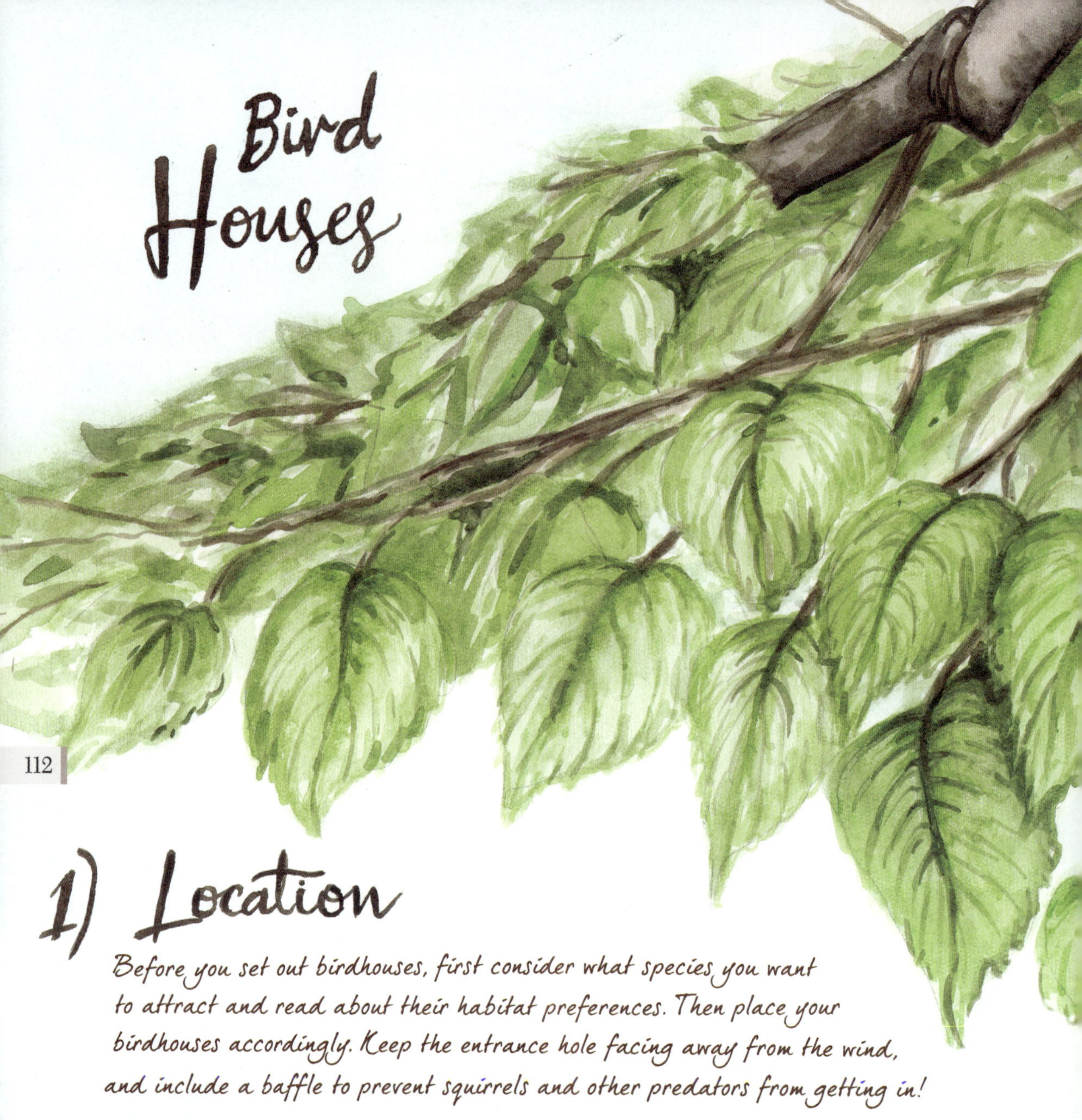

1) Location

Before you set out birdhouses, first consider what species you want to attract and read about their habitat preferences. Then place your birdhouses accordingly. Keep the entrance hole facing away from the wind, and include a baffle to prevent squirrels and other predators from getting in!

Make sure your house has a clean-out door or panel! In the fall, clean it out. This prevents mites/lice or mice from taking up residence!

2) Design

Some birds (like Purple Martins) prefer to live in communities, so they like living apartment style. Others like single-dwelling units. Wood is the best material. Include ventilation on the top and drainage in the floor. The house might sit empty for some time. Have birdhouses up plenty early for the spring!

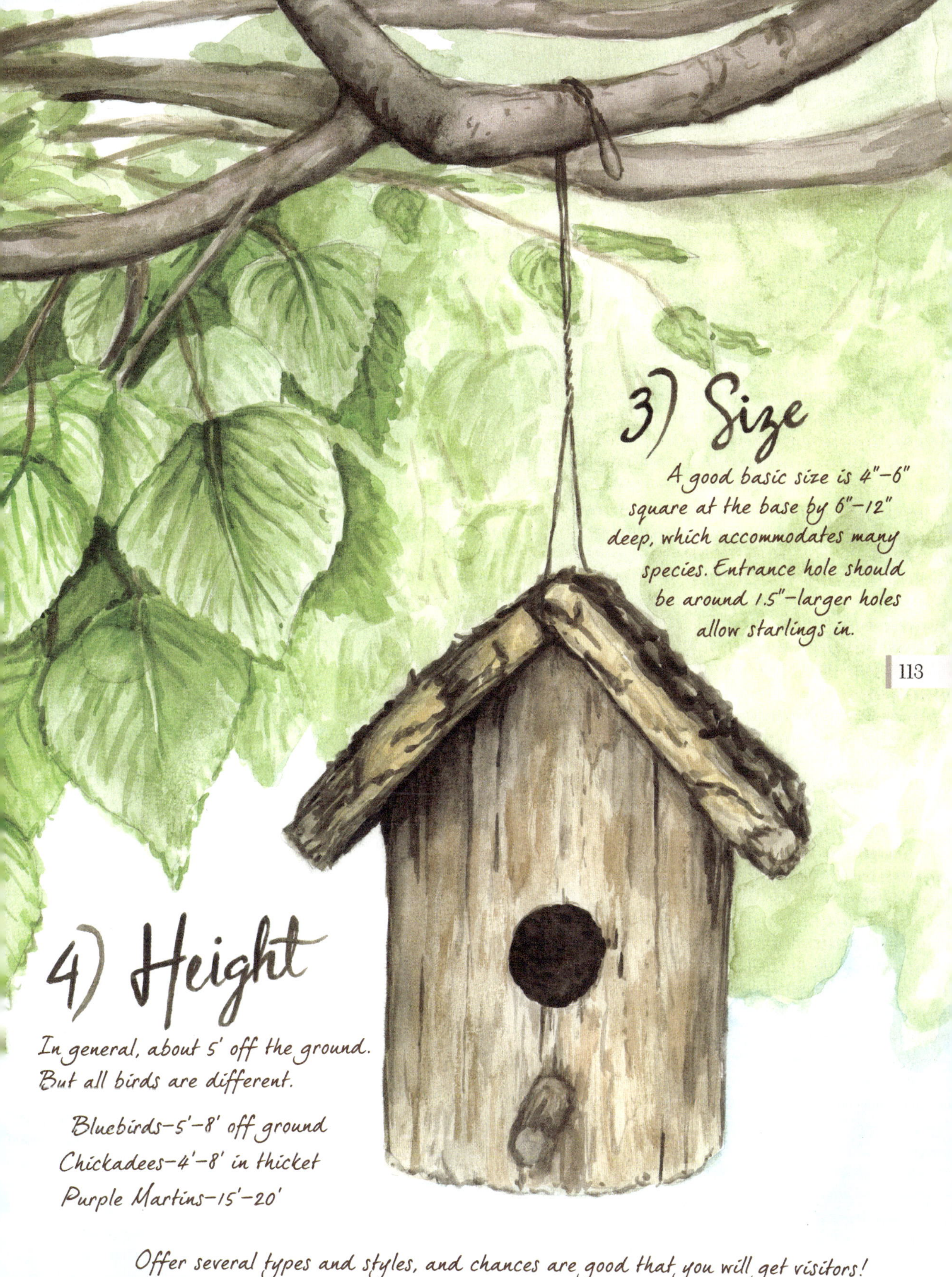

3) Size

A good basic size is 4"–6" square at the base by 6"–12" deep, which accommodates many species. Entrance hole should be around 1.5"–larger holes allow starlings in.

4) Height

In general, about 5' off the ground. But all birds are different.

Bluebirds–5'–8' off ground
Chickadees–4'–8' in thicket
Purple Martins–15'–20'

Offer several types and styles, and chances are good that you will get visitors!

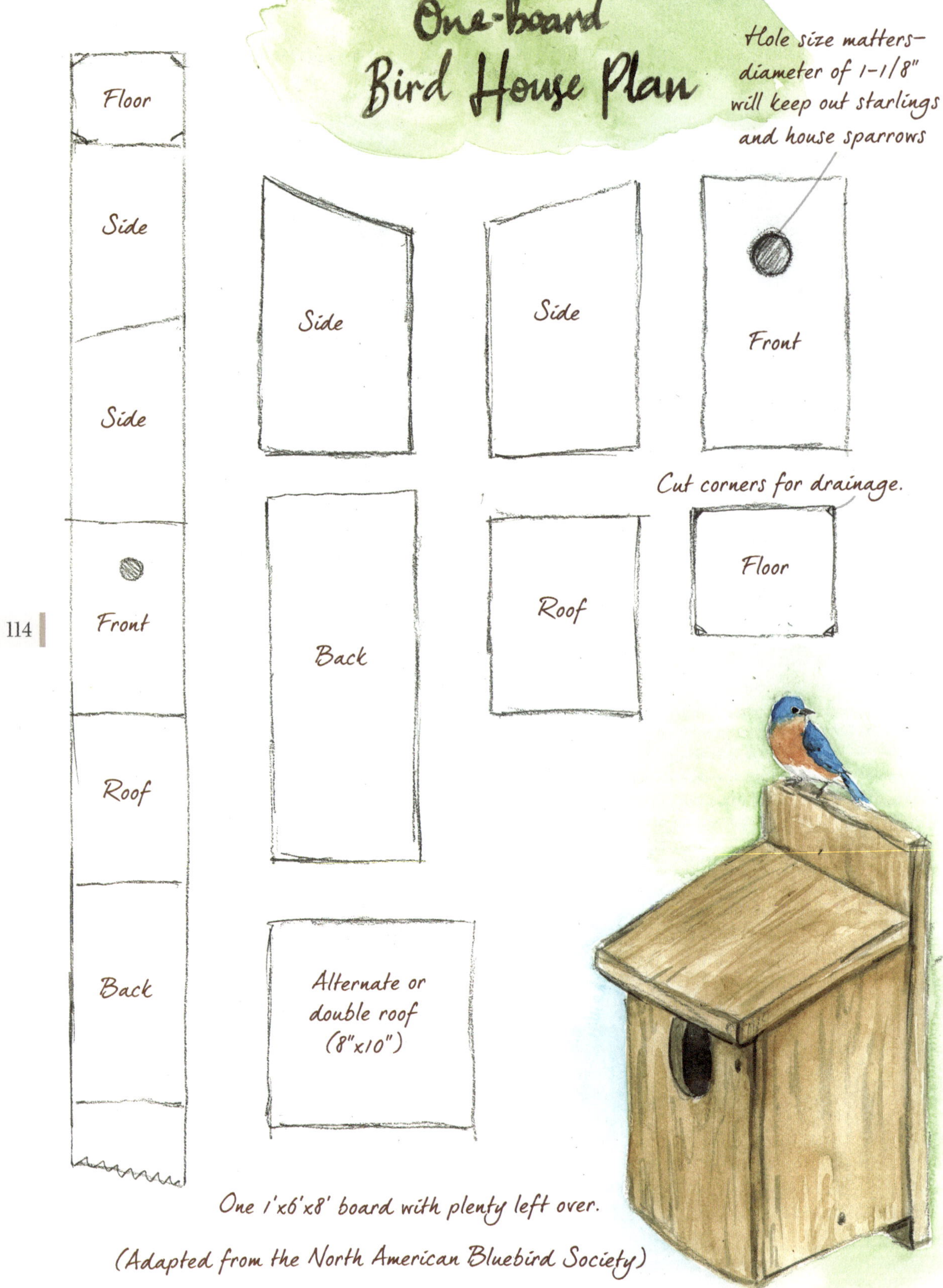
One-board
Bird House Plan
Hole size matters–
diameter of 1-1/8"
will keep out starlings
and house sparrows
Floor
Side
Side
Front
Roof
Back
Side
Side
Front
Back
Roof
Cut corners for drainage.
Floor
Alternate or
double roof
(8"x10")
One 1'x6'x8' board with plenty left over.
(Adapted from the North American Bluebird Society)

the importance of Water!

Birds need water, so consider having a source in your backyard. It helps regulate their bodies, keep them healthy, helps them preen, and keeps them cool on hot days.

Having a water source around will increase how many birds you see in your backyard. Many also like to hear the water, so maybe a fountain/bubbler? Keep it clean to keep them healthy!

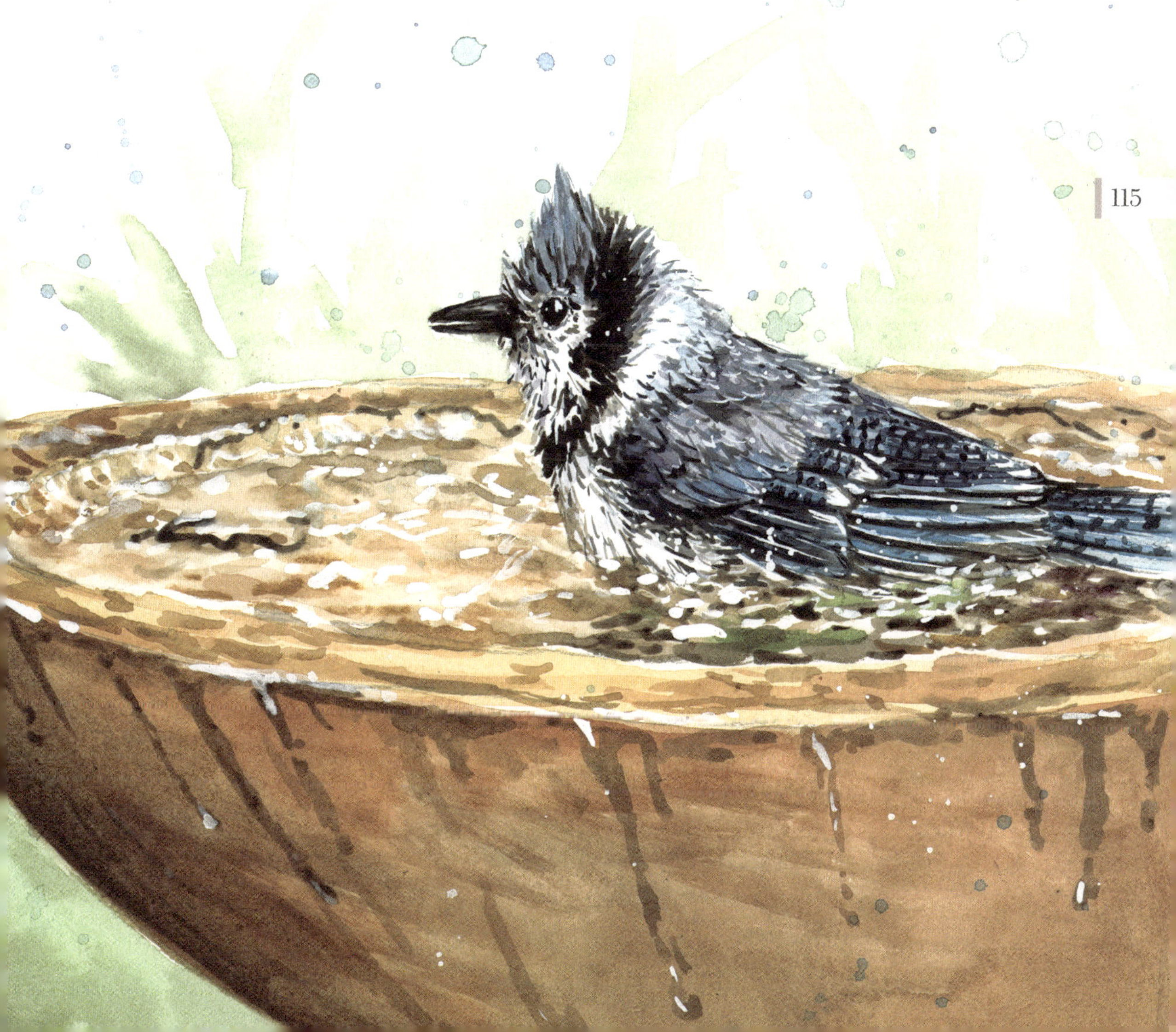

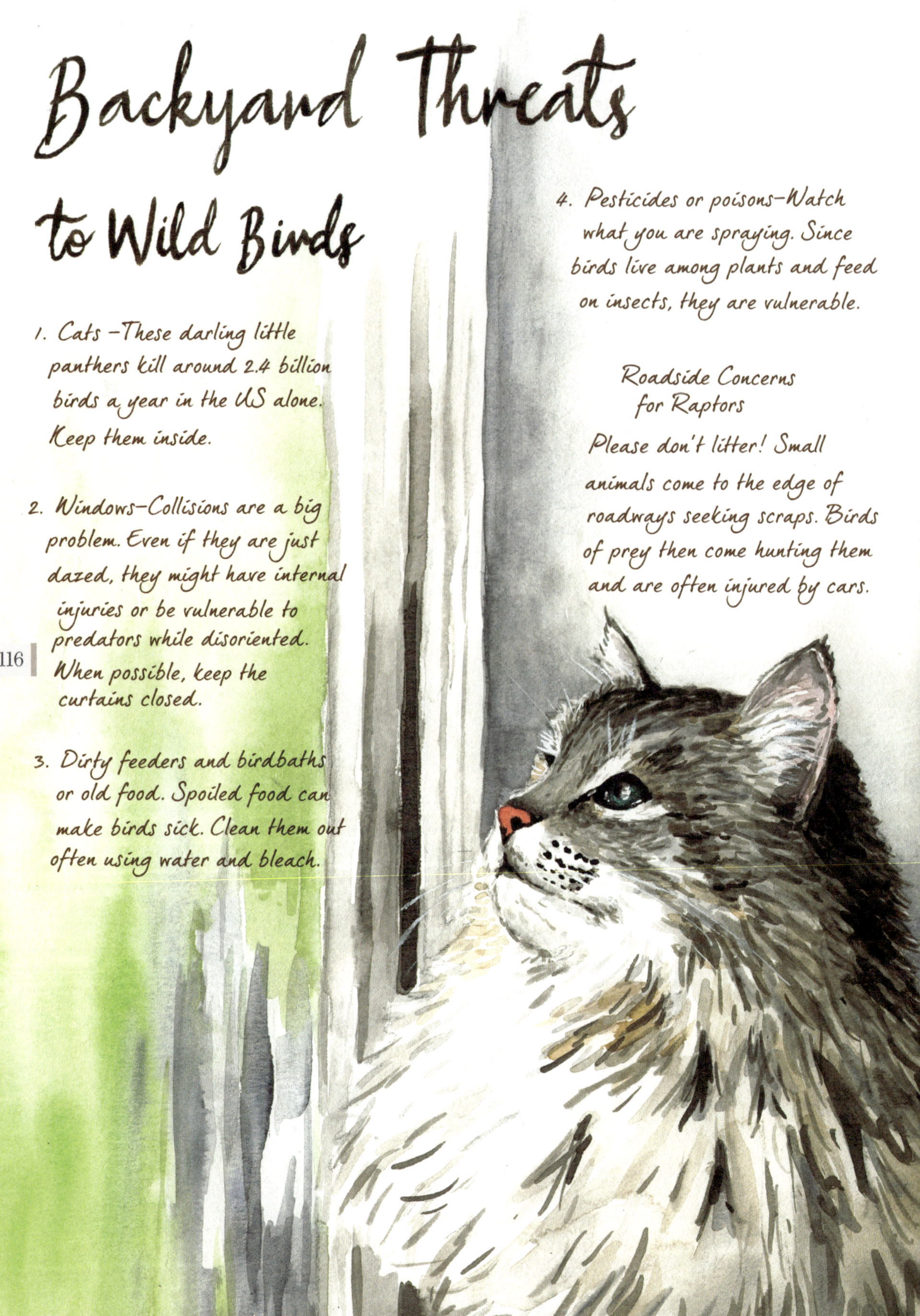

Backyard Threats to Wild Birds

1. Cats –These darling little panthers kill around 2.4 billion birds a year in the US alone. Keep them inside.

2. Windows–Collisions are a big problem. Even if they are just dazed, they might have internal injuries or be vulnerable to predators while disoriented. When possible, keep the curtains closed.

3. Dirty feeders and birdbaths or old food. Spoiled food can make birds sick. Clean them out often using water and bleach.

4. Pesticides or poisons–Watch what you are spraying. Since birds live among plants and feed on insects, they are vulnerable.

Roadside Concerns for Raptors

Please don't litter! Small animals come to the edge of roadways seeking scraps. Birds of prey then come hunting them and are often injured by cars.

What to do if you find an Injured Bird?

The most important step is to determine whether a bird is actually injured or if it's a fledgling. (Fledglings don't need help!)

If you see or hear a bird strike a window, it'll likely be found:

- on the ground, not moving
- motionless, and you can pick it up easily
- with fluffed up feathers, eyes closed/glazed
- with visible injury/wounds

Young birds: Nestlings! Fledglings are often found on the ground, so leave them alone! Many learn to fly from the ground. The parents are nearby watching and they are fine.

Wearing gloves, carefully put it in a cardboard box and put it in a safe/cool place. It might just need time to settle or clear its head. Don't feed it or offer water. Let it rest, but check if it can fly away periodically. If it can't after several hours, find a local wildlife rehabilitator.

Hatchlings/fledglings: (very young, barely any feathers, sometimes eyes not open). Protect the baby while you contact a licensed wildlife rehabilitator immediately.

Raptors—often hit by cars on the roadway. Make sure it and you are safe and away from a roadway. Keep children/pets away. If possible, place a box/basket/blanket over the bird and call a wildlife rehabilitator. If you need to move it, keep a blanket over its head, and use thick gloves.

Note: It is against the law to keep a bird (or other wildlife) without proper permits.

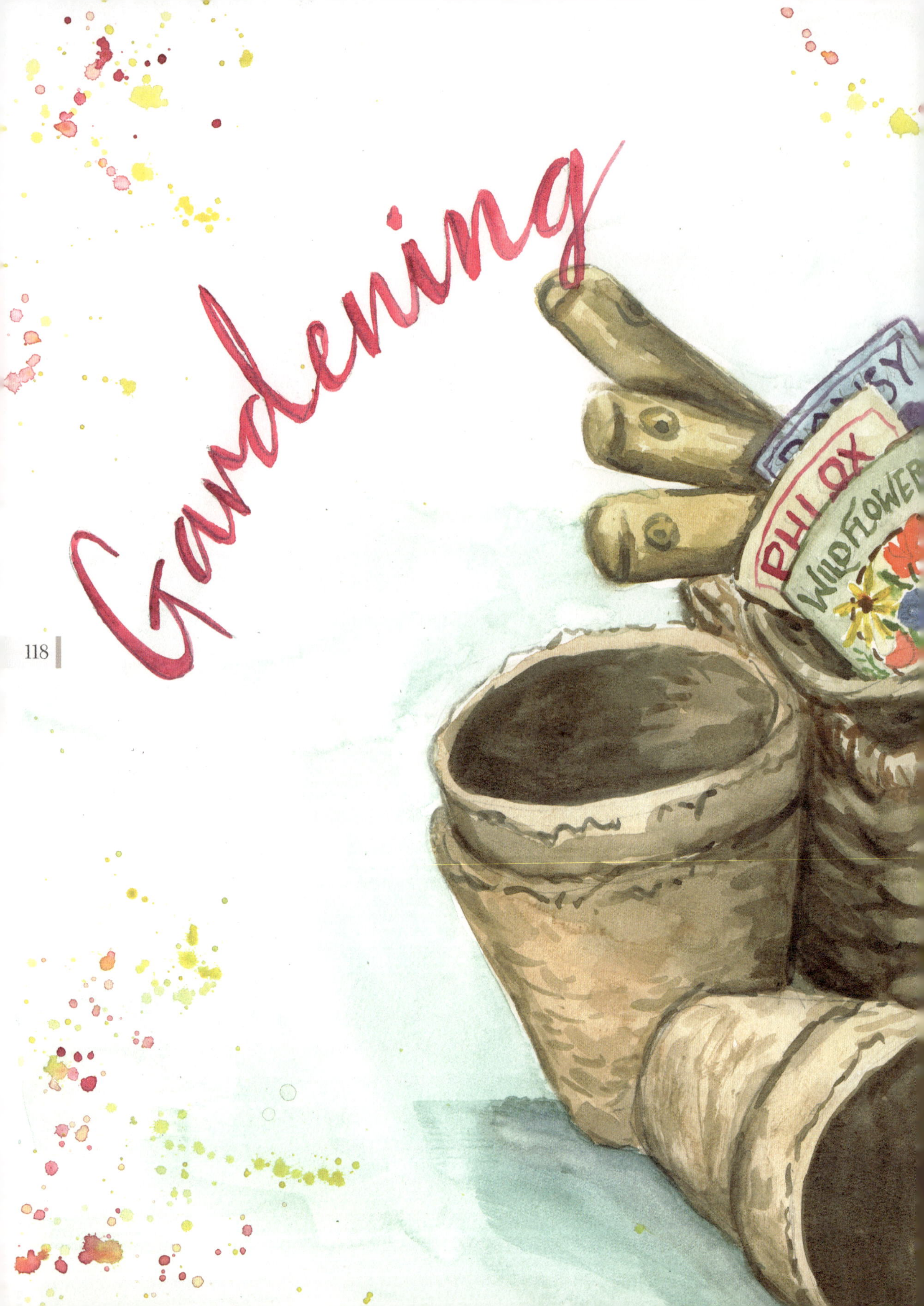
Gardening
PHLOX
WILDFLOWER

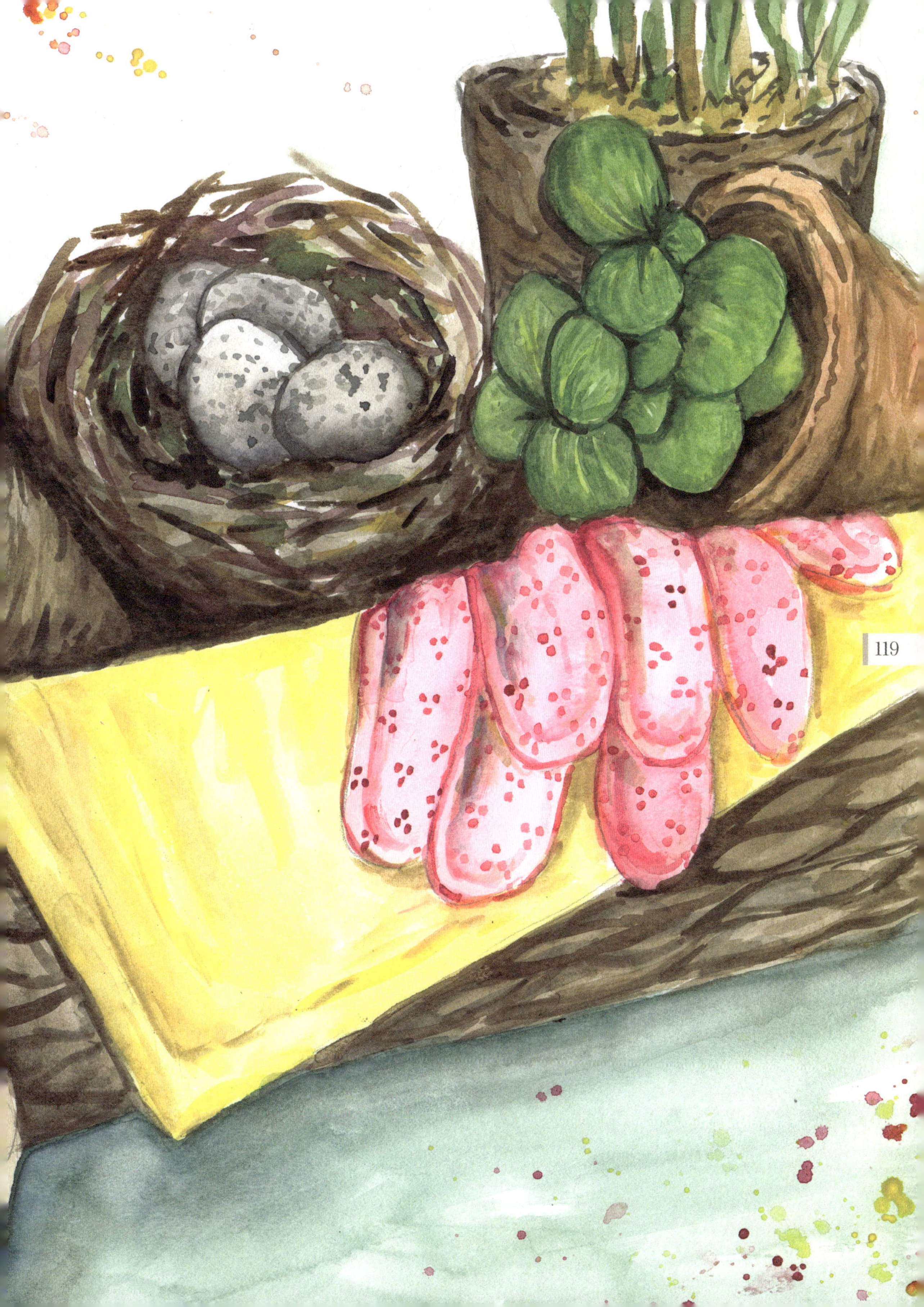

Plant a Pollinator's

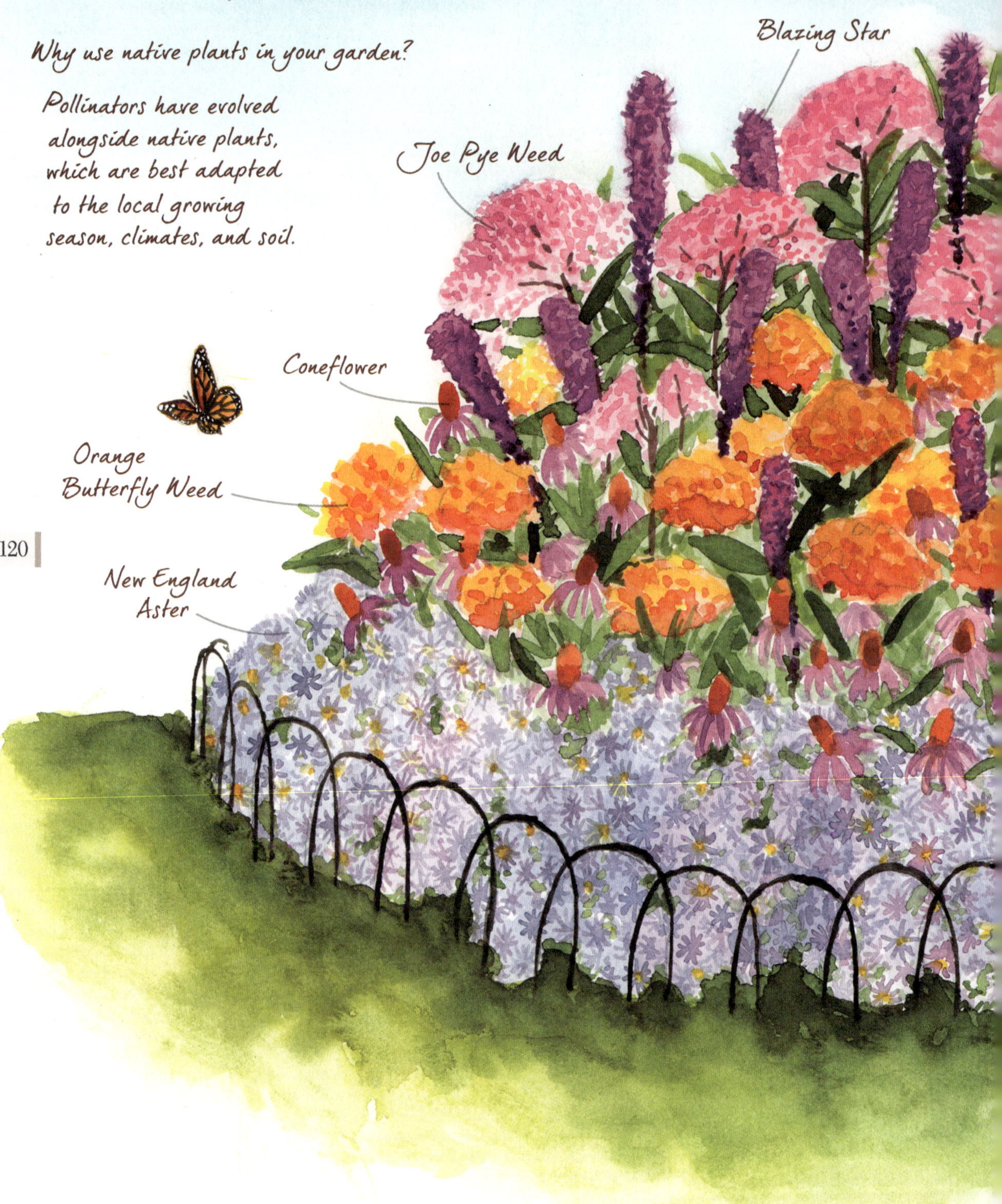

Why use native plants in your garden?

Pollinators have evolved alongside native plants, which are best adapted to the local growing season, climates, and soil.

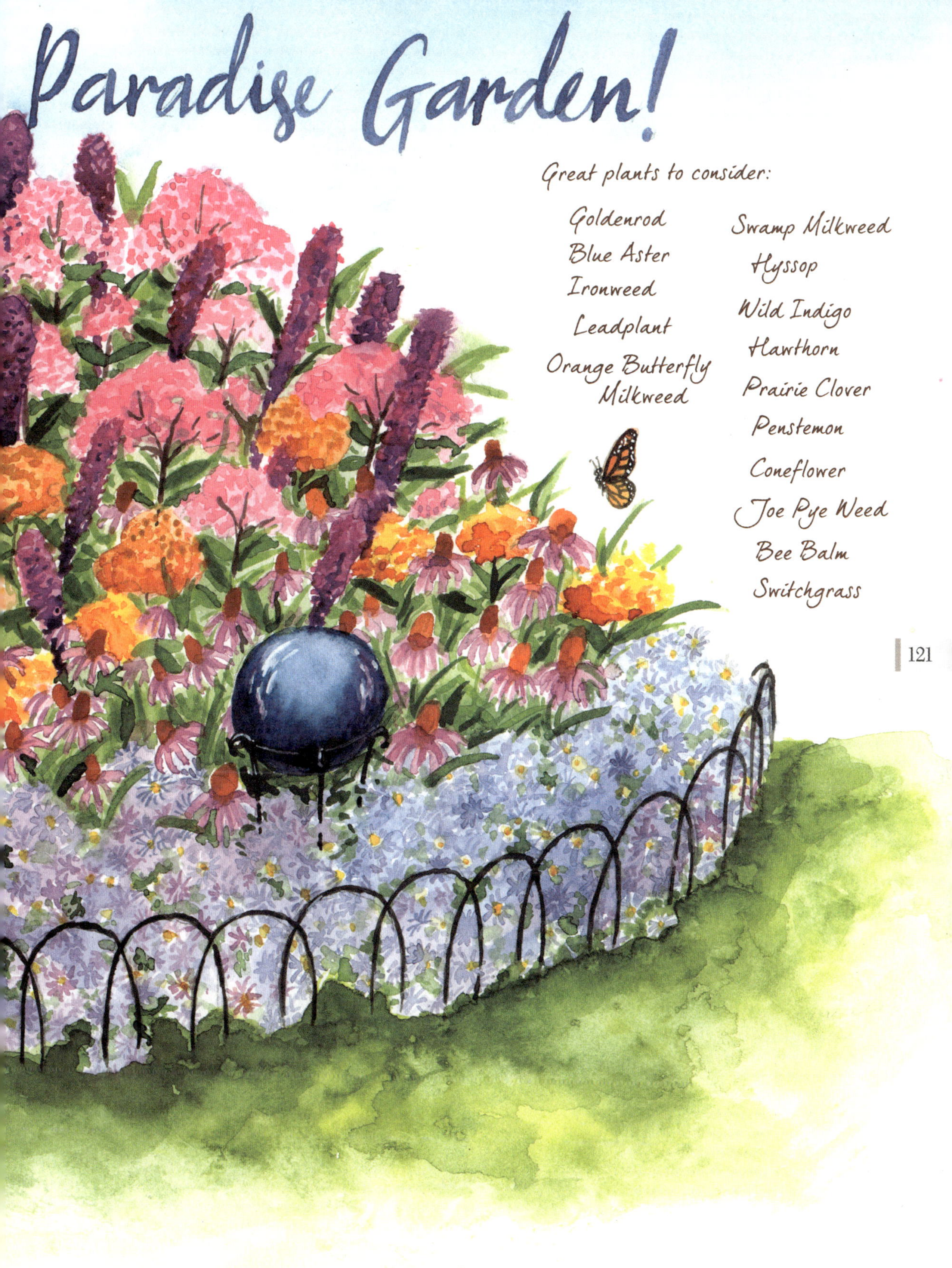
Paradise Garden!
Great plants to consider:
Goldenrod
Blue Aster
Ironweed
Leadplant
Orange Butterfly Milkweed
Swamp Milkweed
Hyssop
Wild Indigo
Hawthorn
Prairie Clover
Penstemon
Coneflower
Joe Pye Weed
Bee Balm
Switchgrass

Gardening for the Birds!

Go Native!

Native plants feed birds all year long and provide the "infrastructure" to support birds. Many birds feed their chicks insects, which in turn often depend on plants. Consider planting a variety of trees/bushes and plants to make your yard as welcoming as possible.

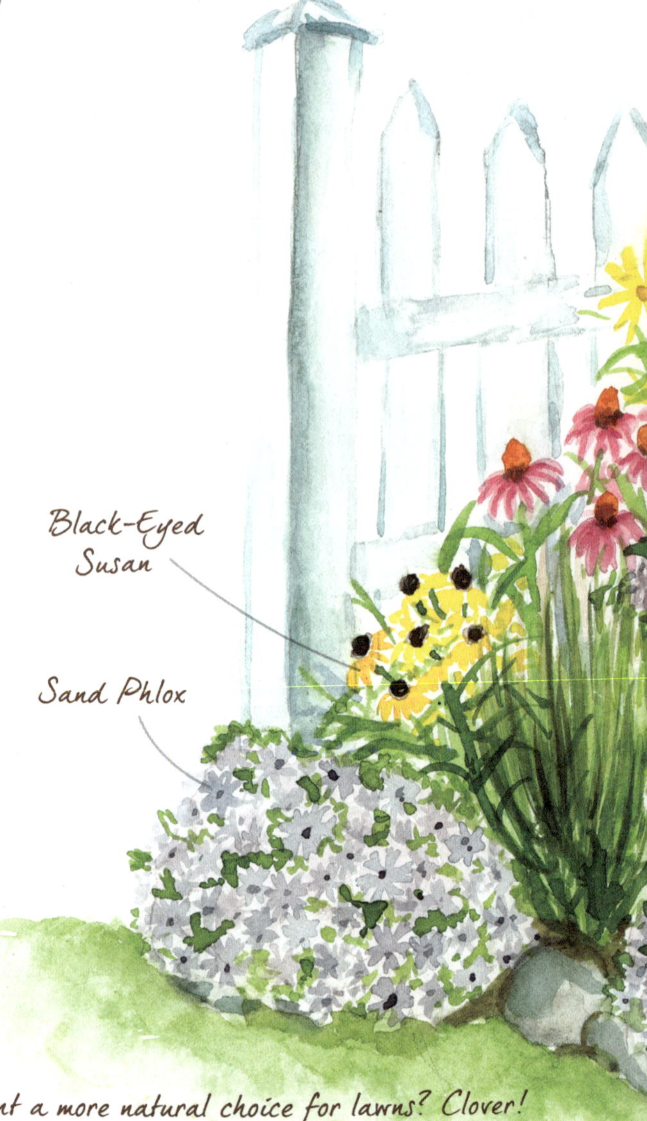

Great Plants for Birds

- Aster
- Native Sunflower
- Coneflowers
- Bee Balm
- Black-eyed Susan
- Michigan Holly
- Black Chokeberry
- Butterfly Weed
- Dogweed
- Elderberry
- Columbine
- Cardinal Flower
- Honeysuckle
- Virginia Creeper *Can spread!
- Buttonbush

Want a more natural choice for lawns? Clover! It needs less water than grass, stays green, and attracts pollinators.

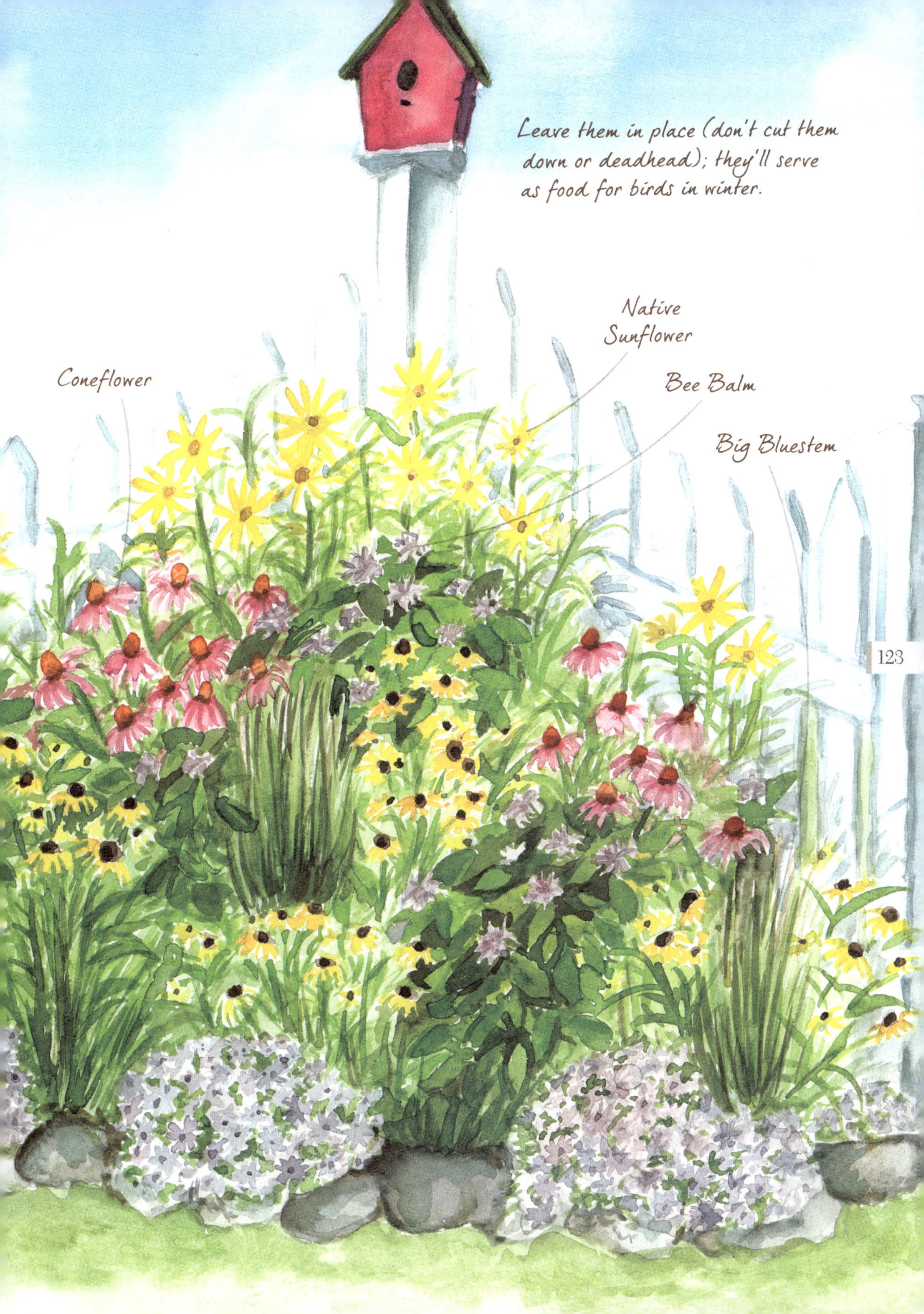
Leave them in place (don't cut them down or deadhead); they'll serve as food for birds in winter.
Native Sunflower
Coneflower
Bee Balm
Big Bluestem

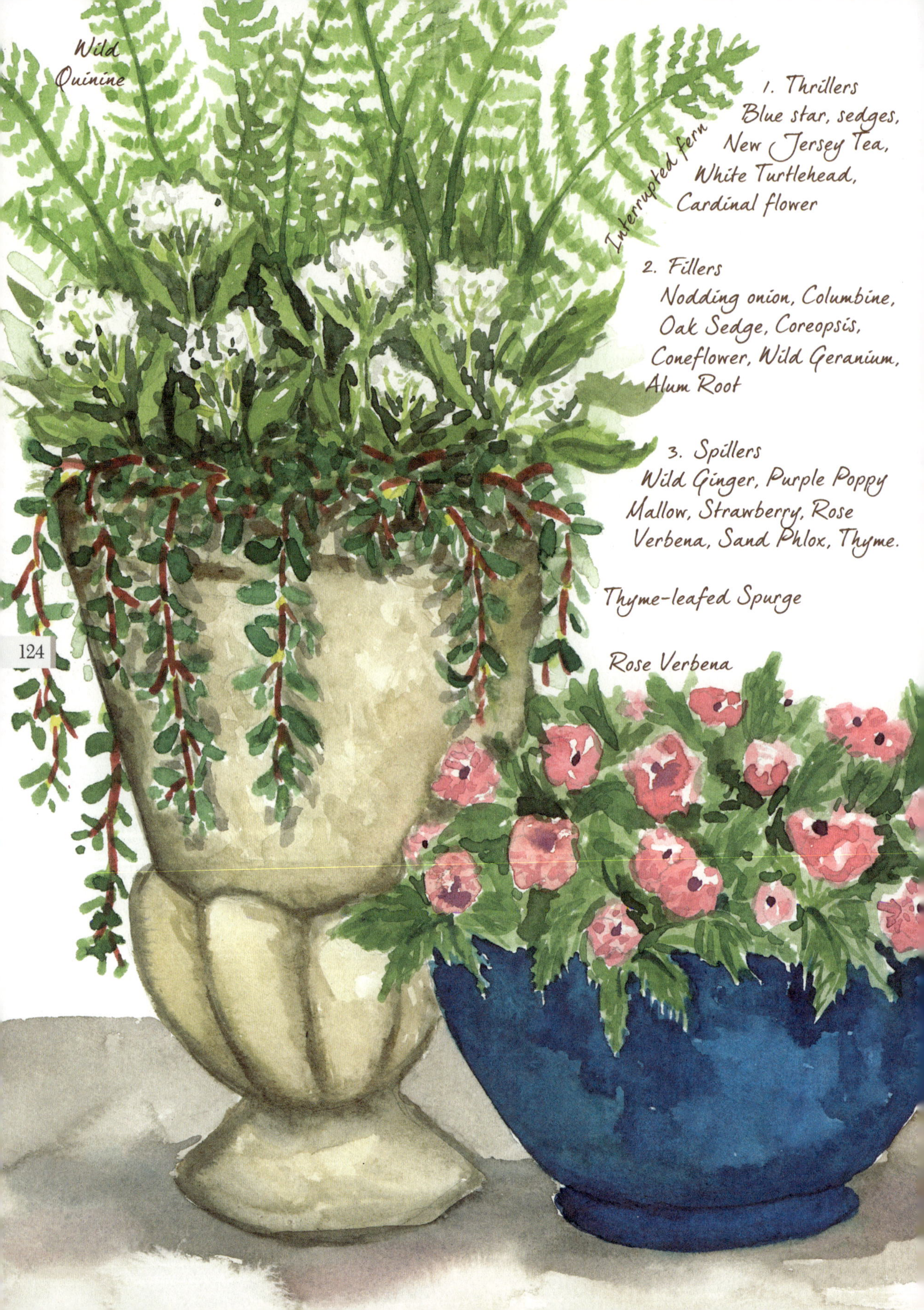
Wild Quinine
Interrupted fern
1. Thrillers
Blue star, sedges, New Jersey Tea, White Turtlehead, Cardinal flower
2. Fillers
Nodding onion, Columbine, Oak Sedge, Coreopsis, Coneflower, Wild Geranium, Alum Root
3. Spillers
Wild Ginger, Purple Poppy Mallow, Strawberry, Rose Verbena, Sand Phlox, Thyme.
Thyme-leafed Spurge
Rose Verbena

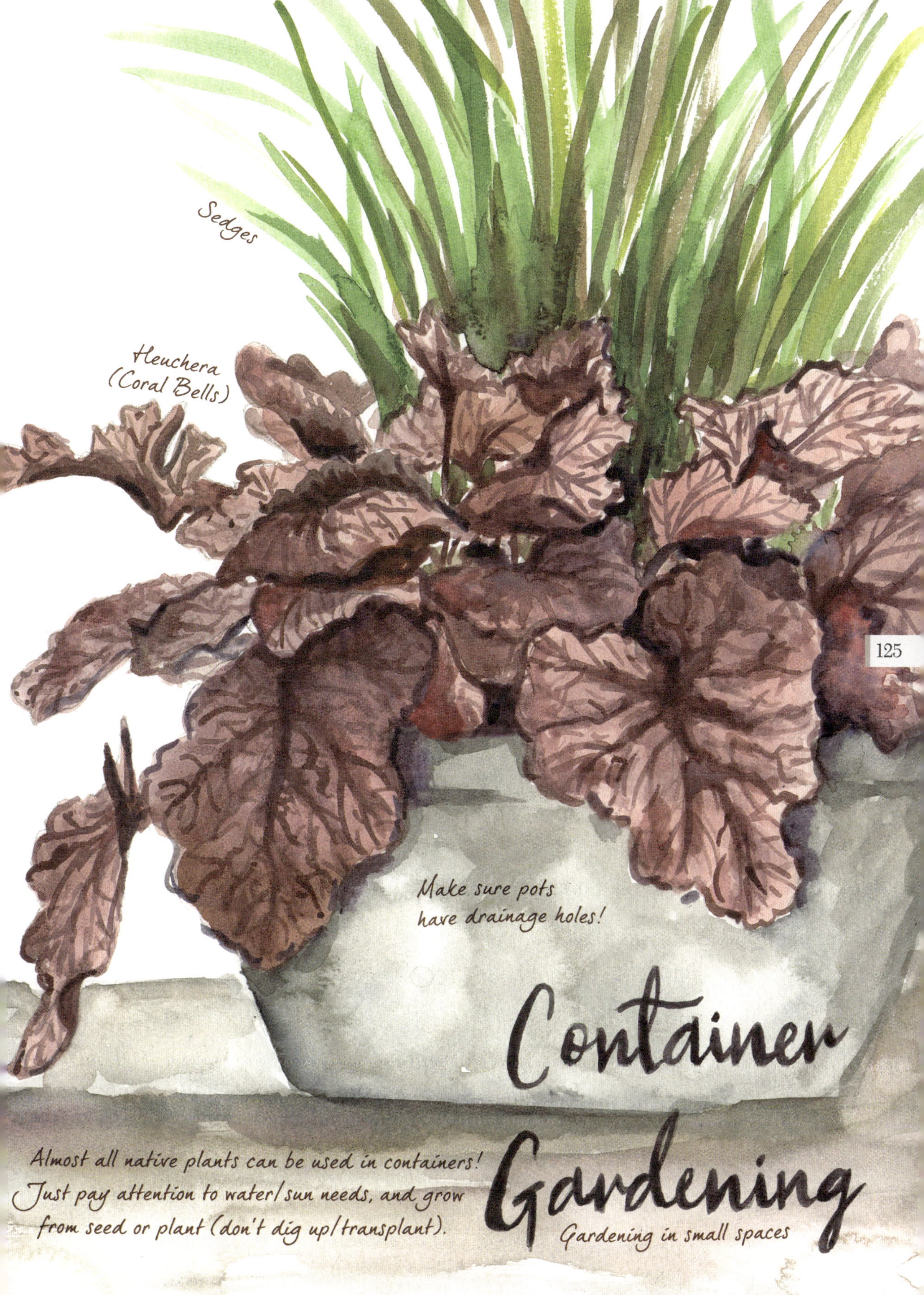
Sedges
Heuchera
(Coral Bells)
Make sure pots
have drainage holes!
Container
Gardening
Gardening in small spaces
Almost all native plants can be used in containers!
Just pay attention to water/sun needs, and grow
from seed or plant (don't dig up/transplant).

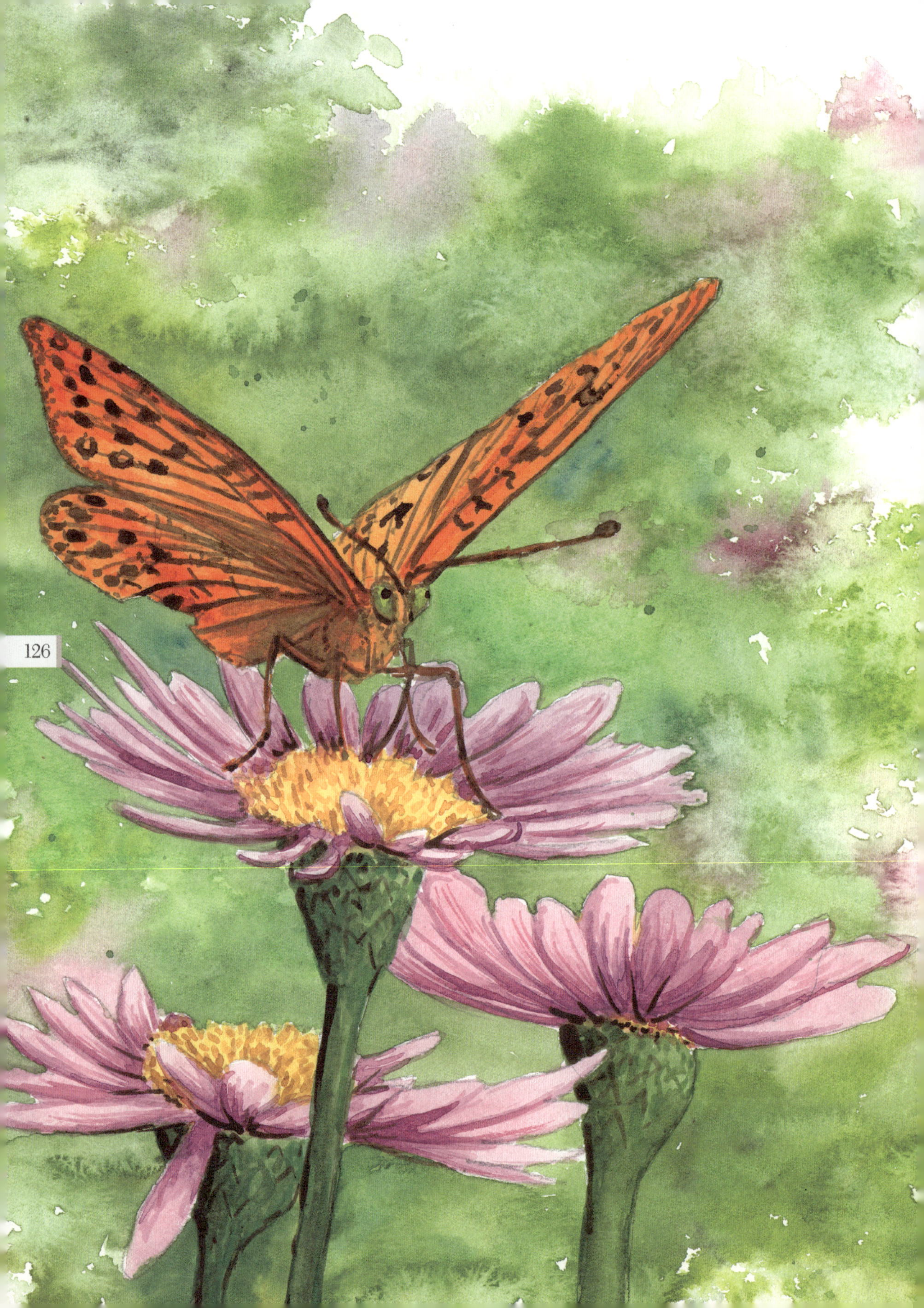

126

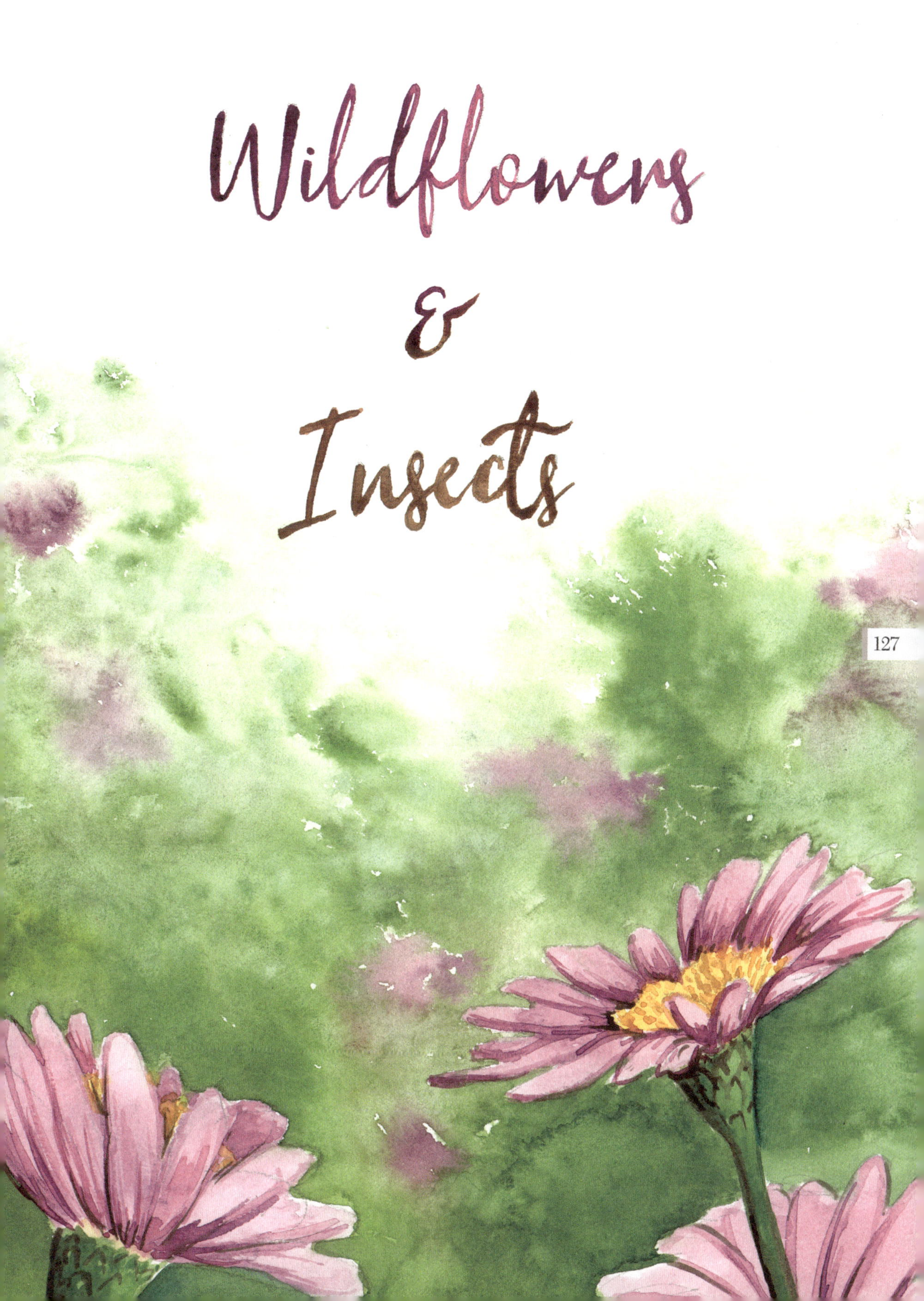
Wildflowers
&
Insects

Wildflowers and Their Uses

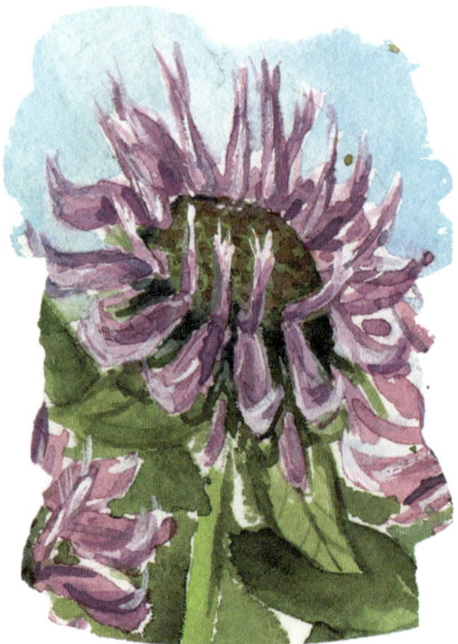

Bee Balm

Sometimes called Bergamot because it smells similar to the citrus tree of the same name. Very popular with pollinators.

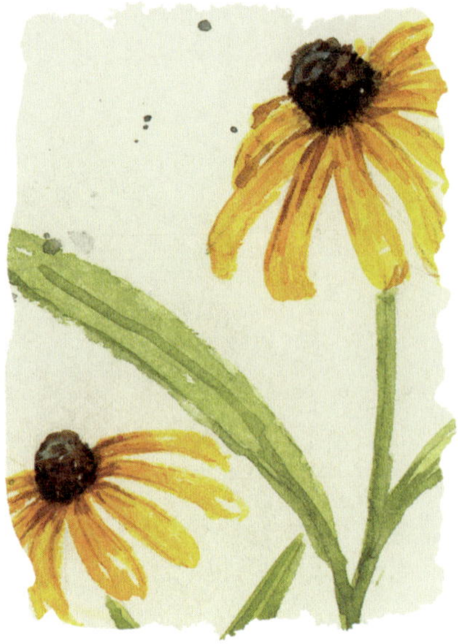

Black-eyed Susan

A cheerful, common wildflower that attracts bees and butterflies.

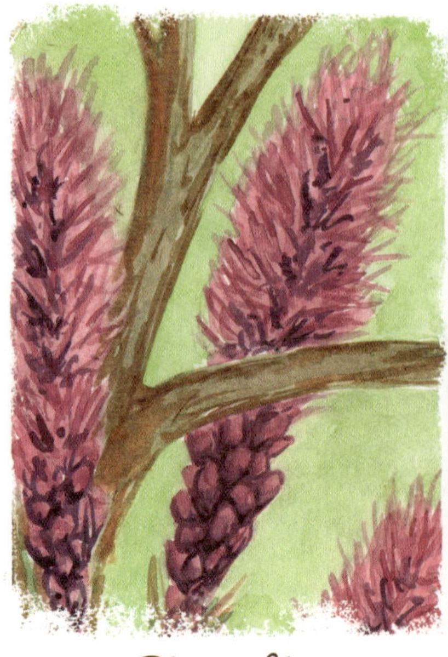

Blazing Star

A beautiful flower that resembles a magic wand in bloom, and a favorite with pollinators.

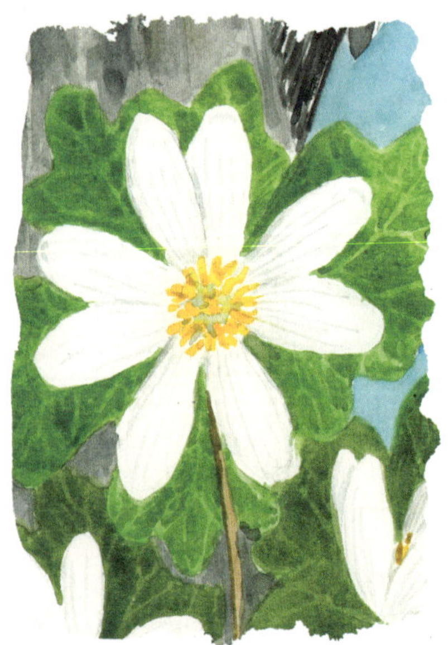

Bloodroot

The red juice from the underground stem gives it its common name, "bloodroot."

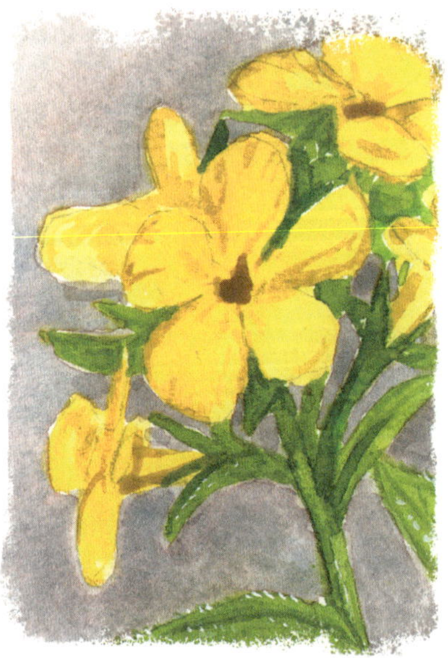

Hairy Puccoon

Its unusual name comes from the downy or hairy appearance of its leaves.

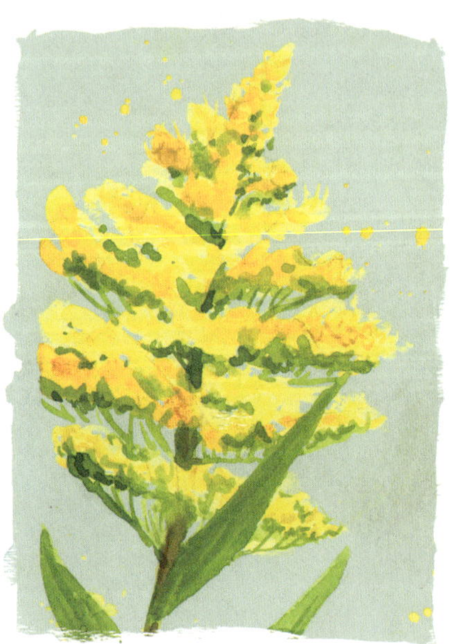

Goldenrod

A great flower for bees and pollinators; doesn't cause allergies (that's ragweed).

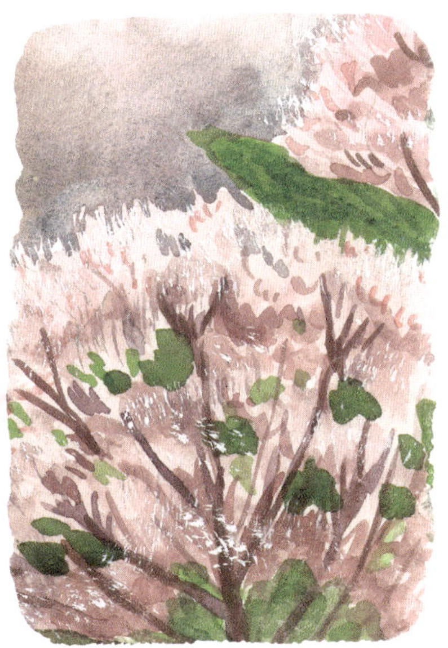

Joe Pye Weed
Attracts birds and butterflies and smells lovely.

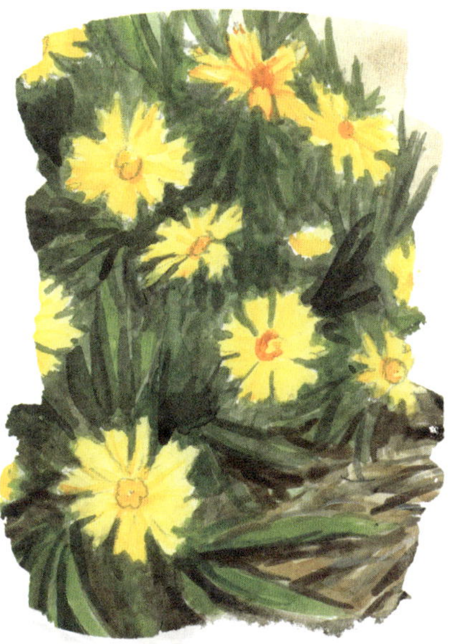

Lanceleaf Coreopsis
Otherwise known as tickseed because the seeds look like ticks. Butterflies love them!

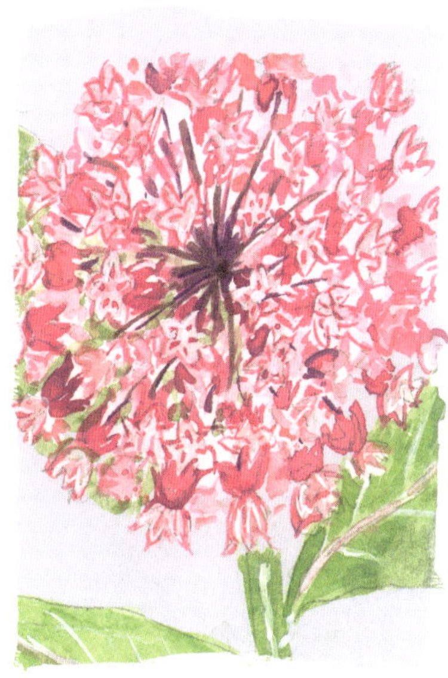

Milkweed
Essential for Monarchs, and a pollen source for many other insects.

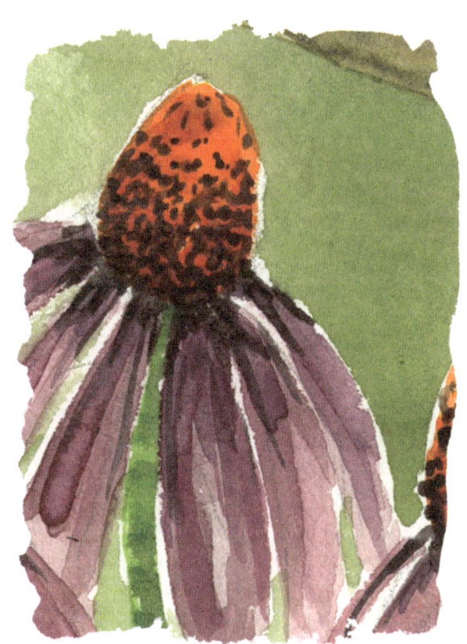

Purple Coneflower
Attracts all types of butterflies and easy to grow.

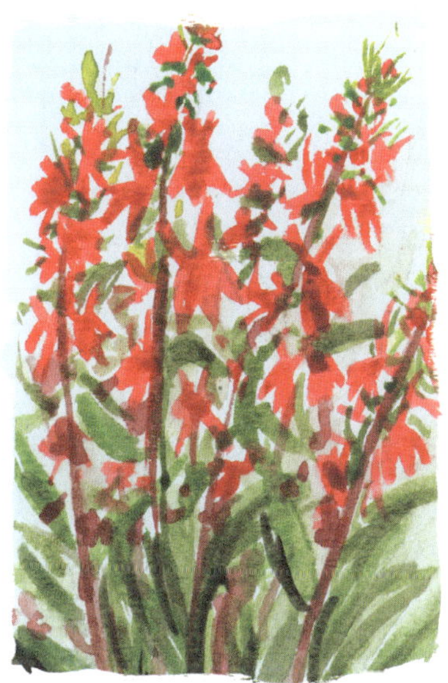

Red Cardinal Flower
Depends on hummingbirds, which feed on the nectar, for pollination.

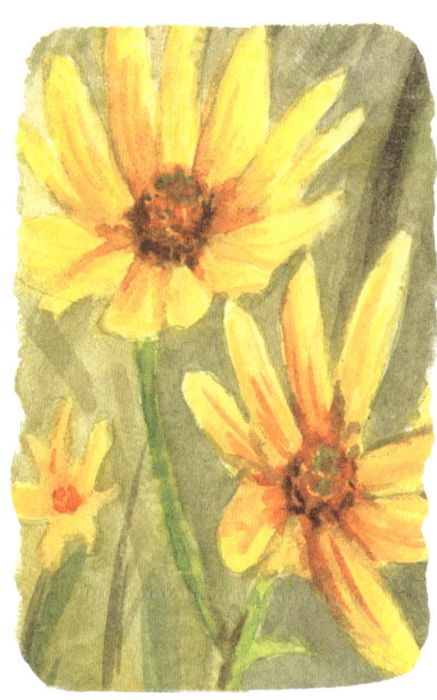

Western Sunflower
A favorite for pollinators and birds, it loves dry soil.

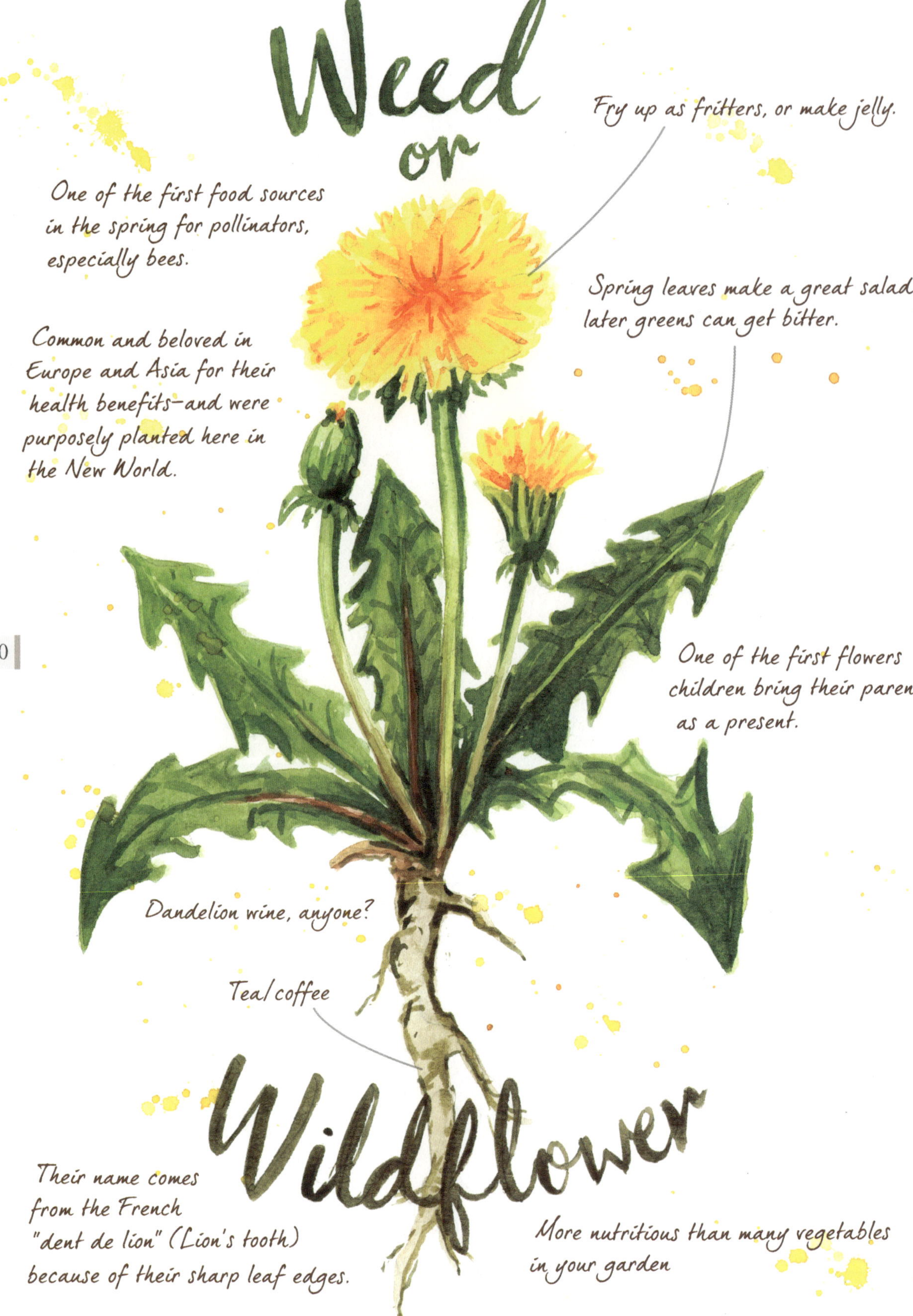
Weed
or
Wildflower
Fry up as fritters, or make jelly.
One of the first food sources in the spring for pollinators, especially bees.
Spring leaves make a great salad, later greens can get bitter.
Common and beloved in Europe and Asia for their health benefits—and were purposely planted here in the New World.
One of the first flowers children bring their parents as a present.
Dandelion wine, anyone?
Tea/coffee
Their name comes from the French "dent de lion" (Lion's tooth) because of their sharp leaf edges.
More nutritious than many vegetables in your garden

Dandelion Jelly:

1 qt. Dandelion blossoms (tightly packed)

2 qt. Water

2 tb. Fresh lemon juice

1-3/4 oz. Powdered pectin

5-1/2 cups Sugar

Rinse well, snip off stem and green collar. Boil in water for 3–4 minutes. Cool and strain, pressing petals out. Measure 3 cups of dandelion liquid, add lemon juice and pectin; stir. Bring to a boil and add sugar. Stir and boil for 2-1/2 minutes. Can be jarred.

Dandelion Coffee:

Use the root! Clean well, chop in food processor. Use a baking sheet and roast in an oven at 300* F for 2 hours. Let it steep in boiling water for 10 minutes before drinking. Yum!

Dandelion Tea:

Steep about 1 tablespoon of the stems and flowers for 30 minutes in 5 oz. boiling water. Strain.

Enjoy!

Violet Jelly:

2 heaping cups of fresh petals
1/4 cup clear lemon juice
2 cups boiling water
4 cups sugar
3 oz. liquid pectin

Wash well; drain. Pour boiling water over, and steep for 30 minutes to 24 hours. Strain. Stir lemon juice and sugar in–bring to rolling boil, and skim off foam. Can be jarred.

Violet flowers can also be candied!

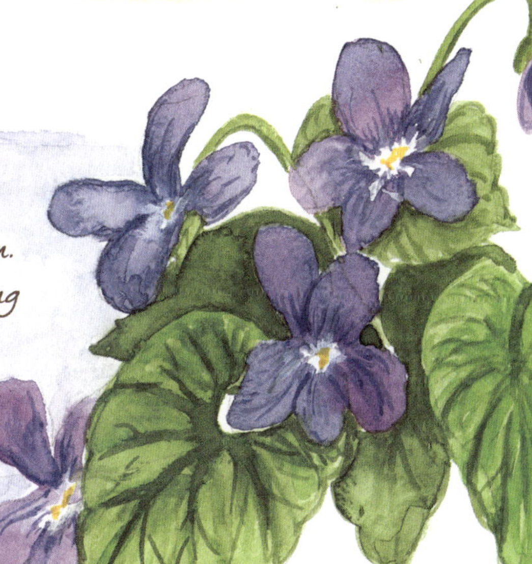

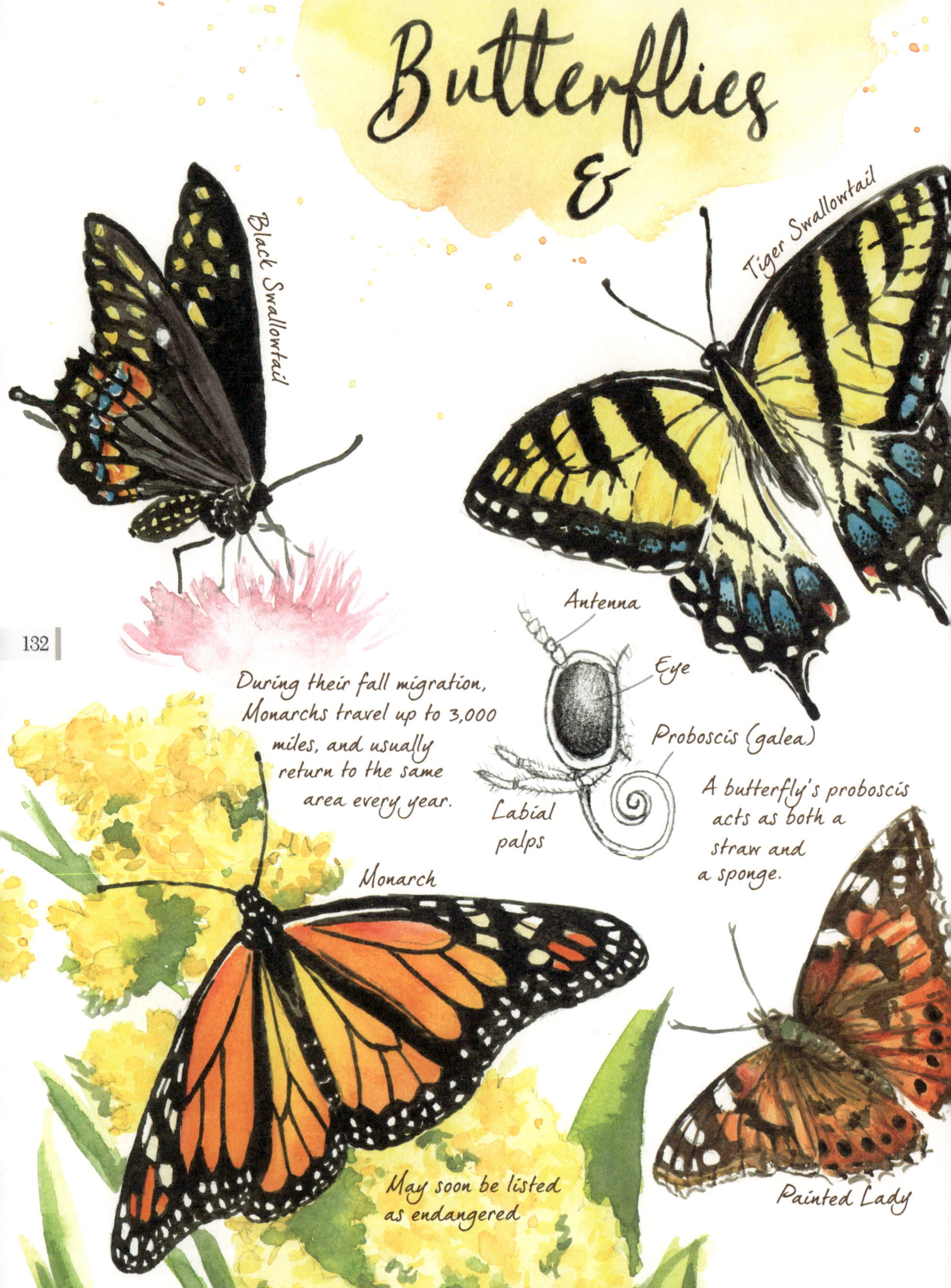
Butterflies
&
Black Swallowtail
Tiger Swallowtail
Antenna
Eye
Proboscis (galea)
Labial palps
During their fall migration, Monarchs travel up to 3,000 miles, and usually return to the same area every year.
A butterfly's proboscis acts as both a straw and a sponge.
Monarch
May soon be listed as endangered
Painted Lady

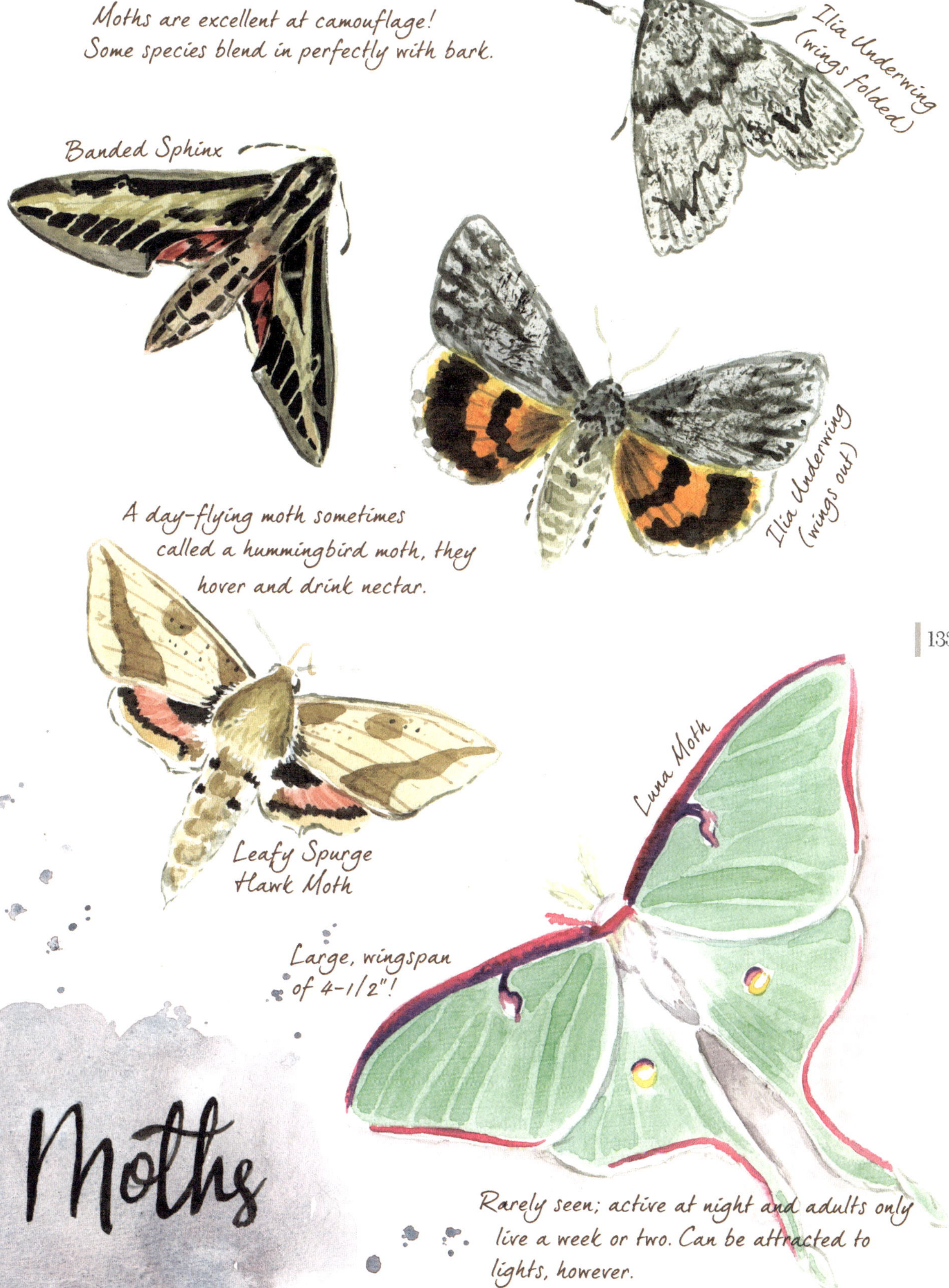
Moths are excellent at camouflage!
Some species blend in perfectly with bark.
Ilia Underwing
(wings folded)
Banded Sphinx
Ilia Underwing
(wings out)
A day-flying moth sometimes
called a hummingbird moth, they
hover and drink nectar.
Luna Moth
Leafy Spurge
Hawk Moth
Large, wingspan
of 4-1/2"!
Moths
Rarely seen; active at night and adults only
live a week or two. Can be attracted to
lights, however.

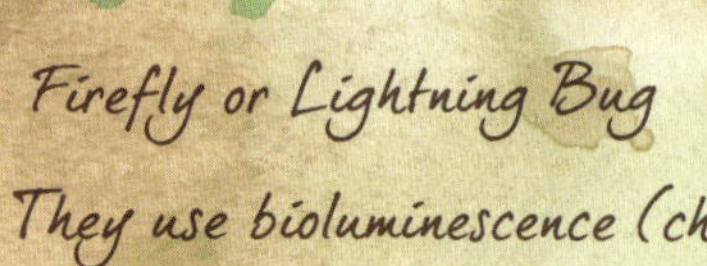

Firefly or Lightning Bug

They use bioluminescence (chemically produced light) during twilight to attract mates. It is known as a "cold light" since it produces almost no heat. The larvae (and even eggs) of many species actually glow too. Up to 25mm in length.

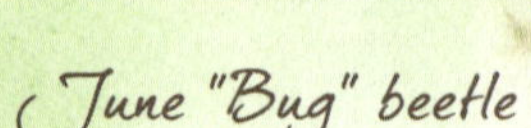

June "Bug" beetle

Related to scarabs. A nocturnal beetle, they can cause a bit of damage in gardens. 12–25mm.

Beet

*not to scale

Dogbane Leaf Beetle

A beautiful metallic beetle that lives on the dogbane plant, which it also eats. 8–11mm.

Stag Beetle (aka Pinching Beetle)

They look intimidating, but they aren't dangerous. 35–75mm.

Soldier Beetle

A common and harmless beetle that eats other harmful bugs. 5–15mm.

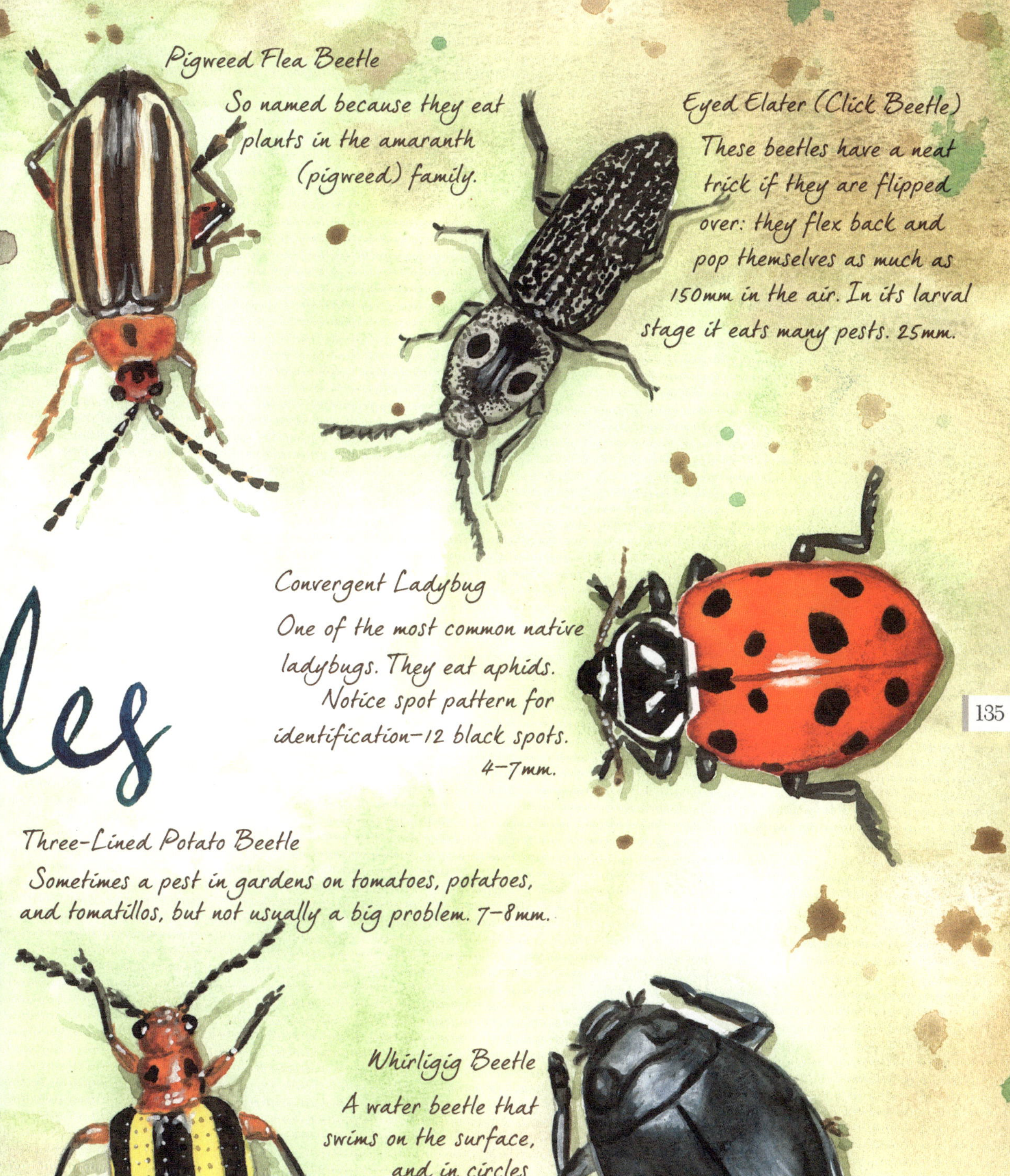
Pigweed Flea Beetle
So named because they eat plants in the amaranth (pigweed) family.
Eyed Elater (Click Beetle)
These beetles have a neat trick if they are flipped over: they flex back and pop themselves as much as 150mm in the air. In its larval stage it eats many pests. 25mm.
Convergent Ladybug
One of the most common native ladybugs. They eat aphids. Notice spot pattern for identification—12 black spots. 4–7mm.
les
Three-Lined Potato Beetle
Sometimes a pest in gardens on tomatoes, potatoes, and tomatillos, but not usually a big problem. 7–8mm.
Whirligig Beetle
A water beetle that swims on the surface, and in circles if alarmed, though they can also swim underwater. They carry a bubble of air to dive and swim for indefinite amounts of time. 3.5–14mm.

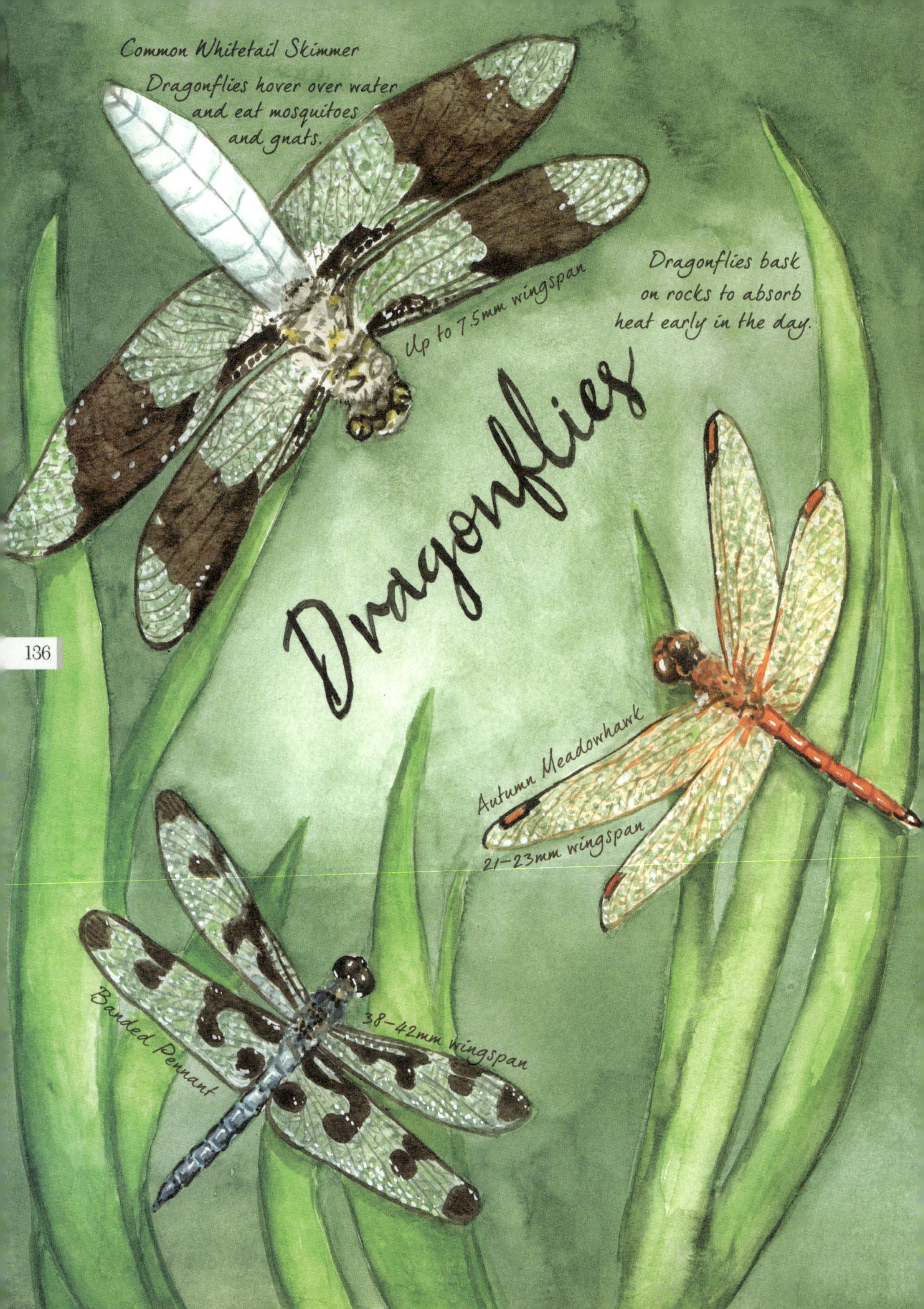
Common Whitetail Skimmer
Dragonflies hover over water and eat mosquitoes and gnats.
Up to 7.5mm wingspan
Dragonflies bask on rocks to absorb heat early in the day.
Dragonflies
Autumn Meadowhawk
21–23mm wingspan
Banded Pennant
38–42mm wingspan

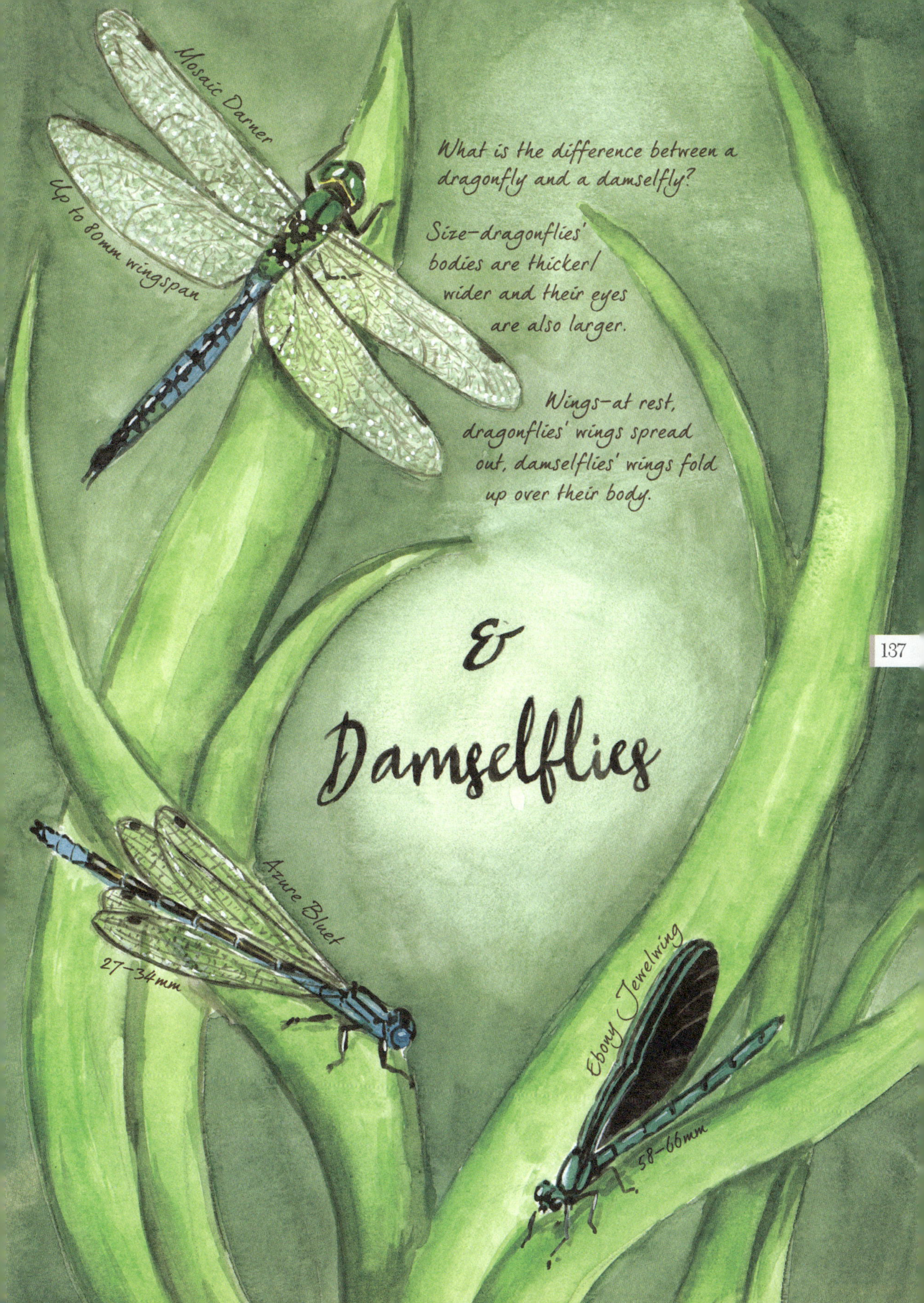
Mosaic Darner
Up to 80mm wingspan
What is the difference between a dragonfly and a damselfly?
Size-dragonflies' bodies are thicker/ wider and their eyes are also larger.
Wings-at rest, dragonflies' wings spread out, damselflies' wings fold up over their body.
&
Damselflies
Azure Bluet
27-34mm
Ebony Jewelwing
58-66mm

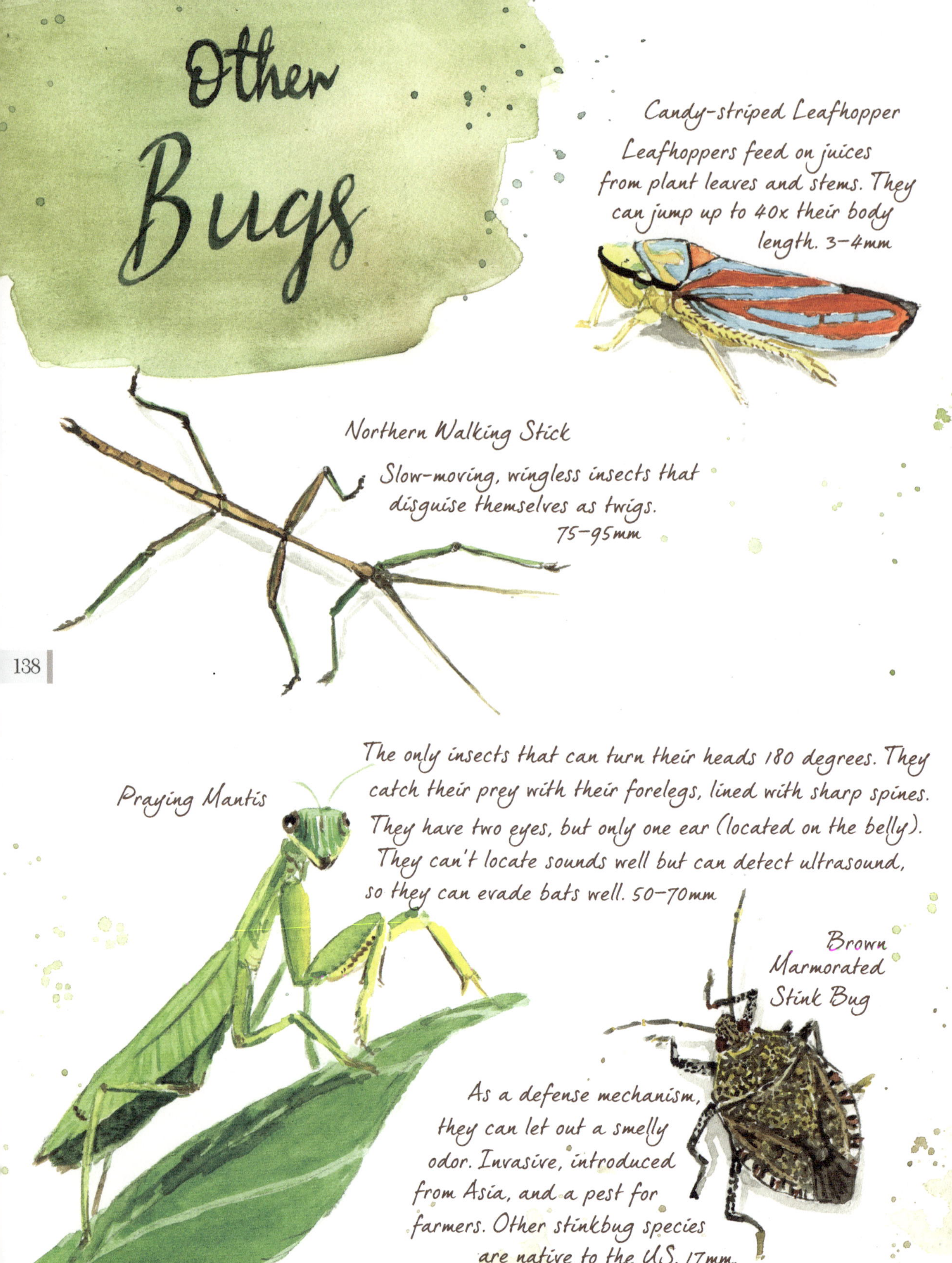
Other Bugs
Candy-striped Leafhopper
Leafhoppers feed on juices from plant leaves and stems. They can jump up to 40x their body length. 3–4mm
Northern Walking Stick
Slow-moving, wingless insects that disguise themselves as twigs. 75–95mm
Praying Mantis
The only insects that can turn their heads 180 degrees. They catch their prey with their forelegs, lined with sharp spines. They have two eyes, but only one ear (located on the belly). They can't locate sounds well but can detect ultrasound, so they can evade bats well. 50–70mm
Brown Marmorated Stink Bug
As a defense mechanism, they can let out a smelly odor. Invasive, introduced from Asia, and a pest for farmers. Other stinkbug species are native to the US. 17mm.

Dog-day Cicada

An annual cicada (unlike the famous periodic cicadas), common during July/August. They have a 2–5 year life cycle. You might find the papery exoskeleton that nymphs emerge from. 27–33mm

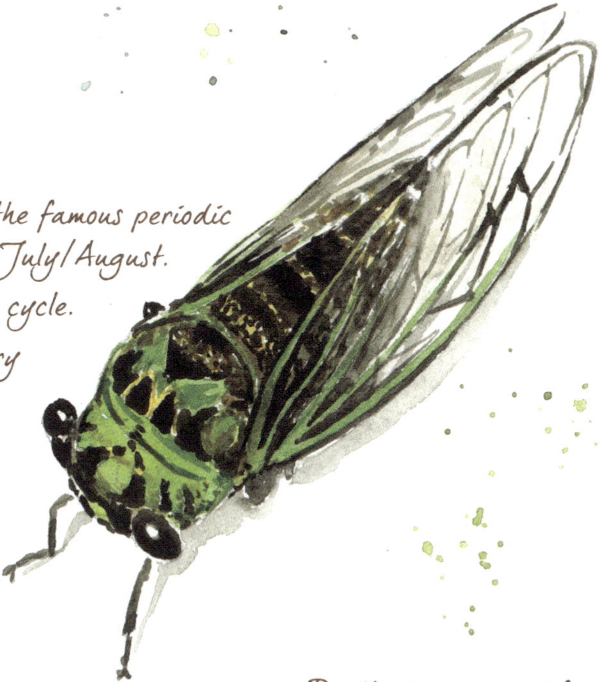

Beetles have a modified front wing that is hard/thick called elytra.

Crane Fly "mosquito hawk"

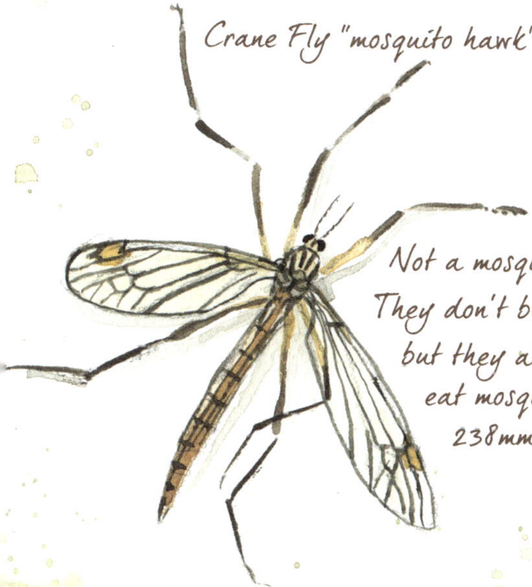

Not a mosquito! They don't bite, but they also don't eat mosquitoes. 238mm.

Katydid

Known for their songs "katydid, katy-didn't". 75mm.

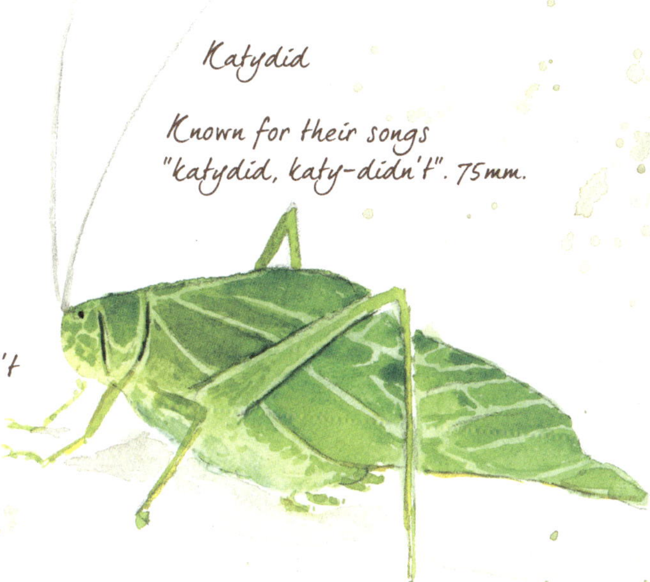

Native Bees

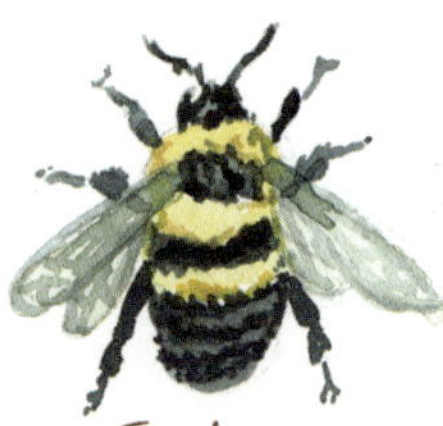
Eastern Bumble Bee

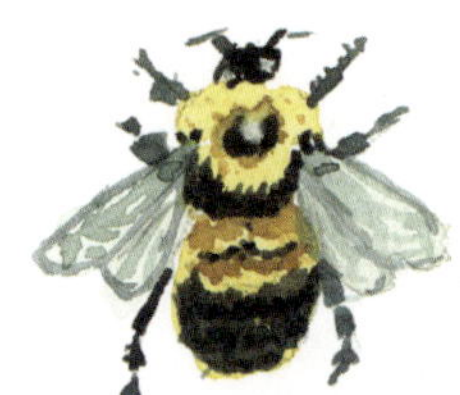
Rusty-patched Bumble Bee

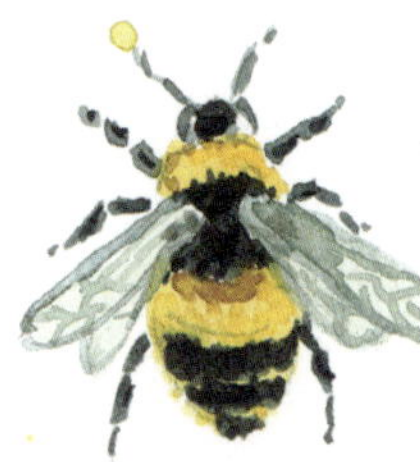
Yellow-banded Bumble Bee

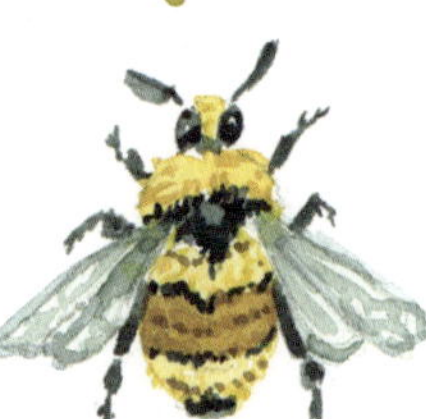
Tri-colored Bumble Bee

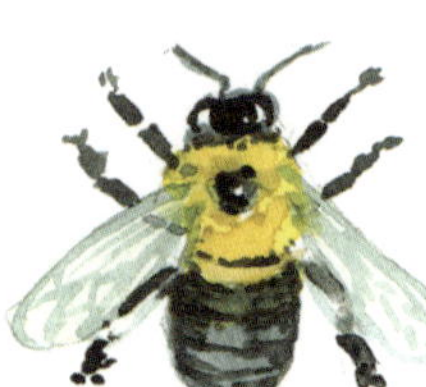
Eastern Carpenter Bee

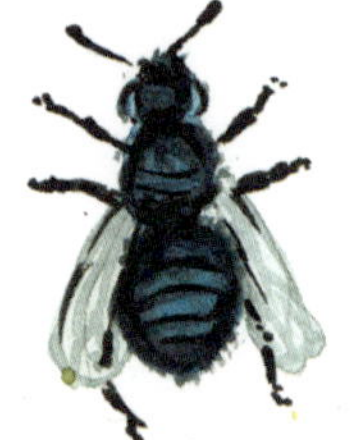
Blue Orchard Mason Bee

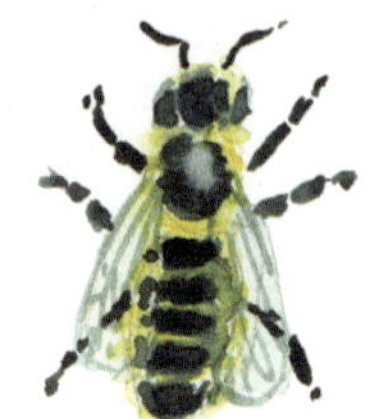
Leafcutter Bee

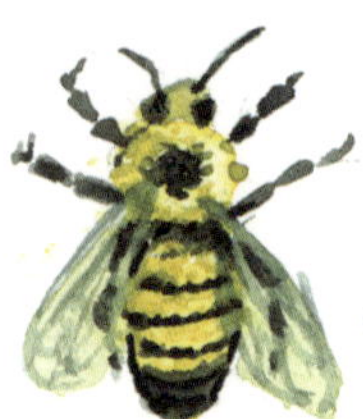
Lemon Cuckoo Bee

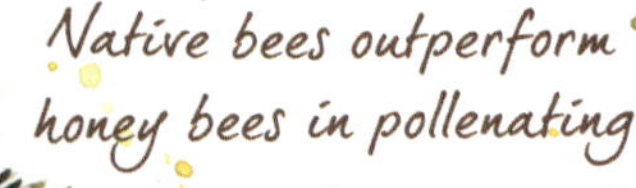
Native bees outperform honey bees in pollenating.

Did you know?

The familiar honey bee is not native to North America. They were introduced to the US by Europeans. They compete with native bees for resources.

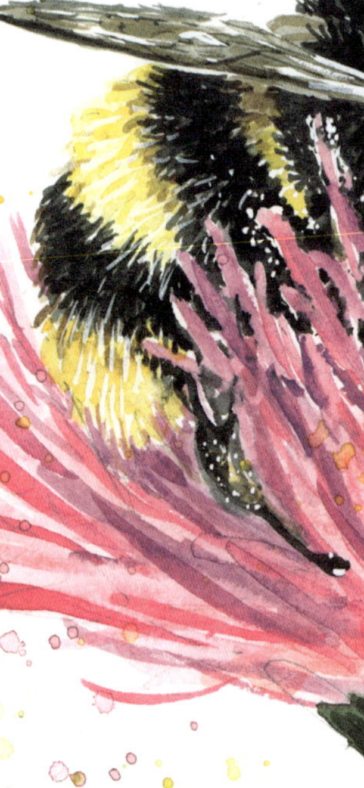

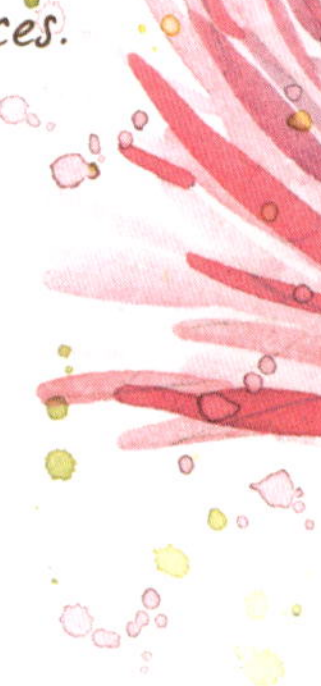

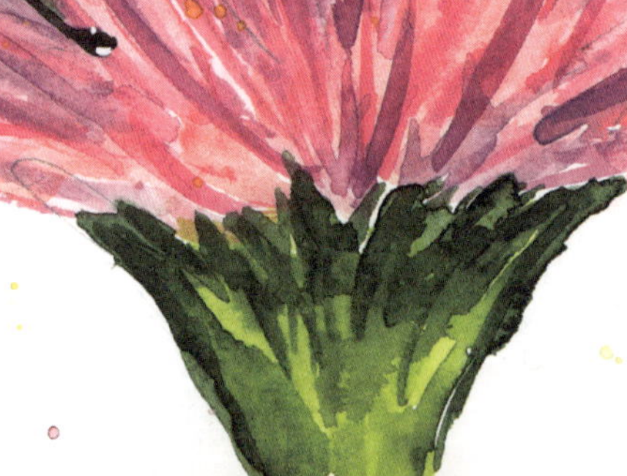

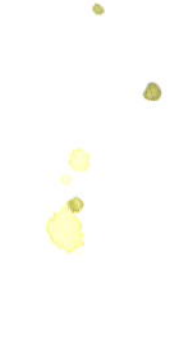

Birding Etiquette & Safety

- Respect the birds and their space- don't chase them or invade their territory.
- Try not to disturb them-stay on the path, keep quiet.
- Don't litter!
- Be aware of other people around you- keep quiet, don't distract or scare birds away. Be polite!
- Bring a friend, or at least tell someone where you will be.
- Avoid conflict.
- Be aware of other wildlife (ticks, bears, etc.) and be prepared
- Have your phone charged and with you, and bring a compass.
- Watch out for weather! Be prepared.

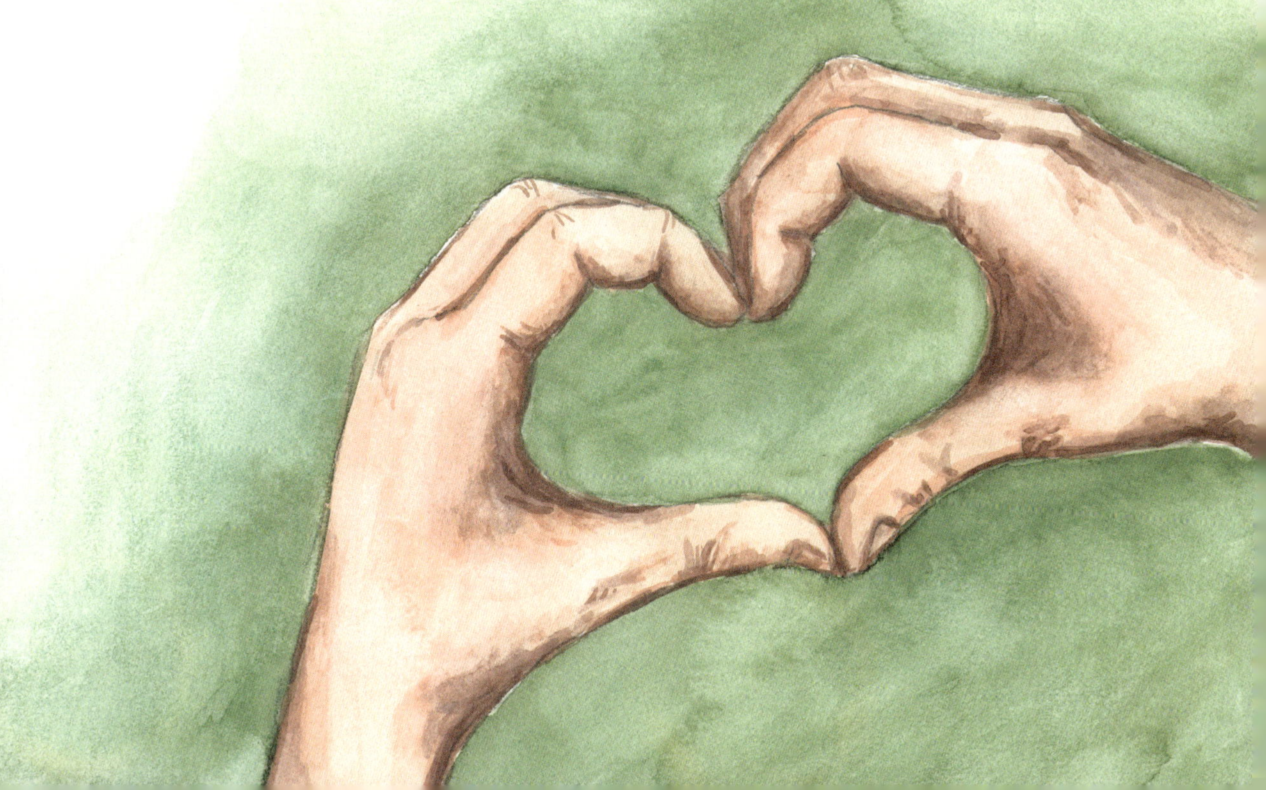

Index/References

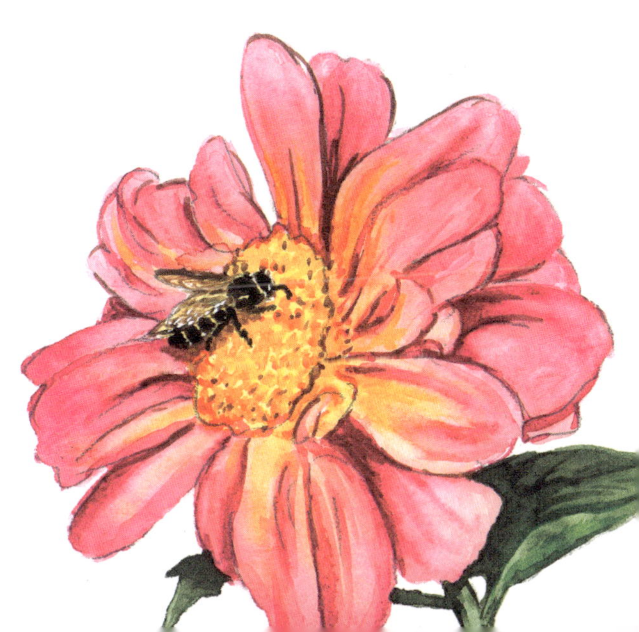

Recommended Reading

Birds *and* Bird-watching

Burton, Robert, and Stephen W Kress. *Audubon North American Birdfeeder Guide.* New York: DK. 2010.

Cornell University. All About Birds. 2021. "Online Bird Guide, Bird ID Help, Life History, Bird Sounds from Cornell." http://www.allaboutbirds.org.

Minetor, Randi. *Backyard Birding and Butterfly Gardening.* S.L.: Lyons Press. 2022.

Sibley, David. *The Sibley Guide to Birds.* New York: Alfred A. Knopf. 2014.

Sibley, David, Chris Elphick, John B Dunning, and National Audubon Society. *The Sibley Guide to Bird Life & Behavior.* New York: Alfred A. Knopf. 2013.

Stokes, Donald W, and Lillian Q Stokes. *The New Stokes Field Guide to Birds. Eastern Region.* New York: Little, Brown. 2013.

Zickefoose, Julie. *Natural Gardening for Birds: Create a Bird-Friendly Habitat in Your Backyard.* New York: Skyhorse Publishing. 2016.

Watercolor *and* Art

AdornThemes. "Let's Make Art: Your Home for Watercolor Painting Tutorials & Supplies." Let's Make Art. https://www.letsmakeart.com.

Edwards, Betty. *Drawing on the Right Side of the Brain.* London: Souvenir. 2016.

Fox, Dana. *Watercolor with Me in the Forest.* Salem, Ma: Page Street Publishing Co. 2018.

O'Connor, Birgit. *Paint Watercolor Flowers: A Beginner's Step-By-Step Guide.* Cincinnati, Ohio: North Light Books. 2018.

Rainey, Jenna. *Everyday Watercolor: Learn to Paint Watercolor in 30 Days.* California: Watson-Guptill. 2017.

Woodin, Mary. *The Painted Garden: A Year in Words and Watercolours.* Philadelphia, Pa.: Courage Books. 2005.

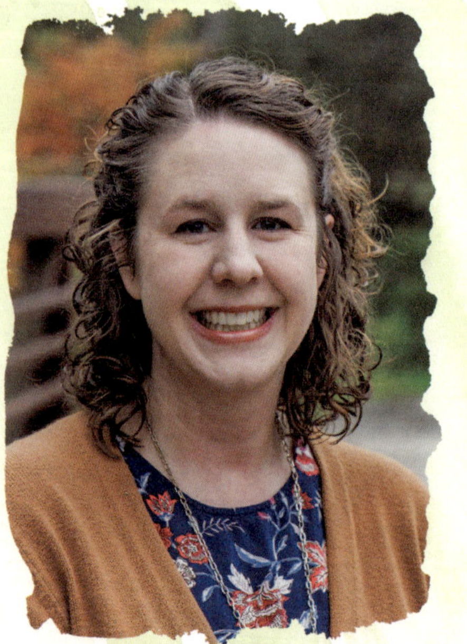

About *the* Artist

Jenny deFouw Geuder is an artist and educator from Michigan. She received her Bachelor's and Master's degrees in Art Education (and minored in English). She has taught art at the middle-school level for 16 years and has continued her own artistic interests on the side, both in commissioned work and personal topics. She primarily works in watercolor, but she also enjoys oils, ceramics, and graphite. She lives in the country with her husband, two small boys, a dog, five cats, a hedgehog, chickens, and occasionally two ponies. She spends most of her summers at a rustic log cabin on a lake in northern Michigan where she hikes and fishes and, in general, enjoys the natural beauty of the area.